Dearest Mun

The Lord is always
at your side -
Trust him
Serve him
Obey him
& above all - Love him.
Seek him daily.

All our love

Nigel & Kathy

x x

FACE to FACE

I saw God face to face.
GENESIS 32:30

A DEVOTIONAL PRAYER JOURNAL

Solly Ozrovech

CHRISTIAN ART
PUBLISHERS

Originally published by Christian Publishing Company
under the title *Van aangesig tot aangesig*
© 2003

English edition © 2003
CHRISTIAN ART PUBLISHERS
PO Box 1599, Vereeniging, 1930

First edition 2003

Translated by Lynette Douglas and Louise Emmerton

Cover designed by Christian Art Publishers

Set in 10 on 12 pt Palatino by Christian Art Publishers

Printed in Singapore

ISBN 1-86920-281-3

03 04 05 06 07 08 09 10 11 12 – 10 9 8 7 6 5 4 3 2 1

PREFACE

D r. Andrew Murray said, "Prayer is the unconditional requirement for all that God wants to do in this world." If we agree with him that these words are undeniably true, we should give earnest attention to our prayer lives.

At the Jabbok River Jacob wrestled all night with God in prayer. Even though Jacob came out of this experience with a dislocated hip, he received the blessing of God that he had pleaded for: *"So Jacob called the place Peniel, saying, 'It is because I saw God face to face, and yet my life was spared'"* (Gen. 32:30).

This incident illustrates a few important issues concerning prayer and emphasizes the urgency with which you should regard prayer. When you use this Devotional Prayer Journal, you will add value to your prayer life – because when God speaks you listen, and when you pray God listens!

Each page has lines where you can make your own notes. These could include the following:

- Your own prayer for that specific day
- Praise to God for prayers that have been answered
- Names of people for whom you want to pray that day
- Your own petitions and requests to God
- Unanswered prayers with which you are still wrestling
- Any thoughts, feelings or reflections on the devotion of the day

If you are serious about your prayer life, each day's prayer time will be a special encounter with a merciful and loving God who will bless you. Peace of mind and tranquility and spiritual growth will be the sure result.

I pray that, through the work of the Holy Spirit who teaches us to pray, this Prayer Journal will inspire and enrich your prayer life.

SOLI DEO GLORIA
26 March 2003

Prayer is not escape – it is victory;
Prayer is not desperation – it is power;
Prayer does not release people from dreadful circumstances –
It prepares each person to cope with every situation.

– William Barclay –

JANUARY

PRAYERS OF PRAISE

When early Christians gathered for worship services, those who led the services used their own words to pray. But set prayers very quickly became part of the discipline of worship. These prayers ensured that the important tenets of the faith were remembered by the worshipers. Some of these prayers were based on prayers of the Bible, while others emerged out of church life.

One of the most well-known prayers of praise in the Bible is Psalm 8:1-9, where David praised the Creator:

O LORD, our Lord, how majestic is your name in all the earth! You have set your glory above the heavens.

From the lips of children and infants you have ordained praise because of your enemies, to silence the foe and the avenger.

When I consider your heavens, the work of your fingers, the moon and the stars, which you have set in place, what is man that you are mindful of him, the son of man that you care for him?

You made him a little lower than the heavenly beings and crowned him with glory and honor.

You made him ruler over the works of your hands; you put everything under his feet: all flocks and herds, and the beasts of the field, the birds of the air, and the fish of the sea, all that swim the paths of the seas.

O LORD, our Lord, how majestic is your name in all the earth!

I will sing to the Lord all my life!

May the glory of the LORD endure forever; may the LORD rejoice in his works – he who looks at the earth, and it trembles, who touches the mountains, and they smoke. I will sing to the LORD all my life; I will sing praise to my God as long as I live. May my meditation be pleasing to him, as I rejoice in the LORD. But may sinners vanish from the earth and the wicked be no more. Praise the LORD, O my soul.

— PSALM 104:31-35 —

There are many different ways to express yourself in prayer to God when you use the Scriptures. This prayer is a wonderful example of how to begin and stimulate your prayer life. Make this prayer part of your meditations and discover the power of the Almighty God who is able to do all things: the glance of His eye can cause the earth to tremble and set the mountains on fire.

Thus, no matter what enemy might confront you, no matter what mountains might block your road, you can be assured that nothing is impossible for our God.

Therefore you can leave your enemies, your worries, and your burdens in His hands: He will handle them for you in His mighty power.

Holy God, I delight in Your power and I want to praise and honor You in song.

Amen

How precious to me are Your thoughts, O God!

For you created my inmost being; you knit me together in my mother's womb. I praise you because I am fearfully and wonderfully made; your works are wonderful, I know that full well. My frame was not hidden from you when I was made in the secret place. When I was woven together in the depths of the earth, your eyes saw my unformed body. All the days ordained for me were written in your book before one of them came to be. How precious to me are your thoughts, O God! How vast is the sum of them!

— Psalm 139:13-17 —

I t is wonderful to be able to enjoy the body that God created for you! In this prayer David expresses his wonder and awe at God's creation of the human body.

Each minute detail contributes to a marvelous whole: brain cells, blood cells, each component of our bodies has been created with intricate care. The eye that is able to observe the wonders of creation, the ear that can hear a pin drop, the nose that can smell the fresh-turned earth.

Think of your Creator when you use your body today, and thank Him for it.

Thank You, Creator God, for the workmanship with which You created me.

Amen

All the earth bows down to You

Shout with joy to God, all the earth! Sing the glory of his name; make his praise glorious! Say to God, "How awesome are your deeds! So great is your power that your enemies cringe before you. All the earth bows down to you; they sing praise to you, they sing praise to your name."

– PSALM 66:1-4 –

The believer needs not have any doubts that God answers prayer! And when He does we should sing His praises and thank Him for His faithfulness.

This psalm was written after Israel had won a war under difficult circumstances. The Israelites wanted to testify to each other, to the world and to God Himself how great and mighty He is – so that everyone would bow before Him.

To be on God's side is the greatest privilege on earth. Let us thank God with our whole heart when He hears our prayers!

We bow in thankfulness before You God. Thank You for everything You have done for us!

Amen

I sing to the honor of my God!

"Hear this, you kings! Listen, you rulers! I will sing to the LORD, I will sing; I will make music to the LORD, the God of Israel. O LORD, when you went out from Seir, when you marched from the land of Edom, the earth shook, the heavens poured, the clouds poured down water. The mountains quaked before the LORD, the One of Sinai, before the LORD, the God of Israel."

– JUDGES 5:3-5 –

Deborah's courage and trust in the Lord inspired Israel to win the battle against the armies of Sisera. Deborah took the lead again at the victory feast. She did not take the honor of the victory for herself, Jael or Balak. Instead, she praised the Almighty God for His astounding victory.

Has God not also given you victory in your life? Has He not revealed His almighty power in your life? Praise and honor God for the work He is doing in your life, and tell others about His greatness.

Lord God Almighty, when you begin to move, the mountains tremble!

Amen

Sing to the Lord a new song!

Praise the LORD. Sing to the LORD a new song, his praise in the assembly of the saints. Let Israel rejoice in their Maker; let the people of Zion be glad in their King. Let them praise his name with dancing and make music to him with tambourine and harp. For the LORD takes delight in his people; he crowns the humble with salvation. Let the saints rejoice in this honor and sing for joy on their beds.

– PSALM 149:1-5 –

This psalm is the prayer of a joyful group of believers. They rejoice because God is their King. They praise God by using the gifts and talents that He gave them: they dance, sing songs, and play various musical instruments.

The message of this psalm is that God takes pleasure in His people and saves those who humble themselves before Him.

Just because someone participates in rendering praise, does not mean that they deserve anything special from Him. It is all about the greatness and goodness of God.

Rejoice in God's goodness in your life and confirm your commitment to worship God in your congregation with the talents that He has given you.

Lord, my God, thank You for the privilege of being able to praise Your name in worship services at church.

Amen

Worship the Lord with gladness

Shout for joy to the LORD, all the earth. Worship the LORD with gladness; come before him with joyful songs. Know that the LORD is God. It is he who made us, and we are his; we are his people, the sheep of his pasture. Enter his gates with thanksgiving and his courts with praise; give thanks to him and praise his name. For the LORD is good and his love endures forever; his faithfulness continues through all generations.

– PSALM 100:1-5 –

Our heartfelt joy in everything that God has given us, in all that He has done for us, is like beautiful, harmonious music that rises up to God. God delights in the joy of people who are thankful for what He has given them.

Joy, happiness and excitement are often associated with earthly pleasures: obtaining a new house or car, a trip to a foreign country, or the birth of a new baby. But in this psalm, joy and happiness are associated with worshiping God and having knowledge of His ways.

Find creative ways to praise and thank God today for His goodness. Delight yourself in all that He has given you and share that joy with friends and everybody you come into contact with!

Holy God, I come before You with utterances of holy joy. Help me to share my joy with others.

Amen

Praise the Lord for His power and His might!

Ascribe to the LORD, O families of nations, ascribe to the LORD glory and strength, ascribe to the LORD the glory due his name. Bring an offering and come before him; worship the LORD in the splendor of his holiness. Tremble before him, all the earth! The world is firmly established; it cannot be moved. Let the heavens rejoice, let the earth be glad; let them say among the nations, "The LORD reigns!"

– 1 CHRONICLES 16:28-31 –

This song of praise was sung when the Ark of the Lord was brought back to Jerusalem after having been captured by the enemies of Israel. David called on the whole of creation to rejoice with him.

God deserves our unreserved praise, because He is the Creator of the whole earth. People like to honor champions and victors and they delight in such rejoicing. God, as Conqueror, deserves our heartfelt songs of praise!

Decide to get out of the city this week and spend some time appreciating nature. See how creation rejoices in the works of God, and add your prayers of praise to the general chorus!

Creator God, as part of Your wonderful creation, I honor and praise You today.

Amen

You give us reason to praise!

O you who hear prayer, to you all men will come. When we were overwhelmed by sins, you forgave our transgressions. Blessed are those you choose and bring near to live in your courts! We are filled with the good things of your house, of your holy temple. You answer us with awesome deeds of righteousness, O God our Savior, the hope of all the ends of the earth and of the farthest seas, who formed the mountains by your power, having armed yourself with strength.

– PSALM 65:2-6 –

God is faithful and eager to answer our prayers and forgive our sins. We need to learn to praise Him with the same enthusiasm we have when we ask for His help. We must also keep the promises we make to God and turn them into deeds of thankfulness.

God is worthy to receive our praise because He does answer our prayers and He forgives our sins. David delights in this assurance and rejoices in the truth that, *"Blessed are those you choose and bring near to live in your courts!"* (v. 4).

David's greatest joy was to spend time with God in prayer. And he makes sure that God knows how much joy it gives him. He bursts forth in joyful songs of praise to God.

Heavenly Father, I will continuously sing Your praises because You always fulfill Your promises.

Amen

You alone are the Lord!

And the Levites – Jeshua, Kadmiel, Bani, Hashabneiah, Sherebiah, Hodiah, Shebaniah and Pethahiah – said: "Stand up and praise the LORD your God, who is from everlasting to everlasting." Blessed be your glorious name, and may it be exalted above all blessing and praise. You alone are the LORD. You made the heavens, even the highest heavens, and all their starry host, the earth and all that is on it, the seas and all that is in them. You give life to everything, and the multitudes of heaven worship you.

– NEHEMIAH 9:5-6 –

There is a specific and fruitful way to approach God in prayer: confess your sins and humble yourself before the Lord. Let your confession of guilt lead to unlimited praise to the One who has forgiven your sins.

This is exactly what the Israelites did in this passage. After the walls of Jerusalem had been rebuilt, they came together for a time of dedication, worship and praise. They expressed sorrow at their sinfulness by fasting and dressing themselves in sackcloth and ashes. They confessed their own sins as well as those of their forefathers.

After that they listened for three hours while the Law was read to them and spent a further three hours in examining themselves and confessing their sins. Only then did the priests ask the people to rise and worship their Creator!

Merciful God, I humble myself before You and thank and praise You for Your grace and forgiveness.

Amen

Come let us kneel before the Lord, our Maker!

Come, let us sing for joy to the LORD; let us shout aloud to the Rock of our salvation. Let us come before him with thanksgiving and extol him with music and song. For the LORD is the great God, the great King above all gods. In his hand are the depths of the earth, and the mountain peaks belong to him. The sea is his, for he made it, and his hands formed the dry land. Come, let us bow down in worship, let us kneel before the LORD our Maker; for he is our God and we are the people of his pasture, the flock under his care.

— PSALM 95:1-7 —

All around us we see evidence of God's mighty and creative power: there is nothing on earth that can be compared to our Creator.

Earthly kings might boast about their kingdoms, their palaces, and their armies but in this prayer we are called to focus on the realm of the King of kings: immoveable mountains, mighty oceans, and fruitful valleys.

The boundaries of His kingdom cannot be measured, and He created it all through His mighty power and He preserves it all each day.

Look around you and notice the evidence of His might and join in the anthem of the hosts of heaven who praise and worship Him with heartfelt thanks.

Great and mighty King, I lift up my voice in prayer and praise to declare Your mighty deeds.

Amen

Make known His Holy Name!

Give thanks to the LORD, call on his name; make known among the nations what he has done. Sing to him, sing praise to him; tell of all his wonderful acts. Glory in his holy name; let the hearts of those who seek the LORD rejoice. Look to the LORD and his strength; seek his face always. Remember the wonders he has done, his miracles, and the judgments he pronounced.

– PSALM 105:1-5 –

The Psalmist leads the people of God in praise and thanksgiving for all the wonderful things that He has done for them. He challenges them to consider all the different ways in which God has worked in their lives, and to offer prayers of praise to Him because of them.

To seek the help and protection of the Lord is the most meaningful endeavor in man's existence. And what a wonderful undertaking it is!

Before you go any further this year, first seek the help and protection of the Almighty; examine your own life to find the countless blessings that the Lord has given to you personally. Then bow before Him in prayer, praise and thanksgiving.

I praise and thank You, Lord, for all the mighty deeds that You have done on my behalf.

Amen

Give thanks to the Lord for His unfailing love!

He led them by a straight way to a city where they could settle. Let them give thanks to the LORD for his unfailing love and his wonderful deeds for men, for he satisfies the thirsty and fills the hungry with good things.

– PSALM 107:7-9 –

This psalm was originally prayed by the Israelites at one of their religious feasts. They were people who really knew what it was to hunger and thirst: they had returned from exile in Babylon.

They could speak from experience and with conviction of God's unfailing love. They had seen how He had made provision for His people in the midst of desperate circumstances.

Many of us can, in some small way or other, identify with the feelings of those exiles. We too have experienced great needs in our lives: physically, spiritually, emotionally, and financially.

You might have an urgent need right now and you can bring it to the Lord in prayer. Ask Him for the profound peace with which He alone is able to satisfy your deepest needs. Praise Him for His peace.

Faithful Father, I trust You to meet my deepest needs.

Amen

Give thanks to the Lord

Give thanks to the LORD, call on his name; make known among the nations what he has done. Sing to him, sing praise to him; tell of all his wonderful acts. Glory in his holy name; let the hearts of those who seek the LORD rejoice. Look to the LORD and his strength; seek his face always. Remember the wonders he has done, his miracles, and the judgments he pronounced.

– 1 CHRONICLES 16:8-12 –

The day on which David first sang this song of praise was an unforgettable one for Israel. Their armies had crushed the Philistines completely. David carried the symbol of God's presence – the Ark of the Covenant – victoriously through the streets of Jerusalem.

He then housed it temporarily in a tent and established a choir of priests to sing praises to God and make known to the nations what the Lord had done. And God received the glory for all these things.

If other people were to listen to our prayers, would they receive an understanding of the greatness of God? When you glorify His name today, do so with courage, thankfulness, and boldness.

Great God, I thank You for Your mighty deeds, and I glorify Your name.

Amen

Our Lord is great and mighty

Praise the LORD. How good it is to sing praises to our God, how pleasant and fitting to praise him! The LORD builds up Jerusalem; he gathers the exiles of Israel. He heals the brokenhearted and binds up their wounds. He determines the number of the stars and calls them each by name. Great is our Lord and mighty in power; his understanding has no limit.

– PSALM 147:1-5 –

The Psalmist delights in singing the praises of God, because he has seen a miracle take place right before his eyes: God's people have returned home from their exile in Babylon; the Lord has rebuilt Jerusalem; and He has gathered those who were scattered.

God's greatness is reflected in His mercy and that is the only way that we can begin to measure the extent of His majesty. He is the God who binds up our wounds and who heals the broken-hearted. He gives each star its name, and yet, in His wisdom and might, each one of us is still special to Him. Therefore the Psalmist declares: *"It is good to sing praises to God."* Can you offer this prayer to Him today?

Meditate once again on the greatness of the God of the universe and reflect on His unfailing love and mercy.

Unchangeable God, it is good to declare Your mercy in prayer.

Amen

Praise the Lord, for He is good

Praise the LORD. Praise the name of the LORD; praise him, you servants of the LORD, you who minister in the house of the LORD, in the courts of the house of our God. Praise the LORD, for the LORD is good; sing praise to his name, for that is pleasant. For the LORD has chosen Jacob to be his own, Israel to be his treasured possession. I know that the LORD is great, that our Lord is greater than all gods.

– PSALM 135:1-5 –

Make sure that some of your prayers in this week are dedicated to thanking God for all that He has done for you and your family. His goodness is evident in so many aspects of our lives. All our blessings come from Him. Therefore, we should take sufficient time to rejoice in His goodness and grace.

The writer of this prayer does exactly that. He calls on the people that have gathered in the temple to worship God and to praise Him for His merciful acts.

Nations and tribes committed themselves to praising God. Some of them helped with the celebrations and offerings. Others were trained as musicians, and led the people in songs of praise. This prayer calls all people to commemorate the goodness of God in joyful prayers and songs.

Loving Father, I praise You because You have been so good to me.

Amen

I stay close to You!

O God, you are my God, earnestly I seek you; my soul thirsts for you, my body longs for you, in a dry and weary land where there is no water. I have seen you in the sanctuary and beheld your power and your glory. Because your love is better than life, my lips will glorify you. I will praise you as long as I live, and in your name I will lift up my hands. My soul will be satisfied as with the richest of foods; with singing lips my mouth will praise you.

— PSALM 63:1-5 —

Our prayers should reflect the joy we find when we come into God's presence; they should echo the delight we find in His love. We give our level best to try and achieve success at work, in sport or in our relationships. We are often disappointed.

In this prayer, David describes a different kind of goal, one that ultimately leads to complete satisfaction. He desires to see God Himself through prayer, to be with God in His holy presence, and thus to experience His strength and His goodness.

And so he achieves the highest goal: a life of meaning and purpose. He discovers that God's love is worth more than life itself!

I pray that you would make the same discovery in your prayer life, even if it means, like David did, that you need to stay up the whole night to honor and praise God in prayer.

Loving Father God, Your love is worth more to me than life itself.

Amen

The Lord is near

I will extol the LORD at all times; his praise will always be on my lips. My soul will boast in the LORD; let the afflicted hear and rejoice. Glorify the LORD with me; let us exalt his name together. I sought the LORD, and he answered me; he delivered me from all my fears. Those who look to him are radiant; their faces are never covered with shame.

— PSALM 34:1-5 —

Our almighty God has the desire and ability to save all those who trust in Him. In this prayer, David extols God because he narrowly escaped from his enemy. King Saul wanted to have David killed, but, through the grace of God, David escaped and he acknowledged his release as an answer to prayer.

Sometimes people act with much bravado, but they are in actual fact very frightened. Their boasting is often a mask for their fear.

There is, however, another kind of boasting that is based in reality, and that is to boast in the Lord. And there is no end to the things of which we can boast in God. Perhaps God has released you from a difficult situation. Extol Him and direct your prayers and praise to Him.

Hearer of prayers, in my need I called to You and You answered me and delivered me. I extol Your great Name.

Amen

Sing a new song to honor the Lord!

Sing to the LORD a new song, for he has done marvelous things; his right hand and his holy arm have worked salvation for him. The LORD has made his salvation known and revealed his righteousness to the nations. He has remembered his love and his faithfulness to the house of Israel; all the ends of the earth have seen the salvation of our God. Shout for joy to the LORD, all the earth, burst into jubilant song with music.

– PSALM 98:1-4 –

It is a good idea to open your hymn book from time to time and to use the hymns in your prayers. Find a song of praise that proclaims God's might, and use it to honor your heavenly Father for His redemption and victory through Jesus Christ.

What we sing, and how we sing, speaks volumes about our true feelings. A depressed face and a half-hearted voice can make the most upbeat lyrics sound like a dirge.

To be able to meditate on and talk about the things that God has done for you, focus on all that is good, true, and praiseworthy. And especially when you sing praise to God, offer Him something that He can truly delight in.

This prayer calls all believers to sing a new song to the Lord. He brings about great victories in our lives through His strength and grace – thank and praise Him for that!

Thank You, Lord Jesus, for the victories that You have wrought in my life.

Amen

Splendor and majesty are before Him!

Sing to the LORD a new song; sing to the LORD, all the earth. Sing to the LORD, praise his name; proclaim his salvation day after day. Declare his glory among the nations, his marvelous deeds among all peoples. For great is the LORD and most worthy of praise; he is to be feared above all gods. For all the gods of the nations are idols, but the LORD made the heavens. Splendor and majesty are before him; strength and glory are in his sanctuary.

— PSALM 96:1-6 —

Make a decision to start every day by thinking of something that God has done for you and praise Him in your prayers for it: the brand new day that He has given you; His mercy and redemption; food and shelter; family ties! Then tell someone about your wonderful God today.

Each day our newspapers are filled with bad news. If the good news of Jesus Christ, who came to save sinners, were proclaimed instead, perhaps our world would be a better place.

The Psalmist undertakes to declare the good news of God's wonderful deeds every day. It is good for us to hear often of the saving grace of God through Jesus Christ, to thank Him for it in prayer, and to declare it to the whole world!

Loving God, I will, as far as I can, proclaim Your mighty deeds. I pray that You will give me strength for the task.

Amen

Praise be to the Lord

Praise be to the Lord, for he has heard my cry for mercy. The Lord is my strength and my shield; my heart trusts in him, and I am helped. My heart leaps for joy and I will give thanks to him in song.

– Psalm 28:6-7 –

When we pray for God's grace we should never forget to sing His praises as well. He is our only hope, our strength, and our shield. Even while we are waiting for Him to deliver us from our present dilemmas, we can praise Him for His faithfulness to us in the past. Then our faith and trust in the mercy of God will be strengthened.

God is merciful! How often have we been on the verge of giving up in despair because our situation seemed completely hopeless, and then God stepped in and acted on our behalf?

David often experienced the might of God, which is why he could so regularly pray this prayer of thanks: "He has been my help! He is the One who protects me, I can trust in Him." And so he closes his song of praise with the statement that, *"I will give thanks to him in song."*

I praise You, Lord because You heard my cry for mercy.

Amen.

There is none like You

No one is like you, O LORD; you are great, and your name is mighty in power. Who should not revere you, O King of the nations? This is your due. Among all the wise men of the nations and in all their kingdoms, there is no one like you.

— JEREMIAH 10:6-7 —

Let us glorify the name of the Lord our God and praise Him. Not only is He the King of the Universe, but also the One who raises up and casts down other kings, presidents, rulers, and even dictators. Honor and praise the Lord in prayer. There is none like Him!

Through the centuries, self-righteous and cruel dictators across the world have dominated nations. These despots live in wealth and luxury while their subjects struggle to survive through hunger and poverty. They act like demi-gods over the people they govern with an iron fist.

But the Bible teaches us that there is only One true King. In his prayer, Jeremiah declares that He alone is worthy to receive love, worship and honor. He alone can hold the title *"King of the nations."* Is He the King on the throne of your heart?

Holy God, there is none like You. You are the King of my heart.

Amen

What god is as great as our God?

I will meditate on all your works and consider all your mighty deeds. Your ways, O God, are holy. What god is so great as our God? You are the God who performs miracles; you display your power among the peoples. With your mighty arm you redeemed our people, the descendants of Jacob and Joseph. The waters saw you, O God, the waters saw you and writhed; the very depths were convulsed.

– PSALM 77:12-16 –

It is wonderful to reminisce about joyful experiences of the past in the company of long-standing friends. Psalm 77 is a prayer in which the wonderful works of God are brought to mind and He is praised for them.

Asaph was in difficulty and desperately needed God's help. By remembering God's great deeds in the past, he is assured that God is faithful and will once again come to his aid.

Don't ever despair: God is always faithful and if we come before Him with prayers and praise, He will give us the solutions we need.

It is good to remind yourself, when you kneel in prayer, of the wonderful things the Lord has done for you. That will cause a spontaneous song of praise to rise from your lips!

Faithful God, I recall all Your wonderful, faithful deeds and thereby find courage for the future.

Amen

Rejoice in the Lord!

Sing for joy to God our strength; shout aloud to the God of Jacob! Begin the music, strike the tambourine, play the melodious harp and lyre. Sound the ram's horn at the New Moon, and when the moon is full, on the day of our Feast.
— PSALM 81:1-3 —

How much joy do you show in your prayer life? When you begin your prayer time today, make an effort to, *"sing for joy to God."* Open a hymn book, or put on a CD of worship music and use it to set the mood for a time of real praise and worship to God. Any celebration, however big or small, makes use of music. Music and singing can express the thoughts and feelings of the heart in ways that few other things can.

That is why believers sing when they come together to worship God. In times of singing together, we remember how majestic God is, and the harmony of our singing tells the world of our gratitude and joy.

In Psalm 81, God's people are called to a time of worship and praise: every joyful song of praise is in itself a prayer! Try it and see how wonderful it is to begin your quiet times with songs of praise. They will bring new meaning to your prayers.

Almighty God, my song is to praise You only.

Amen

Praise God in His sanctuary!

Praise the LORD. Praise God in his sanctuary; praise him in his mighty heavens. Praise him for his acts of power; praise him for his surpassing greatness. Praise him with the sounding of the trumpet, praise him with the harp and lyre, praise him with tambourine and dancing, praise him with the strings and flute, praise him with the clash of cymbals, praise him with resounding cymbals. Let everything that has breath praise the LORD. Praise the LORD.

— PSALM 150:1-6 —

When we call out, *"Praise the Lord!"* in an attitude of prayer, it serves a two-fold purpose. It is an expression of our heartfelt praise for our living God. At the same time, it invites others to do the same. We praise God first of all for who He is: *"His surpassing greatness,"* and then for what He has done; *"His mighty deeds!"* We emphasize our praise and worship of God with music, *"with harp and lyre and tambourine."*

Nothing less than a choir of all the living creatures will be enough to truly sing His praise.

Today, think prayerfully about the depth and enthusiasm of your prayers. Compare your prayers with this unique song of praise and find your own words to praise your Redeemer in song.

Lord God of mercy and love, with all that is within me, I worship and praise Your holy Name.

Amen

The heavens declare His glory

The heavens declare the glory of God; the skies proclaim the work of his hands. Day after day they pour forth speech; night after night they display knowledge. There is no speech or language where their voice is not heard. Their voice goes out into all the earth, their words to the ends of the world. In the heavens he has pitched a tent for the sun, which is like a bridegroom coming forth from his pavilion, like a champion rejoicing to run his course.

— PSALM 19:1-5 —

This overview of creation reveals two aspects of the majesty of God: God is almighty and He alone reigns over everyone and everything. Before you continue with your prayer time today, meditate for a while on the wonders of creation around you. Then join your voice to the "language" of the heavens to bring praise and thanks to your Creator.

For David, the sun and the moon, the stars and the planets, were all evidence of the remarkable workmanship of God. He set everything in order and made all things work together. The heathen nations worshiped the sun, moon, and stars, but David saw the heavenly bodies as objects that brought glory to their Creator simply by doing what they were created to do.

If our ears were always attuned to the praise that creation offers to God, our own prayers would be filled with more praise.

Creator God, help me to testify to Your glory and might, just as creation does.

Amen

The Lord cares for us!

Sing joyfully to the LORD, you righteous; it is fitting for the upright to praise him. Praise the LORD with the harp; make music to him on the ten-stringed lyre. Sing to him a new song; play skillfully, and shout for joy. For the word of the LORD is right and true; he is faithful in all he does. The LORD loves righteousness and justice; the earth is full of his unfailing love.

– PSALM 33:1-5 –

There are few things in this life that we can be absolutely sure of. Change is an inevitable part of life. But God and His Word are eternally trustworthy and true and therefore worthy of our praise.

What does it mean to be faithful and true? We live in a society that regards all truth as relative. Many people have given up hope of finding the truth, or of being able to establish their life on it. But the Scriptures testify that there is something that is absolutely true. God and His Word will always be true.

It is this aspect of God's character that is glorified in this prayer. It encourages believers everywhere to joyfully praise, because their lives are safely founded on the rock of God's eternal truth.

May your prayers also bear witness to His truth!

Oh God, Your Word is the truth and can be trusted.

Amen

The Name of the Lord be praised!

Praise the LORD. Praise, O servants of the LORD, praise the name of the LORD. Let the name of the LORD be praised, both now and forevermore. From the rising of the sun to the place where it sets, the name of the LORD is to be praised.
— PSALM 113:1-3 —

Servants of the Lord, all those who have a relationship with Him, must praise the Lord in prayer. He is worthy of all our praise, which is why He must be worshiped always and everywhere. When you approach God in prayer today, first praise Him because He is God of the whole earth, for all time, and for all people. Meditate on the character of God and His purpose with creation, and praise His name!

The God whom we praise is indeed the Ruler of all the nations. He is the God of the poor and the rich, of all nations and all tribes. He is also the eternal God. He is worthy of our praise because He is *"exalted above all nations"* (v. 4) and His glory reaches to the heavens.

There is no one on earth or in the universe who can be compared to Him. Therefore, let us offer up to Him our enthusiastic praise!

Lord my God, Your glory cannot be described in the words of any earthly language!

Amen

You have upheld my cause!

I will be glad and rejoice in you; I will sing praise to your name, O Most High. My enemies turn back; they stumble and perish before you. For you have upheld my right and my cause; you have sat on your throne, judging righteously. You have rebuked the nations and destroyed the wicked; you have blotted out their name for ever and ever.

– PSALM 9:2-5 –

In the first part of this prayer, the poet boldly declares that he wants to testify to the salvation of God, he wants to be joyful and glad, and he wants to praise God in song. Rather than praying for God's wrath to fall on his enemies, he prays that God's justice will prevail and he leaves the matter in God's hands. If we truly believe that He is almighty, we can also leave our relationships with others in His capable hands.

We often fall into the temptation of complaining about the injustices of life. But we should rather place our trust in God. We should not torment ourselves about the meanness of our enemies or the ways in which we are treated unfairly.

We should rather concentrate on the might of God. How often our prayers are songs of lamentation instead of songs of praise about the greatness and majesty of our God!

Thank You, Lord God Almighty, that You are a God of justice.

Amen

Great is His love toward us!

Praise the LORD, all you nations; extol him, all you peoples. For great is his love toward us, and the faithfulness of the LORD endures forever. Praise the LORD.
— PSALM 117:1-2 —

Think of this for a moment: one day in heaven people of every nation, tribe, and tongue will bow before God in worship and sing His praise (see Rev. 7:9-10). Therefore we should already join with all of God's people across the earth and praise and worship Him.

The Lord is God over every nation, tongue, and tribe, and He is worthy of our praise. Even though Psalm 117 is the shortest chapter in the Bible, it is a simple prayer of praise and encouragement to the people to declare and praise the greatness of God to the uttermost ends of the earth. The Psalmist calls us to do this because He blesses us abundantly every day.

There are two things that the Psalmist says here: all nations and tribes are called to join in the anthem of praise. The second is the declaration that there is no end to the faithfulness of God – He can be trusted forever. How can we do anything else than cry out, *"Praise the Lord!"*

Holy God, I join my voice with all people, of all time, in all places to worship You.

Amen

God's shield of victory

He makes my feet like the feet of a deer; he enables me to stand on the heights. He trains my hands for battle; my arms can bend a bow of bronze. You give me your shield of victory, and your right hand sustains me; you stoop down to make me great. You broaden the path beneath me, so that my ankles do not turn. I pursued my enemies and overtook them; I did not turn back till they were destroyed.

– PSALM 18:33-37 –

David narrowly escaped the plans of Saul to have him killed, and he focused on his military skills: his skillfulness with the bow and his swiftness of foot in mountainous terrain. But David was a man of God and he openly praised God for his strength and ability. No earthly shield could protect him completely from the arrows of his enemies. Only God could surround him with His strength and strengthen him for the battle.

The same is true in the lives of every believer. Come let us bring prayers of praise to God for His protective love and His strength.

Without a doubt, God has supported you in the past when you were in trouble. Have you thanked Him for His support and have you presented all your problems to Him in prayer? Why not do so now?

Heavenly Father, Your right hand has protected me so many times. I thank and praise You for that.

Amen

Living hope and true faith!

Praise be to the God and Father of our Lord Jesus Christ! In his great mercy he has given us new birth into a living hope through the resurrection of Jesus Christ from the dead.

– 1 Peter 1:3 –

Let your anxious heart rejoice with the glorious expectations of all the riches and treasures that await you in heaven. Thank God for that and let this prayer help you to turn your thoughts away from all the burdens and worries of this world. Renew your mind with thoughts of the pure, unspoilt inheritance that is waiting for you – an inheritance that cannot be destroyed. That's worth praising about!

Prayer focuses our hearts on heaven, while our feet are firmly planted on the earth. Peter prays here for Christians who are facing brutal persecution, as well as the rejection of family and friends. Through his prayer he reminds them of the inheritance that is waiting for them in heaven, even though they are involved in such a bitter struggle here on earth.

Make sure that you have laid up treasures in heaven – otherwise your life, seen from the perspective of eternity, is worthless.

I thank and praise You, Holy God, for all the treasures that You have set aside for me in heaven.

Amen

FEBRUARY

PRAYERS OF WORSHIP

Yet a time is coming and has now come when the true worshipers will worship the Father in spirit and truth, for they are the kind of worshipers the Father seeks.

– JOHN 4:23 –

True worship should be offered in Spirit and in Truth. Truth has bearing on those things that truly please God. True worshipers will worship God in righteousness and purity. They will also worship in the Spirit. That speaks of the coming of the Holy Spirit into the lives of believers. The Spirit will lead believers into all truth (see Jn. 14:16, Jn. 16:13). Through the Holy Spirit, God is present in the lives of all true worshipers. God has indeed drawn near to believers. We do not need to seek God in temples or churches built by hand. We are no longer dependent on specific priests to approach God on our behalf. God came to us in the Person of Jesus Christ! Those who follow Jesus know God. Praise the Lord!

A*nd Mary said: "My soul glorifies the Lord and my spirit rejoices in God my Savior … From now on all generations will call me blessed, for the Mighty One has done great things for me – holy is his name. His mercy extends to those who fear him, from generation to generation. He has performed mighty deeds with his arm; he has scattered those who are proud in their inmost thoughts. He has brought down rulers from their thrones but has lifted up the humble. He has filled the hungry with good things but has sent the rich away empty."*

– LUKE 1:46-53 –

To Him be the glory!

Now to him who is able to do immeasurably more than all we ask or imagine, according to his power that is at work within us, to him be glory in the church and in Christ Jesus throughout all generations, for ever and ever! Amen.
— EPHESIANS 3:20-21 —

Notice that Paul builds this worship prayer around the word "more." His song of praise rises to a resounding ovation in honor of the Lord whom he loves and worships.

For Paul, God is not only "more" mighty, He also does "more." We pray for crumbs, and He presents us with an abundant feast. We pray for the strength to get through each day; He answers with eternity.

God answers our prayers with far "more" than we could ever dare to ask or hope for. That is why we worship Him!

Are your prayers of worship also notable for their use of the word "more"? More praise and worship than before? More faith and trust in the eternal and almighty God? Let the glory of God permeate and add meaning to your prayers of worship today.

Dear Lord, I worship You because You do far more than I could ever ask!

Amen

The Lord is strong and mighty!

Sing to the LORD with thanksgiving; make music to our God on the harp. He covers the sky with clouds; he supplies the earth with rain and makes grass grow on the hills. He provides food for the cattle and for the young ravens when they call. His pleasure is not in the strength of the horse, nor his delight in the legs of a man; the LORD delights in those who fear him, who put their hope in his unfailing love.

– PSALM 147:7-11 –

God is not impressed by the things that people consider highly valuable. People are inclined to regard material riches, power and prestige very highly, while God seeks for those people who trust and honor Him.

This psalm was written after the exiles had returned from Babylon. They were people who had learned the hard way that the highest calling in life is to worship God, delight in Him, and yield to Him.

The writer reminds us that the whole of creation is dependent on Him. He provides the rain. He makes the grass grow and makes sure the animals have sufficient food.

Thank God in your time of worship today for the provision He has made for your needs and acknowledge your deep dependence on Him, *"If that is how God clothes the grass of the field, which is here today, and tomorrow is thrown into the fire, how much more will he clothe you, O you of little faith!"* (Lk. 12:28).

Merciful God, I place my trust in Your never-ending love.

Amen

The Lamb that was slain!

And they sang a new song: "You are worthy to take the scroll and to open its seals, because you were slain, and with your blood you purchased men for God from every tribe and language and people and nation. You have made them to be a kingdom and priests to serve our God, and they will reign on the earth." Then I looked and heard the voice of many angels, numbering thousands upon thousands, and ten thousand times ten thousand. They encircled the throne and the living creatures and the elders. In a loud voice they sang: "Worthy is the Lamb, who was slain, to receive power and wealth and wisdom and strength and honor and glory and praise!"

– REVELATION 5:9-12 –

My deepest prayer is that you will be one of the multitude of people, described in this passage, who will worship and praise God forever. The Scriptures encourage Christians to continuously offer prayers of worship, praise and thanksgiving to God (see 1 Thes. 5:17-18).

We will miss out on an important aspect of our Christian lives if we do not worship with others. To be caught up in worship together with other believers, is the fulfillment of our calling to be worshipers.

When the Lord comes, His people will respond with a united song of praise and worship in which the Lord God and the Lamb will be glorified.

Eternal God, honor, glory and might belong to You alone.

Amen

The Lord reigns!

Ascribe to the LORD, O families of nations, ascribe to the LORD glory and strength. Ascribe to the LORD the glory due his name; bring an offering and come into his courts. Worship the LORD in the splendor of his holiness; tremble before him, all the earth. Say among the nations, "The LORD reigns." The world is firmly established, it cannot be moved; he will judge the peoples with equity.

— PSALM 96:7-10 —

Our typical response in the presence of powerful people is awe. How much more should we then come in holy respect and fear before the Almighty God of the whole universe! That is the center of all our worship.

Throughout the Scriptures we read of people, who, when they caught a glimpse of God's glory, fell prostrate before Him in worship. This prayer calls us to honor Him in all things. We do this through bringing Him offerings and worshiping Him openly and so bringing the good news that the Lord reigns to other people.

When you kneel in worship before the Lord today, think of the fact that He reigns over all the earth. Worship Him and express your wonder at His greatness and might. Ask Him to lead all people in all places to the knowledge that He rules as King.

Almighty God of Creation, You reign over the whole universe, but also in my heart and life.

Amen

Lord, God Almighty, who is like You?

For who in the skies above can compare with the Lord*? Who is like the* Lord *among the heavenly beings? In the council of the holy ones God is greatly feared; he is more awesome than all who surround him. O* Lord *God Almighty, who is like you? You are mighty, O* Lord*, and your faithfulness surrounds you. You rule over the surging sea; when its waves mount up, you still them.*

– PSALM 89:6-9 –

Imagine for a moment what it will be like to be part of the choirs of angels and worshipers who worship God without ceasing in heaven.

People have always been fascinated by angels. The thought of kindly spiritual beings watching over us is a comfort to many. But when the Scriptures describe the encounters of people with angels, they are usually shocked and awestruck.

Nonetheless, the glory and might of angels is but a shifting shadow compared to the glory and might of their Creator.

Angels also worship the Lord Almighty of Heaven. In this prayer of worship, the writer considers the throne room of God in heaven, where all the heavenly beings bow in awe before God. Let your time of worship today link with the worship of the angels.

Almighty God, let my praise join that of the choir of angels. There is none like You.

Amen

O Lord my God, You are very great!

Praise the LORD, O my soul. O LORD my God, you are very great; you are clothed with splendor and majesty. He wraps himself in light as with a garment; he stretches out the heavens like a tent and lays the beams of his upper chambers on their waters. He makes the clouds his chariot and rides on the wings of the wind. He makes winds his messengers, flames of fire his servants. He set the earth on its foundations; it can never be moved.

— PSALM 104:1-5 —

We are so often busy rushing feverishly from task to task, without ever becoming still to meditate on the greatness of God. But then every so often we are suddenly overwhelmed by the magnitude of His creation: a sudden clap of thunder, a field of sunflowers, a breathtaking sunset.

Then we are reminded of how worthy our God is, the One who created all these things. In the above prayer, nature and the wonders of creation are the starting point for the writer's worship. Why don't you follow his example?

Praise and worship God today for His strength and wisdom. Remind yourself of all the ways that you have witnessed His greatness in creation.

O Lord my God, how great You are!
Amen

Lord, You are more majestic than the mountains

You are resplendent with light, more majestic than mountains rich with game. Valiant men lie plundered, they sleep their last sleep; not one of the warriors can lift his hands. At your rebuke, O God of Jacob, both horse and chariot lie still. You alone are to be feared. Who can stand before you when you are angry? From heaven you pronounced judgment, and the land feared and was quiet – when you, O God, rose up to judge, to save all the afflicted of the land.

— Psalm 76:4-9 —

Anyone who has spent time in the mountains develops an admiration for the power of nature. We sometimes feel so small and unworthy in the presence of magnificent rock formations. God created the mountains in this way so that we could catch just a glimpse of His glory. This prayer of worship asks, *"You alone are to be feared. Who can stand before You?"* If the whole of creation falls silent in fear and trembling before the Lord, how much more should we worship Him with awe and holy reverence? We do not want to be counted as one of His enemies when He comes to judge the world!

Worship the Almighty God for His power and strength. Give God the honor and the glory that are due to Him. Today, esteem the Lord through offering your time and possessions to Him. He is after all the awesome King of kings!

O God, You are more wonderful and more mighty than the mountains in all their majesty. I worship You as the King of my heart.

Amen

May His name be exalted forever!

May his name endure forever; may it continue as long as the sun. All nations will be blessed through him, and they will call him blessed. Praise be to the LORD God, the God of Israel, who alone does marvelous deeds. Praise be to his glorious name forever; may the whole earth be filled with his glory. Amen.

– PSALM 72:17-19 –

The word "bless" is usually a part of our vocabulary of prayer when we plead with God to bless us or others. But what Solomon is actually doing here is calling on his fellow worshipers to bless God. He means that they should glorify God and worship Him for everything that He has done. He praised the God of Israel because *"He alone does mighty deeds"*.

That is the essence of the prayer of Solomon, in which he asks God to bless his people and his government. He has received so much from the hand of God that he wants to worship and praise Him. Each of us has so very much for which we can worship, praise and thank God.

When you, during your times of worship, ask God to bless you and your family, make sure that you have glorified and worshiped Him sufficiently for His support in the past.

God of mercy and love, I praise and worship You for all the wonderful deeds You have done for me and those close to me.

Amen

The Lord our God is Holy!

The LORD reigns, let the nations tremble; he sits enthroned between the cherubim, let the earth shake. Great is the LORD in Zion; he is exalted over all the nations. Let them praise your great and awesome name – he is holy. The King is mighty, he loves justice – you have established equity; in Jacob you have done what is just and right. Exalt the LORD our God and worship at his footstool; he is holy.

– PSALM 99:1-5 –

Every worshiper should delight in being a servant of the great King of all kings. But far too often we want to place ourselves on the throne and enforce our own will. Follow the example of the Psalmist today and bow low in worship before the King of all kings!

The Lord reigns! The Psalmist's heart breaks out in thankful worship before God's righteous rule.

The people of Israel knew through experience what it meant to be under the yoke of unrighteous and imperfect kings. When law and order break down, anarchy, fear and terrorism reign in a land. But God's reign brings righteousness, peace, and life for all. Praise the Lord. Worship His holy name!

Lord my God, I bow before You as the only King in heaven and on earth.

Amen

I call to God and He hears my voice!

He said: The LORD is my rock, my fortress and my deliverer; my God is my rock, in whom I take refuge, my shield and the horn of my salvation. He is my stronghold, my refuge and my savior – from violent men you save me. I call to the LORD, who is worthy of praise, and I am saved from my enemies. The waves of death swirled about me; the torrents of destruction overwhelmed me. The cords of the grave coiled around me; the snares of death confronted me. In my distress I called to the LORD; I called out to my God. From his temple he heard my voice; my cry came to his ears.

– 2 SAMUEL 22:2-7 –

When God delivers us out of desperate situations, we should remember to come quietly before Him for a while and thank Him for what He has done.

There is no greater feeling than arriving home safely after a dangerous journey. We like to tell others about our adventures, but we often forget to worship God with prayers of praise for granting us safe passage.

When David was able to relax in complete safety, he still remembered to thank God for delivering him from King Saul. He acknowledges that it was God and not his own military ingenuity that saved him.

How many evils does God protect us from daily? How can we then forget to thank Him in prayerful worship?

I worship You, Lord my God, because You have saved me from so much evil.

Amen

I stand in awe!

LORD, I have heard of your fame; I stand in awe of your deeds, O LORD. Renew them in our day, in our time make them known; in wrath remember mercy.
– HABAKKUK 3:2 –

In the times of your greatest difficulty, your prayers should always begin and end with praise and worship to the God who is worthy of all praise and thanksgiving. Habakkuk was a prophet of God in a time of desperate need: when God's people were staring humiliation and defeat in the face and it seemed that evil had overcome good.

But Habakkuk was not discouraged by these events. He reminded himself of how mighty God is and encouraged himself by thinking of the awesome deeds that God had done in the past. God's wrath toward His people is justified, but he also knows that God can save His people. God is merciful. Therefore he pleads with God by worshiping His greatness.

It would be good if individuals and nations were to take this into consideration in their prayers today.

Almighty God, I am filled with awe when I think of Your almighty deeds.
Amen

I will proclaim the name of the Lord!

Listen, O heavens, and I will speak; hear, O earth, the words of my mouth. Let my teaching fall like rain and my words descend like dew, like showers on new grass, like abundant rain on tender plants. I will proclaim the name of the LORD. Oh, praise the greatness of our God! He is the Rock, his works are perfect, and all his ways are just. A faithful God who does no wrong, upright and just is he.

– DEUTERONOMY 32:1-4 –

The theme of this prayer is that God is perfect and is worthy of our worship. No person, no matter how morally upright his life, can achieve perfection. But everything that God does is righteous and just.

If we believe this, we need to adjust our perspective on the trials and tests of life. From our imperfect standpoint, we cannot always understand why certain things happen to us and what purpose they have in our lives.

But in such troubling times, we especially need to remind ourselves that God cannot make any mistakes or do anything wrong. He is perfect, faithful, righteous, and just. Therefore, you can with thousands of other faithful believers through the centuries, join in the prayer of Moses.

Praise and worship our perfect and holy God and "proclaim the name of the Lord."

We worship and proclaim Your name, merciful God. Everything that You do is perfect and just.

Amen

I love the house where You live

I wash my hands in innocence, and go about your altar, O LORD, proclaiming aloud your praise and telling of all your wonderful deeds. I love the house where you live, O LORD, the place where your glory dwells.

– PSALM 26:6-8 –

Far too often we approach worship on Sundays with little enthusiasm. In this prayer of worship, David finds many reasons to be joyful in the sanctuary of the Lord. He describes what he did in the tabernacle.

After he had washed his hands and his heart before God, he approached the altar. There he sang songs of worship and thanksgiving and testified before other worshipers of God's wonderful deeds. He loved to join together with the people of God and to worship the God of the universe with them.

David could think of no place he would rather be than in the presence of God, praising Him for all that He had done for him.

Let David's prayer inspire us to renew our covenant with God and with fellow-believers.

I love the house where You live, Lord, for there I can tell others of Your wonderful deeds, and worship You with a sincere heart.

Amen

I rejoice in the Lord!

The LORD brings death and makes alive; he brings down to the grave and raises up. The LORD sends poverty and wealth; he humbles and he exalts. He raises the poor from the dust and lifts the needy from the ash heap; he seats them with princes and has them inherit a throne of honor. For the foundations of the earth are the LORD's; upon them he has set the world.

– 1 SAMUEL 2:6-8 –

When difficult situations and circumstances come their way, some people become bitter and say blasphemous things. Others, though, turn to prayer and worship. Rather be like Hannah and talk to the Lord about your problems. It would have been very easy for her to use the birth of Samuel as a weapon of personal triumph and pride. She could so easily have been vindictive and smug toward Peninnah. Not only did Hannah now have a son, but also the love of the husband that they shared.

But instead of revenge against Peninnah, under whose scorn she had suffered for many years, she offered her thanks to God in worship because He had heard and answered her prayer. In His love and mercy He raised her up out of her misery.

It is a great mercy to be able to forget your own misery and bow in worship before God.

Lord, and Father God, I praise You that You have shown me great mercy before so many others and have lifted me up.

Amen

Praise the Lord!

Who is like the LORD our God, the One who sits enthroned on high, who stoops down to look on the heavens and the earth? He raises the poor from the dust and lifts the needy from the ash heap; he seats them with princes, with the princes of their people. He settles the barren woman in her home as a happy mother of children. Praise the LORD.

— PSALM 113:5-9 —

It is impossible to compare anything to the Lord. Comparisons can only be made between things in the same category. It would be silly to try to compare the speed of a marathon runner with the speed of an ice-skater because they compete in completely different kinds of races. We find that the same applies when it comes to God: there is no one strong, wise, or loving enough to be compared to Him.

We can only celebrate His glory and uniqueness through testifying to what He has done for us personally. He raised the needy up out of their poverty; He gave children to the barren. Who else can do such things? We can only cry out in worship, *"Praise the Lord!"*

Consider all the times and ways in which He has worked in your life and in the lives of others. Worship Him in spirit and in truth for His love and concern for you.

Merciful God, You are incomparable in mercy and love. Your might knows no limits and Your wisdom is above our understanding. Praise the Lord!

Amen

Hosanna in the highest

A very large crowd spread their cloaks on the road, while others cut branches from the trees and spread them on the road. The crowds that went ahead of him and those that followed shouted, "Hosanna to the Son of David!" "Blessed is he who comes in the name of the Lord!" "Hosanna in the highest!"

— MATTHEW 21:8-9 —

Make your times of worship a celebration of the glory of God and of His Son, Jesus Christ.

Use the words of the people of Jerusalem to glorify Jesus. The Jews had gathered to celebrate the Passover Feast, and they understood what it meant to glorify the One who had delivered them.

Every year they came to the temple in Jerusalem to commemorate their deliverance from slavery in Egypt. During these times they would sing Psalms 113-118 as praise songs to their Deliverer. Therefore it was completely natural for them to praise Jesus with the words of these psalms (see Ps. 118:26).

Why should they not have enthusiastically welcomed Jesus, who came in the name of the Lord? Let us too worship Him with the same enthusiasm and excitement!

Father God, I worship You because You sent Your Son to set me free from slavery to sin.

Amen

Praise and glory, wisdom and honor to God

All the angels were standing around the throne and around the elders and the four living creatures. They fell down on their faces before the throne and worshiped God, saying: "Amen! Praise and glory and wisdom and thanks and honor and power and strength be to our God for ever and ever. Amen!"

— REVELATION 7:11-12 —

This excerpt gives us a quick glimpse into God's throne room in heaven. In the apostle John's vision he sees both the believers and the awe-inspiring heavenly beings as they bow before the throne of God and praise and worship Him for everything that He has done. Such deep reverence for God contrasts greatly with the easy familiarity with which we often approach God. We need to remember who it is we speak to when we worship.

When we come before God in prayer we would do well to remember that He is the ruler of the universe. How can we be forward with the Holy One? We should remove our shoes, for the place where we stand is holy ground.

The angelic beings in Revelation express their humility and honor for God by prostrating themselves before Him. Join them today by offering your deepest worship to Your Creator.

Holy God, I come before You with reverence and humility because You are the King of the universe.

Amen

His name alone is exalted!

Praise the LORD from the earth, you great sea creatures and all ocean depths, lightning and hail, snow and clouds, stormy winds that do his bidding, you mountains and all hills, fruit trees and all cedars, wild animals and all cattle, small creatures and flying birds, kings of the earth and all nations, you princes and all rulers on earth, young men and maidens, old men and children. Let them praise the name of the LORD, for his name alone is exalted; his splendor is above the earth and the heavens.

— PSALM 148:7-13 —

We are given the opportunity here to consider the infinite diversity of the creation of God, and to bow in worship and adoration before the Creator. People these days are able to go to the bottom of the oceans or through undiscovered jungles and there they discover many species of animals previously unknown. Spending time meditating on how God rules all the magnificent diversity of creation should lead us to heartfelt worship.

This prayer calls all of God's creation to worship Him and to declare His praise. It encourages the mighty elements of nature – wind, snow, hail, and fire – to add their voices to the choir. No human choir is able to surpass the combined praise of God's creation.

All people, old and young, big and small, must worship the Creator. He created each one of us and sustains us in His love.

Holy God, I join with all of creation to sing Your praises and to worship You.

Amen

By Your will all things were created

Whenever the living creatures give glory, honor and thanks to him who sits on the throne and who lives for ever and ever, the twenty-four elders fall down before him who sits on the throne, and worship him who lives for ever and ever. They lay their crowns before the throne and say: "You are worthy, our Lord and God, to receive glory and honor and power, for you created all things, and by your will they were created and have their being."

— REVELATION 4:9-11 —

Some people are privileged enough to be able to examine the luxuries of a king's palace, but nobody is able to imagine exactly what God's throne room looks like. Revelation gives us a glimpse into it: a throne of glittering gem stones, a sea of crystal glass; and a glow like that of a rainbow that fills the whole palace.

In spite of all this, the central focus of the throne room of God is the worship of His people. Angelic beings, elders, and exotic living creatures combine their voices in eternal and continuous songs of worship and praise that glorify God and declare that all of creation was made for His honor and glory.

If creation exists to honor God, our part is clear. We must give to God the worship that is due to Him. Let your voice be heard with the heavenly multitudes in worship and praise to the Creator.

Creator God, You are worthy to receive our glory and praise because You created all things.

Amen

The Lord will provide!

By the word of the LORD were the heavens made, their starry host by the breath of his mouth. He gathers the waters of the sea into jars; he puts the deep into storehouses. Let all the earth fear the LORD; let all the people of the world revere him. For he spoke, and it came to be; he commanded, and it stood firm.

– PSALM 33:6-9 –

As a point of departure for your prayers today, focus on a particular element of creation that has deeply impressed you. Worship and praise God for it: an enthralling sunrise, a snow-capped mountain peak, undulating wheat fields.

Can you remember when you last consciously admired nature? The resplendence of the starry heavens, the ocean that crashes against the rocks, the majestic mountains with their steadfast immovability! All reasons to worship the God of Creation.

He spoke but a word, and creation came into existence. And He sustains it all day by day. How small and worthless we feel before all this, how we are compelled to worship God!

Come let us kneel in worship before Him!

I praise and thank You, Creator God, that You not only created all things, but that You provide for all things daily.

Amen

From everlasting to everlasting You are God

LORD, you have been our dwelling place throughout all generations. Before the mountains were born or you brought forth the earth and the world, from everlasting to everlasting you are God. You turn men back to dust, saying, "Return to dust, O sons of men." For a thousand years in your sight are like a day that has just gone by, or like a watch in the night. You sweep men away in the sleep of death; they are like the new grass of the morning.

— PSALM 90:1-5 —

We never seem to have enough time to do all that we want to do. We often hear the words, "Where did the time go?" Minutes, days, weeks, and years slip by unnoticed.

In this prayer of worship, Moses meditates on the brevity of life. He praises God because for Him a thousand years are but as a day. God is not limited by time in the ways that we are. He is never hasty or agitated. He is without beginning and end, for He is the one who created time.

When you become acutely aware of your own limitations, seek for peace in the Lord. Submit each moment of your life to His care and allow Him to bring an eternal meaning to your temporal efforts. Worship Him as the Timeless and Eternal God!

Eternal God, teach me to number my days so that I can live with wisdom.

Amen

Who is a God like You?

Shepherd your people with your staff, the flock of your inheritance, which lives by itself in a forest, in fertile pasturelands. Let them feed in Bashan and Gilead as in days long ago. Who is a God like you, who pardons sin and forgives the transgression of the remnant of his inheritance? You do not stay angry forever but delight to show mercy. You will again have compassion on us; you will tread our sins underfoot and hurl all our iniquities into the depths of the sea.

— MICAH 7:14, 18-19 —

Micah, as a prophet called to the people of Judah, often spoke *to* God about the people and *for* God to the people. He knew how much God hates sin and so he could warn the people in no uncertain terms about the coming judgment of God.

At the same time he was also well acquainted with God's compassionate and merciful heart. Even though God would be justified in wiping out the whole nation, He did not stop extending forgiveness to those who repented of their sins. He cast the sins of His people into the depths of the sea.

We are still able to approach and worship this same God. He longs to forgive those who turn away from their sinful ways.

Merciful God, through Your compassion and mercy, I have been restored to favor with You through the forgiveness of sins.

Amen

The Lord is with me, I will not be afraid!

Give thanks to the LORD, for he is good; his love endures forever. Let Israel say: "His love endures forever." Let the house of Aaron say: "His love endures forever." Let those who fear the LORD say: "His love endures forever." In my anguish I cried to the LORD, and he answered by setting me free. The LORD is with me; I will not be afraid. What can man do to me?

– PSALM 118:1-6 –

What qualities do we look for in our friends? Faithfulness, trustworthiness and integrity: faithfulness when things go wrong, trustworthiness when we need to depend on them, and integrity in all circumstances.

This worship prayer declares that all these qualities are found perfectly in God. He came and saved us when we were caught in the claws of sin and could do nothing to help ourselves.

Such faithful love is something to celebrate and worship the Creator for, because His love endures forever.

Worship and praise God for His faithfulness. Meditate on the many ways in which God, in His love, has blessed you and your loved ones. Thank Him and worship Him with songs of praise.

Lord my God, Your faithful love sets me free and gives me joy!

Amen

Heavenly worship for the Lamb!

After this I looked and there before me was a great multitude that no one could count, from every nation, tribe, people and language, standing before the throne and in front of the Lamb. They were wearing white robes and were holding palm branches in their hands. And they cried out in a loud voice: "Salvation belongs to our God, who sits on the throne, and to the Lamb."

– REVELATION 7:9-10 –

Our prayers often focus on this life and the battles that we are engaged in here and now. But our worship should also concentrate on the wonderful victory that Christ shares with us.

In Revelation, God gives us a glorious picture of that final victory. John sees an unbelievable scene: A multitude of people who worship the Lamb of God in joyful celebration. They wave palm branches, a traditional symbol of victory. People from across the whole world worship God and praise Him for the redemption that He has wrought through His Son.

As followers of Christ, we are part of this triumphal procession through the ages. Through the death of Christ, a new life was made possible for us. We can praise God for this and worship the Lamb with all that is within us!

Lamb of God, thank You that I too can be part of Your triumphal procession through the ages.

Amen

His faithfulness endures forever!

Praise the LORD. I will extol the LORD with all my heart in the council of the upright and in the assembly. Great are the works of the LORD; they are pondered by all who delight in them. Glorious and majestic are his deeds, and his righteousness endures forever. He has caused his wonders to be remembered; the LORD is gracious and compassionate. He provides food for those who fear him; he remembers his covenant forever.

– PSALM 111:1-5 –

It is human for our thoughts to dwell on the unpleasant experiences of our lives. We ponder on them and try to make sense of them. But the Psalmist encourages us to rather worship God for His wonderful deeds.

The worship that we offer in the privacy of our inner rooms should also be expressed openly in public. Other believers should be encouraged through our testimony of the goodness of God toward us. God feeds us, He keeps His covenant with us, He demonstrates His love and power through the infinite gifts of grace He gives us. Truly we can rejoice: "His deeds are full of glory and majesty! His faithfulness endures forever!"

Let your voice be joined to those of the countless throngs who sing this song of worship. Let this be your prayer both in private devotions and when you pray with other believers.

Lord, Your deeds are awesome! Your acts of mercy will never be forgotten.

Amen

Holy! Holy! Holy!

Each of the four living creatures had six wings and was covered with eyes all around, even under his wings. Day and night they never stop saying: "Holy, holy, holy is the Lord God Almighty, who was, and is, and is to come."

— REVELATION 4:8 —

Be still and listen with your heart. Can you hear it: the worship of the heavenly choir resonates across the borders of time itself: *"Holy, Holy, Holy!"* This song of worship was first heard by the prophet Isaiah. He heard the throngs of angels around the throne of God singing this song (see Is. 6).

Hundreds of years later, while John was in exile on the Isle of Patmos, God also allowed him to hear the angel choir singing, *"Holy, holy, holy is the Lord God Almighty!"*

When the insignificant things of life get you down, and when life seems to be meaningless, listen to this refrain from heaven, *"Holy, holy, holy is the Lord God Almighty!"* The song of worship never ceases.

Join the heavenly choir today as they honor and worship God, because He is holy!

You are holy, Lord my God, You are the Almighty who was and is and is to come.

Amen

Worship the Lord with gladness!

Shout for joy to the LORD, all the earth. Worship the LORD with gladness; come before him with joyful songs. Know that the LORD is God. It is he who made us, and we are his; we are his people, the sheep of his pasture. Enter his gates with thanksgiving and his courts with praise; give thanks to him and praise his name. For the LORD is good and his love endures forever; his faithfulness continues through all generations.

— PSALM 100:1-5 —

Imagine that you are one of the singing crowd surging toward the gates of the temple on the way to worship God. You get caught up in the excitement and carried along with the words: *"Enter His gates with thanksgiving!"*

This is a call to worship that helps people to focus their hearts and thoughts on God and to meditate on all the good gifts He has given to us. It helped to create the right attitude in the people's hearts for when worship really began.

Let the words of this worship prayer help you to focus your thoughts and your heart on the goodness of God toward you. Come before Him with thanks and praise on your lips.

Ever-loving Lord, I come into Your presence with thanksgiving and praise.

Amen

Your name is the Lord Almighty!

"Ah, Sovereign Lord, you have made the heavens and the earth by your great power and outstretched arm. Nothing is too hard for you. You show love to thousands but bring the punishment for the fathers' sins into the laps of their children after them. O great and powerful God, whose name is the Lord Almighty, great are your purposes and mighty are your deeds. Your eyes are open to all the ways of men; you reward everyone according to his conduct and as his deeds deserve."

— Jeremiah 32:17-19 —

If you have looked at your situation from every angle, and weighed up all the possibilities, and still feel that it is hopeless, then it is likely that you have made the mistake of leaving God out of your reckoning. Even if your current position is hopeless, and it poses a challenge to your ability to trust God, you should once again place your hope in God. You will be rewarded in inconceivable ways.

Just before the Israelites were taken into exile by the Babylonians, God instructed Jeremiah to buy a piece of land. In that way God guaranteed that they would return. God is faithful and He will never leave you at a loose end. Let us always bear in mind the words of worship spoken by Jeremiah: *"Nothing is too hard for You!"* Worship and trust God in all circumstances – He will take care of your future!

Beloved Lord, nothing is impossible for You;
You name is the Almighty Lord! And that
is why we worship You.

Amen

When You hear, forgive

Yet give attention to your servant's prayer and his plea for mercy, O LORD my God. Hear the cry and the prayer that your servant is praying in your presence this day. May your eyes be open toward this temple night and day, this place of which you said, 'My Name shall be there,' so that you will hear the prayer your servant prays toward this place. Hear the supplication of your servant and of your people Israel when they pray toward this place. Hear from heaven, your dwelling place, and when you hear, forgive.

– 1 KINGS 8:28-30 –

We each have places in our lives that remind us of the presence of God. When Solomon stood before the magnificent and splendid temple in Jerusalem, he realized how foolish it is for man to equate a building of wood and stone with God.

Solomon knew his temple was really an insignificant offering to God, the One who cannot be contained in the whole universe! Solomon also realized that setting a place aside for worship does not mean that God is confined to that place.

Places of worship are only reminders and symbols of our relationship with God. Church buildings cannot grant us forgiveness or bring us into the right relationship with God – it is the God whom we meet there who forgives us! Make sure that your worship is always directed to God.

Merciful God, hear my prayer, and forgive my sins.

Amen

MARCH

PRAYERS OF REPENTANCE AND FORGIVENESS

Sin is an awful reality in human existence. Paul laments his sinfulness in Romans 7:21: *"So I find this law at work: When I want to do good, evil is right there with me."* But forgiveness is a wonderful reality too. Paul groans under the weight of his sins: *"What a wretched man I am! Who will rescue me from this body of death?"* (Rom. 7:24). And then he rejoices in his forgiveness through Jesus Christ: *"Therefore, there is now no condemnation for those who are in Christ Jesus, because through Christ Jesus the law of the Spirit of life set me free from the law of sin and death"* (Rom. 8:1-2). This month, our prayers from the Bible will concentrate on repentance and forgiveness.

Wash *away all my iniquity and cleanse me from my sin. For I know my transgressions, and my sin is always before me. Against you, you only, have I sinned and done what is evil in your sight, so that you are proved right when you speak and justified when you judge. Restore to me the joy of your salvation*

and grant me a willing spirit, to sustain me. Then I will teach transgressors your ways, and sinners will turn back to you. Save me from bloodguilt, O God, the God who saves me, and my tongue will sing of your righteousness.

— PSALM 51:2-4, 12-14 —

You forgave the guilt of my sin

When I kept silent, my bones wasted away through my groaning all day long. For day and night your hand was heavy upon me; my strength was sapped as in the heat of summer. Then I acknowledged my sin to you and did not cover up my iniquity. I said, "I will confess my transgressions to the LORD" – and you forgave the guilt of my sin.

– PSALM 32:3-5 –

David discovered the freedom there is in confessing sin. We find many ways to avoid confessing our sins: we rationalize our sinfulness, we try to reason sin away by giving it euphemistic names (a weakness, a psychological aberration), but we never use the word "sin." And by doing this, our prayer life becomes weak and loses its impact.

David was intimately aware of the multitude of ways in which we hide our sins. He exhausted himself trying to cover up his sins! But everything changed as soon as he stopped trying to run away from the consequences of his sins.

He admits, *"Then I confessed my sin!"* And he adds, with new-found joy, *"You forgave my sin!"*

Why don't you confess your hidden sins to God right now and enjoy the freedom it brings?

Merciful God, I want to confess my sins to You and so live freely and enjoy a powerful prayer life.

Amen

Grace has come to us!

O my God, I am too ashamed and disgraced to lift up my face to you, my God, because our sins are higher than our heads and our guilt has reached to the heavens. From the days of our forefathers until now, our guilt has been great. Because of our sins, we and our kings and our priests have been subjected to the sword and captivity, to pillage and humiliation at the hand of foreign kings, as it is today. But now, for a brief moment, the LORD our God has been gracious in leaving us a remnant and giving us a firm place in his sanctuary, and so our God gives light to our eyes and a little relief in our bondage.

– EZRA 9:6-8 –

To confess guilt is often embarrassing and uncomfortable for us. It is in times like these that we should remember that God is compassionate and full of mercy and that He longs to forgive those who draw near to Him in humility and awareness of their sin.

Even though the sins of the Israelites were piled high, God was still merciful. He allowed a remnant to survive the exile in Babylon and return to Jerusalem. But the remnant in Israel did not seem to have learned their lesson. They were immediately disobedient to God.

It was a great embarrassment to the prophet Ezra to have to approach God on their behalf. But the merciful God listened, and once again heard their confession and forgave them!

Holy God, I am ashamed of my sins, but I know that You will never leave me. The riches of Your grace are available to me if I confess my sins.

Amen

My family and I have sinned!

Then I said: "O LORD, God of heaven, the great and awesome God, who keeps his covenant of love with those who love him and obey his commands, let your ear be attentive and your eyes open to hear the prayer your servant is praying before you day and night for your servants, the people of Israel. I confess the sins we Israelites, including myself and my father's house, have committed against you. We have acted very wickedly toward you. We have not obeyed the commands, decrees and laws you gave your servant Moses. Remember the instruction you gave your servant Moses, saying, 'If you are unfaithful, I will scatter you among the nations, but if you return to me and obey my commands, then even if your exiled people are at the farthest horizon, I will gather them from there and bring them to the place I have chosen as a dwelling for my Name.'"

– NEHEMIAH 1:5-9 –

When Nehemiah heard how his own people were suffering in the desolate province of Judea, he grieved, he mourned, he fasted, and he prayed.

He knew that unconfessed sins are a stumbling block in the way of prayers rising to God. Only after he had confessed his own, his family's and his nation's sins, did he ask God to give him favor with the king. God answered Nehemiah's prayer. He moved the king's heart to send Nehemiah back to Jerusalem and to rebuild the walls of the destroyed city.

Are you concerned about the spiritual condition in our own country? First confess your own sins and those of your people before God, and then ask God to intervene in the land.

Merciful God, I confess my own sins to You and plead for the welfare of our people.

Amen

Joy in God's Comfort

May God arise, may his enemies be scattered; may his foes flee before him. As smoke is blown away by the wind, may you blow them away; as wax melts before the fire, may the wicked perish before God. But may the righteous be glad and rejoice before God; may they be happy and joyful. Sing to God, sing praise to his name, extol him who rides on the clouds – his name is the LORD – and rejoice before him.

– PSALM 68:1-4 –

Far too often we approach our times of prayer with hesitation or reluctance. It is almost as if we want to say, "Not again! I am too busy to find time for God." As the above mentioned prayer shows, David nurtured an attitude of joy when he came before God in prayer. He understood what a great privilege it is to talk to the Almighty God.

He knew that his enemies wouldn't even be able to stand in the presence of God. Although David was overwhelmed at the power of God, he was filled with joy because he was allowed to enter into the presence of God. He saw himself as one of God's dedicated children.

When you enter into the realm of prayer, thank God abundantly for the privilege of speaking to Him and having Him listen to you.

Almighty and loving God and Father, I am filled with joy in Your presence. Thank You for listening and talking to me.

Amen

Our hope is in You

O LORD, we acknowledge our wickedness and the guilt of our fathers; we have indeed sinned against you. For the sake of your name do not despise us; do not dishonor your glorious throne. Remember your covenant with us and do not break it. Do any of the worthless idols of the nations bring rain? Do the skies themselves send down showers? No, it is you, O LORD our God. Therefore our hope is in you, for you are the one who does all this.

— JEREMIAH 14:20-22 —

If you experience pain and adversity as a result of sin, then follow the example of Jeremiah and surrender yourself to the mercy of God. When Jeremiah prayed for the welfare of Judah, he first confessed their sins. Sin brings inevitable pain and suffering.

Often when Jesus healed someone from a physical condition, He first addressed the sick person's sinfulness. When the friends of the paralyzed man lowered him through the roof of the house where Jesus was preaching, He said, *"Your sins are forgiven you"* (Lk. 5:20).

Jeremiah confessed the sins of his people in an attitude of utter helplessness and dependence on God. His only hope was the One true God and that was why he was prepared to wait for the Lord to take action. If you are suffering as the result of sin, do as Jeremiah did, and take comfort in the grace of God.

Holy God, I confess my sins, with deep remorse, and know that You will not cast me away.

Amen

Help me, for You are faithful

O LORD, do not rebuke me in your anger or discipline me in your wrath. Be merciful to me, LORD, for I am faint; O LORD, heal me, for my bones are in agony. My soul is in anguish. How long, O LORD, how long? Turn, O LORD, and deliver me; save me because of your unfailing love.

— PSALM 6:1-4 —

When you find yourself in a pickle through your own foolishness, follow David's example and pour your heart out in prayer before God.

Just like children, we often find ourselves in difficult situations from which it is difficult to extricate ourselves. We know that our predicament is the result of our own sin and foolishness. Holy wrath is the natural reaction we could expect from our Heavenly Father.

In David's prayer of confession, he found himself in such a situation. But he also knew that God was the only one to whom he could turn for mercy and that is why he was able to pray so openly to God.

God is just, merciful and loving. He does discipline us, but He also offers us forgiveness.

Loving God, be merciful to me because I have sinned and I need Your forgiveness.

Amen

We have sinned and we are guilty

When they sin against you – for there is no one who does not sin – and you become angry with them and give them over to the enemy, who takes them captive to a land far away or near; and if they have a change of heart in the land where they are held captive, and repent and plead with you in the land of their captivity and say, "We have sinned, we have done wrong and acted wickedly"; and if they turn back to you with all their heart and soul; then from heaven, your dwelling place, hear their prayer and their pleas, and uphold their cause. And forgive your people, who have sinned against you.

– 2 CHRONICLES 6:36-39 –

If we are truly honest with ourselves, we will realize that, in spite of our most noble intentions, we are still disobedient to the Lord. We should pray like Solomon that we would truly grieve over our sinfulness and repent and turn to God so that He can forgive us.

Solomon was given the great honor of being allowed to build the temple where Almighty God could be worshiped. His prayer to God during the consecration of the temple is an indication of his wisdom and insight.

He anticipates the day when God will need to discipline His people because of their persistent sinfulness. But he also realizes that their exile to a foreign land could bring them to their senses. He pleads with God to hear their prayers when that happens and to forgive them.

God of mercy, hear my prayer of remorse when I have sinned, and be merciful to me.

Amen

Your judgment is righteous

Have mercy on me, O God, according to your unfailing love; according to your great compassion blot out my transgressions. Wash away all my iniquity and cleanse me from my sin. For I know my transgressions, and my sin is always before me. Against you, you only, have I sinned and done what is evil in your sight, so that you are proved right when you speak and justified when you judge.

– PSALM 51:1-4 –

When you become aware that the Holy Spirit is convicting you of sin, your first concern should be the disruption it brings to your relationship with God. Accept the judgment of God, as David accepted it, and surrender yourself to His grace. He is the only one who can purify and cleanse you.

Sometimes prayers for forgiveness of sins seem so inadequate. Our sins seem to us like ugly stains. When the prophet Nathan confronted David with the fact of his adultery with Bathsheba and the murder of her husband, David was deeply conscious of his sin. In spite of the injustices that he had brought against others, his greatest concern was the effect his sin would have on his relationship with God.

Let us listen to our conscience, to the voice of the Holy Spirit and cast ourselves on the mercy of God. He forgives us in His mercy and love if we truly repent and confess our sins.

Lord, my God, cleanse me from my sin. You know the depths of my heart's wrongdoing. Be merciful to me in Your great love.

Amen

I dedicate myself to You again

Restore to me the joy of your salvation and grant me a willing spirit, to sustain me. Then I will teach transgressors your ways, and sinners will turn back to you. Save me from bloodguilt, O God, the God who saves me, and my tongue will sing of your righteousness.

— PSALM 51:12-14 —

The prophet Nathan exposed a swamp of selfishness, hypocrisy, betrayal, lies, and murder. In that moment of piercing self-examination, David saw the sinfulness of his own heart. Rather than withdrawing into a cocoon of self-pity, he turned to God in repentant prayer.

At this point in his prayer, David moved from ruthless self-examination to hopeful meditation. He considers his sins, but also God's grace. He knew that his healing from guilt did not lie in decisions of his own will to make things right.

David knew that his only way out was through God, that He alone could cleanse him from his sin and sort out the mess he had made in his life.

Perhaps, just like David, you urgently need to ask God to examine your heart. Whatever the condition of your heart, God is the only doctor with a reliable cure for all your shortcomings.

Create in me a clean heart, O God.

Amen

But You, O Lord, show mercy to us

I prayed to the LORD my God and confessed: "O Lord, the great and awesome God, who keeps his covenant of love with all who love him and obey his commands, we have sinned and done wrong. We have been wicked and have rebelled; we have turned away from your commands and laws. Lord, you are righteous, but this day we are covered with shame – the men of Judah and people of Jerusalem and all Israel, both near and far, in all the countries where you have scattered us because of our unfaithfulness to you. The Lord our God is merciful and forgiving, even though we have rebelled against him."

– DANIEL 9:4-5, 7, 9 –

If we pay careful attention when we read the Word of God, our consciences will be affected by what we read. At times we will be moved to sing songs of praise, while at other times we will grieve over our sins and repent because of what we read. Like Daniel, we will discover how great and awesome God is, but also how merciful and compassionate He is toward those who turn to Him in repentance.

When Daniel prayed this prayer, he had already lived a rich and full life. And now his days were filled with unusual visions of God's plans for the world. When he read the prophecies of Jeremiah, he was overwhelmed at the faithfulness and justice of God and sinfulness of Israel. Our nation needs intercessors such as Daniel at this time too.

Holy God, You are a great and awesome God! You are merciful and compassionate and You hear our prayers.

Amen

God listens

Come and listen, all you who fear God; let me tell you what he has done for me. I cried out to him with my mouth; his praise was on my tongue. If I had cherished sin in my heart, the Lord would not have listened; but God has surely listened and heard my voice in prayer. Praise be to God, who has not rejected my prayer or withheld his love from me!

– PSALM 66:16-20 –

Confession is a necessary precursor to petition. It attunes our hearts to the truth of God. It reminds us of our own unworthiness and the holiness of God. Before you present any requests to God today, take time to humbly confess your sins to Him. Then praise and thank God for hearing your prayer.

Like the Psalmist, we often need to ask God for help, and this psalm is a good model for such prayers. The Psalmist first praises God for who He is. God is naturally always worthy of our praise and we often need to remind ourselves of the greatness of God. After that, and more importantly, the Psalmist confesses his own sins. He goes so far as to suggest that unless he confesses his sins, God will not hear his prayer.

Make confession of sins a priority in your prayer life and you will find that God does not only listen to your prayers, but He will also answer them!

Lord God, I praise and thank You because You listen to my confession and hear my prayers.

Amen

Keep me from intentional sins

Keep your servant also from willful sins; may they not rule over me. Then will I be blameless, innocent of great transgression. May the words of my mouth and the meditation of my heart be pleasing in your sight, O LORD, my Rock and my Redeemer.

— PSALM 19:13-14 —

The closer we come to God, the more aware we are of our own unworthiness and sinfulness. David begins this psalm by proclaiming the greatness of God. *"The heavens declare the glory of God; the skies proclaim the work of his hands"* (v. 1).

While he is worshiping God, David becomes aware of the sin in his own life. He pleads with God to cleanse him from all sin: even those that are hidden in his heart.

In spite of his weaknesses and failures, David wants his whole life, everything that he says and thinks, to be acceptable to God. That is a good example to follow.

Begin your time of prayer today by meditating on God's perfection and holiness. Then confess your shortcomings and sins. Ask God to cleanse your heart.

Merciful God, reveal my sins through Your Holy Spirit and cleanse me so that my thoughts and my words will be acceptable to You.

Amen

Examine all that we do thoroughly

Is it not from the mouth of the Most High that both calamities and good things come? Why should any living man complain when punished for his sins? Let us examine our ways and test them, and let us return to the LORD. Let us lift up our hearts and our hands to God in heaven, and say: "We have sinned and rebelled and you have not forgiven."

— LAMENTATIONS 3:38-42 —

If you read through Lamentations without being convicted of pride, it is possible that you have hardened your heart against God. Jeremiah addresses the arrogant attitude that criticizes God for His actions while not even considering the sinfulness in one's own life.

We often want to preside as Judge over the actions of God while we ignore our own sinful condition. The weeping prophet shows us the cost of such an attitude: we miss out on God's forgiveness!

The problem is not God's judgment and punishment, but our reluctance to confess our sins to Him!

Today, consider the ways in which you have been disobedient to God. Open your heart to God and confess all the things that the Holy Spirit reveals to you.

Lord, my Father God, with sorrow in my heart I confess my sins and plead for Your forgiveness.

Amen

O God, be merciful to me, a sinner

"The Pharisee stood up and prayed about himself: 'God, I thank you that I am not like other men – robbers, evildoers, adulterers – or even like this tax collector. I fast twice a week and give a tenth of all I get.' But the tax collector stood at a distance. He would not even look up to heaven, but beat his breast and said, 'God, have mercy on me, a sinner.'"

– Luke 18:11-13 –

These two prayers stand in stark contrast with one another. The Pharisee acknowledges God only in passing. He uses his prayer time to justify himself in God's eyes.

In the pretence of worshiping God, he congratulates himself on the things he has done and looks down condescendingly on others. There was no humility in him at all.

The tax collector, on the other hand, was more than aware of his own sinfulness before God. He asks nothing for himself and does not try to justify himself. He confesses that he is a sinner. Jesus explains that the contrite tax collector, not the self-righteous Pharisee, was justified in God's eyes.

Take time to meditate on the holiness of God and stop trying to justify yourself. Humbly submit yourself to the grace of God as you confess your sins.

O God, be merciful to me, a sinner.
Amen

Let us experience Your faithful love

You showed favor to your land, O LORD; you restored the fortunes of Jacob. You forgave the iniquity of your people and covered all their sins. You set aside all your wrath and turned from your fierce anger. Will you not revive us again, that your people may rejoice in you?

– PSALM 85:1-3, 6 –

It has become common nowadays to deny sin and its consequences. But there are millions of people who live under the burden of sin.

A feeling of guilt is often a gift of God's grace to give our lives new meaning, to lead us to a new and more productive life. But an even greater gift from God is His grace that allows us to move in a new direction.

The Psalmist thanks God that He has forgiven His people. From experience, he learned that if people confess their sin and ask for forgiveness, God is merciful and forgives them.

Remind yourself of all the ways in which God has forgiven you and renewed your life. Praise and thank Him for each one.

I thank and praise You, Lord, my God, that in Your mercy You have forgiven all my sins and help me to bear fruit to Your glory.

Amen

Heal us, O God

When the cloud lifted from above the Tent, there stood Miriam – leprous, like snow. Aaron turned toward her and saw that she had leprosy; and he said to Moses, "Please, my lord, do not hold against us the sin we have so foolishly committed. Do not let her be like a stillborn infant coming from its mother's womb with its flesh half eaten away." So Moses cried out to the LORD, "O God, please heal her!"

– NUMBERS 12:10-13 –

The Israelites had set up camp in the wilderness near Hazeroth. Aaron and Miriam criticized Moses because he had married a Cushite woman. As punishment, God struck Miriam with leprosy.

Aaron begged Moses to intercede with God for her, and Moses did so without delay. He earnestly prayed that God would heal her and God responded to Moses' prayer.

Even though Miriam was banished outside the camp for seven days, God did heal her of leprosy. Our prayers and intercession can mean a lot to those we pray for.

Are you, like Moses, prepared to intercede for someone before God, even when that person has wronged you? In your prayer time today, intercede for someone who has caused you pain.

Dear Lord, help me to intercede for others, even though they have harmed me.

Amen

Search me, O God

*Search me, O God, and know my heart; test me and know my anxious thoughts.
See if there is any offensive way in me, and lead me in the way everlasting.*
– Psalm 139:23-24 –

We all need to pray this prayer of Psalm 139. Here, David praises God because of His intimate knowledge of his life and actions, because, *"Your eyes saw my unformed body. All the days ordained for me were written in your book before one of them came to be"* (v. 16).

In prayer, David admits that God knows everything he thinks and does. That is why David pleads with God in prayer to cleanse and purify him. He knows that his own perception of his sinfulness is limited. There could be areas in his life where he has unconsciously sinned against God. That is why he prays, *"See if there is any wicked way in me."*

We need to confess our sins to God so that He can show us where we have disobeyed Him. Spend some time in silence before God today and ask Him to examine your heart and to show you where you have wandered from the path of truth.

Holy and merciful God, search me and see if there is anything in my life that does not honor You.

Amen

You keep no records of my sins

Out of the depths I cry to you, O Lord; O Lord, hear my voice. Let your ears be attentive to my cry for mercy. If you, O Lord, kept a record of sins, O Lord, who could stand? But with you there is forgiveness; therefore you are feared. I wait for the Lord, my soul waits, and in his word I put my hope. My soul waits for the Lord more than watchmen wait for the morning, more than watchmen wait for the morning.

— Psalm 130:1-6 —

Even people who keep careful financial records don't like going through the ordeal of an audit! They feel uncomfortable having every detail of their finances scrutinized and having to give account of every cent they have spent.

The Psalmist rejoices in the fact that God does not keep account of all his sins and that he won't be called to give account of every sin he has committed in his life. God forgives us as soon as we confess our sins, and wipes the record clean! That should fill us with gratitude and worship.

God is waiting to hear from you, to forgive your sins, and to restore and renew your life.

Thank God today that He does not keep a record of your sins.

I praise You, O God, that You forgive me, because if You were to keep a record of my sins, I would not be able to live!

Amen

We are like clay in Your hands

All of us have become like one who is unclean, and all our righteous acts are like filthy rags; we all shrivel up like a leaf, and like the wind our sins sweep us away. No one calls on your name or strives to lay hold of you; for you have hidden your face from us and made us waste away because of our sins. Yet, O Lord, you are our Father. We are the clay, you are the potter; we are all the work of your hand. Do not be angry beyond measure, O Lord; do not remember our sins forever. Oh, look upon us, we pray, for we are all your people.

— ISAIAH 64:6-9 —

We must all, like Isaiah, recognize that we are sinful through and through. But before we give up in despair, we must remember that God forgives us and can restore us.

There are times when we are overwhelmed by the unpleasant truth of our sinfulness and like Isaiah must confess: *"We have all become as people who are unclean. Our righteous deeds are as filthy rags and like leaves blown about in the autumn winds."* None the less, the Israelites refused to call on God for help. And so God gave them over to their sins. In spite of that, Isaiah was bold enough to remind God that they were His chosen people and he begged God not to wipe them out.

Awareness of sin, confession of sin, and forgiveness are all active terms that we should not neglect in our prayers.

Eternal Father, we are sinful people, but You are compassionate and merciful.

Amen

Compassionate and merciful is the Lord

The LORD is compassionate and gracious, slow to anger, abounding in love. He will not always accuse, nor will he harbor his anger forever; he does not treat us as our sins deserve or repay us according to our iniquities. For as high as the heavens are above the earth, so great is his love for those who fear him; as far as the east is from the west, so far has he removed our transgressions from us.
— PSALM 103:8-12 —

We often pray for our family, loved ones and friends, missionaries and people in need, but some of our prayers need to be exclusively about God. That was the case when David prayed Psalm 103. He praised the un-equivocal love of God.

David praises God because He does not remain angry forever, and He does not punish us as we deserve. His love is as great as the span of the heavens above the earth. He removes our sins from us as far as the east is from the west!

With this vivid metaphor, David expresses his gratitude and admiration for God's greatness. Come, let us follow David's example.

Spend the next few minutes express-ing your gratitude to God in prayer.

Lord, our Lord, You are compassionate and merciful, long-suffering and full of love. For that, we praise and thank You.

Amen

Lord, do not hold this sin against them

While they were stoning him, Stephen prayed, "Lord Jesus, receive my spirit."
Then he fell on his knees and cried out, "Lord, do not hold this sin against them."
When he had said this, he fell asleep.

– Acts 7:59-60 –

Stephen was a deacon in the early church and he boldly declared the deity of Jesus Christ to the Jews, explaining the purpose of His death and His resurrection. He was stoned for his powerful testimony of the Good News.

When the crowds began throwing the stones at him, Stephen began to pray. Firstly, he surrendered himself to the mercy of God, convinced that God would receive him into His kingdom. Before he died, his prayer surprised his murderers when he asked that God would forgive them.

He simply followed the example of the great Intercessor who prayed for His enemies to be forgiven while He was dying on the cross.

Many times in our lives we receive injustice and humiliation at the hands of others – even when we make a stand for the Lord. May God so compel us with His love and grace that we, like Stephen, will pray for those who come against us and persecute us.

Lord Jesus, help me to forgive others as You did.

Amen

Forgive all my sins

For the sake of your name, O LORD, forgive my iniquity, though it is great. Turn to me and be gracious to me, for I am lonely and afflicted. The troubles of my heart have multiplied; free me from my anguish. Look upon my affliction and my distress and take away all my sins.

– PSALM 25:11, 16-18 –

When we, as a result of our sins, are separated from God, it is imperative that we repent and confess our sins, and in remorse ask for our sins to be forgiven. Then we can come before Him with a pure heart and ask for His help. He will hear you and forgive you, for His name's sake.

Has your life ever seemed like a house of cards? When one card falls, it sets off a chain reaction and the whole house of cards collapses in a heap.

David felt that his problems were going from bad to worse: his enemies had surrounded him and were waiting for his final destruction. He could see no way out.

But even in his despair, he knew that there was One whom he could trust for help. He turned to God, confessed his sins, asked for forgiveness and begged for mercy. May you, in your day of trial, also simply turn to God.

Compassionate God, be merciful to me for the sake of Your name and forgive my many sins.

Amen

We have sinned against You

Then the Israelites cried out to the LORD, "We have sinned against you, forsaking our God and serving the Baals." But the Israelites said to the LORD, "We have sinned. Do with us whatever you think best, but please rescue us now." Then they got rid of the foreign gods among them and served the LORD. And he could bear Israel's misery no longer.

— JUDGES 10:10, 15-16 —

Sometimes it requires more than words to prove to others that you have had a change of heart. Words must be underlined by corresponding actions. This is the situation that the Israelites found themselves in. Time after time they turned to foreign gods. This ignited the wrath of God against them and led to the neighboring nations attacking them.

When the Israelites later begged God for deliverance, they realized that their prayers needed to be backed up by actions of confession and remorse. They needed to remove the foreign gods from among them and once again serve and worship the one true God.

Examine your heart so that you can identify any idols that may dwell there – the temporal things to which you offer your time and possessions. Cast them away and reaffirm your trust in God alone.

Lord, the Almighty God, I deserve Your punishment for my sins, but I ask that You would deliver me today from the situation that I find myself in.

Amen

Do not punish me in Your wrath

O LORD, do not rebuke me in your anger or discipline me in your wrath. For your arrows have pierced me, and your hand has come down upon me. Because of your wrath there is no health in my body; my bones have no soundness because of my sin. My guilt has overwhelmed me like a burden too heavy to bear. I confess my iniquity; I am troubled by my sin.

— PSALM 38:1-4, 18 —

Sometimes the seriousness of our sins can overwhelm us. The physical and emotional suffering can feel like the hand of God's judgment against us.

That was how David felt when he prayed this prayer to God. He spoke of God's anger and wrath, of the arrows of God that penetrated deep into his heart and wounded him. But David also realized that his suffering was his own fault and he knew where to turn for help and mercy. He confessed his sins to God and knew that he would be forgiven.

May we be just as remorseful over our sins as David was – and may the Holy Spirit guide us to handle our sin in the right way.

Let us learn from David, who immediately turned to God. Confess your sins with true remorse and bring an end to the spiral of sin that whirls you away from the presence of God.

Holy God, I confess my sins with remorse to You and say that I am sorry for what I have done. Please forgive me, Lord.

Amen

Hear my prayer and supplication

Now, our God, hear the prayers and petitions of your servant. For your sake, O Lord, look with favor on your desolate sanctuary. Give ear, O God, and hear; open your eyes and see the desolation of the city that bears your Name. We do not make requests of you because we are righteous, but because of your great mercy. O Lord, listen! O Lord, forgive! O Lord, hear and act! For your sake, O my God, do not delay, because your city and your people bear your Name.
— Daniel 9:17-19 —

The Lord will discipline His people if they refuse to walk in His ways. In this sense, "God's people" refers to the church rather than to a nation. Most of us can think of at least one or two "inherited consequences" in our lives.

That is what Daniel experienced in Babylon. He knew that he was in exile because the nation of Israel was being punished for the sins of previous generations. That is why he prayed for his nation, God's people.

From his place in exile he pleaded for the forgiveness of God. His appeal for mercy was based entirely on the compassion of God.

Are you aware of the consequences of sin in your own congregation? Spend some time on your knees today and pray for God's forgiveness and guidance.

Merciful God, because of Your great mercy, look with favor on Your people once more, and on those who worship You.

Amen

God walks in the paths of truth and love

Remember not the sins of my youth and my rebellious ways; according to your love remember me, for you are good, O LORD. Good and upright is the LORD; therefore he instructs sinners in his ways. He guides the humble in what is right and teaches them his way. All the ways of the LORD are loving and faithful for those who keep the demands of his covenant.

— PSALM 25:7-10 —

Each of us has things hidden deep in our past that still cause us sorrow: a cutting, loveless remark, or a selfish action. It sometimes happens that such incidents hinder our prayers in the present. We think that we should not dare to ask too much from God, because we know that we disappointed Him deeply.

Even David, the man of God, harbored such thoughts. But rather than allowing the past to limit his future, David prayed for God's forgiveness, and he believed that God's people can learn to live in a way that is pleasing to Him.

What sins are still haunting you? Ask God today to forgive your sins of the past and to cast them away. But don't stop there: ask God to show you, through His Holy Spirit, how to live in a way that will please Him.

Lord, my Father God, forgive my sins of the past and teach me today to live righteously.

Amen

We have sinned against You

Although our sins testify against us, O LORD, do something for the sake of your name. For our backsliding is great; we have sinned against you.

— JEREMIAH 14:7 —

When God brought drought upon the land of Judah, the people became aware of the extent of their sin and prayed to God in their need. They were literally caught in their sin. It was only when they could no longer deny the reality of their sin that they approached God in prayer.

They prayed that God would deliver them for the sake of His own honor and reputation. God would not want to wipe out His own chosen people.

Sometimes we are confronted with the disastrous consequences of our sins and we realize too late that our sins have caught up with us. Don't let your sorrow and repentance toward God be half-hearted.

Pray that sincere sorrow will take root in your heart so that God can bring about continuous change in your life. May our prayers of repentance and appeals for forgiveness be sincere and pure.

Holy God, my sins have caught up with me, and it is only with You that I can find mercy and forgiveness.

Amen

You surround me on all sides

You hem me in – behind and before; you have laid your hand upon me. Such knowledge is too wonderful for me, too lofty for me to attain. If I say, "Surely the darkness will hide me and the light become night around me," even the darkness will not be dark to you; the night will shine like the day, for darkness is as light to you.

– Psalm 139:5-6, 11-12 –

Because we know that God has knowledge of all things, His presence can be either a source of comfort or a source of fear. Just as Adam and Eve hid from the presence of God after they had eaten the forbidden fruit (see Gen. 3: 10), we try to hide our sins from God.

At the same time it can be comforting to know that the darkness – symbol of danger and hopelessness – is as light to God.

No sin of our own or of others is too big for God to forgive as long as we yield to His mercy. Through the resurrection of Christ, the darkness was destroyed forever, and was transformed into the clear light of grace.

Take heart when you draw near to God in prayer today. Remind yourself of God's intimate knowledge of you and His promise to lead you from darkness into His eternal light.

Holy God, even in the darkness I cannot hide from You. I admit my guilt and, full of sorrow for my sins, pray for forgiveness.

Amen

I will heal their waywardness

Take words with you and return to the LORD. Say to him: "Forgive all our sins and receive us graciously, that we may offer the fruit of our lips. … We will never again say 'Our gods' to what our own hands have made, for in you the fatherless find compassion." "I will heal their waywardness and love them freely."
– HOSEA 14:2-4 –

After the prophet Hosea had depicted God's wrath because of the idols of Israel, he explained that God would still take them back if they came to Him in humility and remorse. He even taught them the prayer that they should pray when they returned to God. They needed to cast away their idols and confess that only the One true God was able to save them.

Only the true God was worthy of their worship and praise. This is still true today: God will forgive everyone who trusts in Him with their whole heart.

When you are tempted to depend on your own strength and abilities, turn immediately in humility to God. Surrender yourself to Him again and pray for forgiveness. Know that He, in His mercy, will receive all those who turn to Him with sincere hearts.

Lord, my Lord, forgive me in Your mercy for all my trespasses and receive me back so that I can once again live as Your child.

Amen

Father, forgive them

When they came to the place called the Skull, there they crucified him, along with the criminals — one on his right, the other on his left. Jesus said, "Father, forgive them, for they do not know what they are doing."

No matter how impossible it might sound, we need to pray the same prayer that Jesus prayed for His enemies.

It is difficult enough to forgive those who have humiliated and hurt us, but it is even more difficult to forgive those who mock and ridicule us when we suffer.

His opponents did not know that Jesus is the Lord of glory, or that they were helping to fulfill the prophecies of the Messiah by putting Jesus to death. Even so, the compassion of Jesus and His willingness to forgive shone through clearly even while He was being mocked and scorned. It is here, on the cross, that we clearly see who Jesus truly is.

This prayer demonstrates His divine love more than anything else. We, as followers of Jesus should pray the same prayer for our enemies no matter how difficult it might be.

Loving Lord Jesus, help me to forgive those who hurt me, just as You have forgiven me.

Amen

You do not require a sacrifice

You do not delight in sacrifice, or I would bring it; you do not take pleasure in burnt offerings. The sacrifices of God are a broken spirit; a broken and contrite heart, O God, you will not despise.

– Psalm 51:16-17 –

God does not want half-hearted, hypocritical sacrifices from us. We need to offer Him a heart of humility and sorrow. This is our most difficult challenge: to humble ourselves before God in sincere repentance. But it is also an inescapable challenge. It is the point at which our spiritual life with God is made or broken. It is only after we have repented that we will know God's goodness and love and God will be prepared to receive our offerings again. We cannot bribe God with our offerings, but His mercy is without end toward those who confess their sins with humility and remorse.

Accept His forgiveness as a gift of mercy to you and spend some time today reviewing all that we have been considering about prayers of confession and forgiveness. Let the message sink into your spiritual life and become a reality. There is no other way that will bring God's grace into our lives and allow us to experience His forgiveness.

Merciful and compassionate God, in humility and remorse I ask for Your forgiveness and mercy. I praise and worship Your name for that.

Amen

APRIL

PRAYERS FOR PROTECTION AND PROVISION

I love the LORD, for he heard my voice; he heard my cry for mercy.
Because he turned his ear to me, I will call on him as long as I live.
— PSALM 116:1-2 —

Prayer is one of the greatest mysteries of life. Why would the Almighty God choose to bend down and listen to the petitions of insignificant human beings? Why would the Creator of the universe, the King of kings, answer us when we call on Him?

Praying gives us access to God; it allows us to talk to the One who through His spoken word brought the whole world into existence; the One who can, in an instant, change us and the world in which we live.

God invites us to talk to Him (see 2 Chr. 7:14); He takes pleasure in answering the prayers of His people: *The LORD detests the sacrifice of the wicked, but the prayer of the upright pleases him* (Prov. 15:8).

We often tend to neglect our conversations with God: we are too busy, we do not know exactly how to pray, we are reluctant to lay before God those things that really bother us.

T*he LORD is near to all who call on him, to all who call on him in truth. He fulfills the desires of those who fear him; he hears their cry and saves them.*
— PSALM 145:18-19 —

From where does my help come?

I lift up my eyes to the hills – where does my help come from? My help comes from the LORD, the Maker of heaven and earth. He will not let your foot slip – he who watches over you will not slumber; indeed, he who watches over Israel will neither slumber nor sleep. The LORD watches over you – the LORD is your shade at your right hand.

– PSALM 121:1-5 –

The function of security guards is extremely important for protecting buildings from intruders. If guards do not pay attention to their surroundings, they could allow an intruder to slip in unnoticed.

In the same way, the Psalmist describes the Lord as the One who never loses concentration while He watches over you. He watches over you to make sure that you do not stumble or fall. Our God never loses focus and will be our protective covering, day in and day out.

The one who prays knows that God will protect him because God, who made the heavens and the earth, is able to protect His children perfectly at all times.

Remember during your time of prayer today that God – who neither slumbers nor sleeps – keeps watch over you.

I thank You, Almighty God, that You watch over me day and night and keep me safe from all the dangers that threaten me.

Amen

Trust in the Lord forever

We have a strong city; God makes salvation its walls and ramparts. Open the gates that the righteous nation may enter, the nation that keeps faith. You will keep in perfect peace him whose mind is steadfast, because he trusts in you. Trust in the LORD forever, for the LORD, the LORD, is the Rock eternal. The path of the righteous is level; O upright One, you make the way of the righteous smooth.

— ISAIAH 26:1-4, 7 —

We all want to feel safe from the attack of strangers and enemies. In Israel, safety meant being able to live in a city with strong walls that would keep the enemy out.

In this prayer of praise, believers declare that their safety is in the Lord. While it is possible that walls of stone can collapse, God will be able to protect and guard the righteous forever. Therefore, believers need never fear anyone!

This song of prayer encourages us to always focus our thoughts on the Almighty God. Reconfirm your trust in God today and experience the peace that this kind of trust can bring.

Sovereign God, help me to focus my thoughts on You and to trust You at all times, because You are my Protector and my eternal Rock.

Amen

Holy Father, protect them in Your name

I will remain in the world no longer, but they are still in the world, and I am coming to you. Holy Father, protect them by the power of your name – the name you gave me – so that they may be one as we are one. While I was with them, I protected them and kept them safe by that name you gave me. None has been lost except the one doomed to destruction so that Scripture would be fulfilled. I am coming to you now, but I say these things while I am still in the world, so that they may have the full measure of my joy within them. I have given them your word and the world has hated them, for they are not of the world any more than I am of the world.

– John 17:11-14 –

Just before Jesus was taken into custody by the Roman soldiers, He took time to pray for His disciples. He asked the Father to protect those for whom He would die the following day.

Jesus' prayer revealed the attitude of His heart; He cares for His disciples and desires that they will live together in peace and unity.

Jesus cares for those who follow Him today, just as He cared for His disciples when He was on earth. Meditate with gratitude and awe on the fact that Jesus cares for you personally. Ask Him to help you live in peace and unity with your fellow Christians.

Lord Jesus, thank You that You care for me, an insignificant person and that You intercede for me before the Father.

Amen

Thanks to God, our hiding place

He will judge the world in righteousness; he will govern the peoples with justice. The LORD is a refuge for the oppressed, a stronghold in times of trouble. Those who know your name will trust in you, for you, LORD, have never forsaken those who seek you.

– PSALM 9:8-10 –

David went through intense suffering and trouble in his life. He was a fugitive from King Saul, the mightiest man in the land (see 1 Sam. 23:25). On another occasion, David's own son turned against him (see 2 Sam. 15:14).

Therefore, when David praised God for being a refuge for people in danger, he was not dealing with hypothetical or abstract concepts. Placing his trust in God was a matter of life or death for him. God never let him down.

In times of trial and tribulation remember that God always watches over you. He will never forsake those who call upon Him, nor let them down.

Thank You, mighty God, that we can find a safe refuge in You and that we can hide in You. Thank You that You never turn away those who come to You.

Amen

Where is the God of Israel?

Let the priests, who minister before the LORD, weep between the temple porch and the altar. Let them say, "Spare your people, O LORD. Do not make your inheritance an object of scorn, a byword among the nations. Why should they say among the peoples, 'Where is their God?'"

– JOEL 2:17-18 –

When we experience difficulties, we are quick to call out, "Lord, save me!" Sometimes these words roll off our tongues too easily. Even though Joel encouraged the Israelites to pray to God to save them, he first explained how they should approach God (see Joel 2:12-13).

Their pleas for mercy should be accompanied by sincere remorse. Rather than just tearing their clothes as an outward sign of sorrow, their hearts should be broken by the sorrow they feel at their sinfulness when they realize that they have trespassed against God. They needed to draw near to Him through fasting, weeping, and sorrow.

God was willing to forgive His people in those days, and He will forgive us today if we show the same repentance for our sins.

In your prayers today, praise God for the abundant grace and wonderful compassion that He shows to sinners.

Forgive me Lord! Forgive my conscious and unconscious sins. You who know my heart, know how sincerely I repent.

Amen

He carries us day by day

Save your people and bless your inheritance; be their Shepherd and carry them forever.

– Psalm 28:9 –

In the presence of God, meditate on the image presented in this passage. Place yourself in David's position. When you begin to talk to God about your needs and concerns, imagine that God's arms surround you with loving protection and allow His encompassing presence to comfort you.

What images do you have in your mind when you pray? Do you have a picture of a loving Father who listens to His child? Or of a mighty warrior who has charge over countless legions of angels who are ready to respond to His bidding?

Your answer will probably depend on what it is that you are asking for at this time. David's prayer provides an intimate image of a God who carries His child in His loving arms.

Thank You, Lord my God, that You carry me safely in Your eternal arms and that I am always safe with You.

Amen

How wonderful are Your thoughts toward me, O God

Your eyes saw my unformed body. All the days ordained for me were written in your book before one of them came to be. How precious to me are your thoughts, O God! How vast is the sum of them! Were I to count them, they would out-number the grains of sand. When I awake, I am still with you.

— PSALM 139:16-18 –

When a couple falls in love, they spend a lot of time thinking of each other. They long for the times when they can be together. When they are apart from each other, they think often of what the other would be do-ing at that moment. They take note of experiences that they want to share with each other. If lovers are so occupied with thoughts of each other, how much more are God's thoughts focused on us – the people whom He loves with an unfath-omable love!

God's thoughts about you, an indi-vidual whom He has created, are "pre-cious" and "vast" and more than the grains of sand on the seashore. How wonderful are Your thoughts toward me, O God!

Meditate on the enormity of God's love for you. Thank Him for caring for you so much.

Holy God, I thank and praise You for Your immeasurable love for me who am not worthy of it! Help me to love You with an unchanging love.

Amen

Your dominion endures through all generations

The LORD is gracious and compassionate, slow to anger and rich in love. The LORD is good to all; he has compassion on all he has made. All you have made will praise you, O LORD; your saints will extol you. They will tell of the glory of your kingdom and speak of your might, so that all men may know of your mighty acts and the glorious splendor of your kingdom. Your kingdom is an everlasting kingdom, and your dominion endures through all generations. The LORD is faithful to all his promises and loving toward all he has made.

– PSALM 145:8-13 –

David could not refrain from singing of the goodness of God. God's might is so impressive that David could not imagine that only people should praise God's goodness.

In his prayer, David describes how the whole creation praises the Lord: *"All that you have made, will praise you, O Lord."* He imagines how all those God has saved, together with the whole of creation, come together to praise God. They can't wait to tell others of the wonderful deeds of God. Are you ready to do so, too?

Look around you with new eyes today. See how the whole of creation, even the flowers in the field, in their own way give their praise to God. Join that choir and bring your own expressions of thanks to the Creator.

Creator God, I joyfully join the whole of creation to declare Your praises and to honor Your name.

Amen

The Lord is near to all those who call on Him

The LORD is near to all who call on him, to all who call on him in truth. He fulfills the desires of those who fear him; he hears their cry and saves them. The LORD watches over all who love him, but all the wicked he will destroy. My mouth will speak in praise of the LORD. Let every creature praise his holy name for ever and ever.

– PSALM 145:18-21 –

Does it sometimes seem to you that God is far away and distant from you? In this prayer, David reminds himself that God is near to all those who call on Him in righteousness.

He continues by praising God because he knows that He always hears and answers his prayers. He fulfills the needs of those who fear Him.

Sometimes, like David, we need to remind ourselves of God's great love and compassion, and how He has always fulfilled the needs and desires of those who love and fear Him.

If we consider how the Lord answers the petitions of His people, and has saved them, we will also call on God in faith more often. Even though we sometimes doubt, it is undeniable that God watches over those who truly love Him.

Thank You, Lord God, that You are near to those who call on You in faith.

Amen

I found rest

My heart is not proud, O LORD, my eyes are not haughty; I do not concern myself with great matters or things too wonderful for me. But I have stilled and quieted my soul; like a weaned child with its mother, like a weaned child is my soul within me. O Israel, put your hope in the LORD both now and forevermore.

— PSALM 131:1-3 —

We have all seen it before: a small child in the arms of his mother. He is content to rest there, feeling secure and loved. Tears, worries and fears, even desires, are forgotten for a while. He lies safe in the embrace of his mother's arms.

In this prayer, David describes himself as such a child – at rest and secure in the embrace of God. David quiets his own soul enough in the presence of God to be able to accept his circumstances, as well as the problems that he cannot find solutions for.

He does not worry about the big things. He leaves the things that are beyond his control in God's capable hands. He simply trusts in Someone bigger and mightier than he is to take care of his interests.

Be still before God in your prayer time, as David was. You can trust your life into the loving hands of God.

Loving Father, I find rest and peace in You, just as a child is calm and peaceful in his mother's arms.

Amen

God's love is unchangeable!

Praise the LORD, O my soul; all my inmost being, praise his holy name. Praise the LORD, O my soul, and forget not all his benefits – who forgives all your sins and heals all your diseases, who redeems your life from the pit and crowns you with love and compassion, who satisfies your desires with good things so that your youth is renewed like the eagle's.

— PSALM 103:1-5 —

Most large businesses that have a large number of employees, provide benefits of one sort or another for their workers. These often include medical care and pension funds.

David describes God's "benefit package." At the head of the list is his life and his health, that come directly from the hand of God. Along with that, God fills David's life with other good things. He realizes that the key gift of God's grace is forgiveness: the grace of God that has broken down the wall of separation between God and man. The Psalmist acknowledges in prayer that his life is completely dependent on God, the merciful giver of life.

During your prayer time, make a list of all the blessings and gifts of grace that you have received from the hand of God. Then think about these during the day, and when you do, praise the Lord!

God of mercy how can I ever find the words to express my gratitude for Your gifts of grace. I want to praise and thank You, however inadequate my words!

Amen

Lord Almighty, Your justice is righteous

I hear many whispering, "Terror on every side! Report him! Let's report him!" All my friends are waiting for me to slip, saying, "Perhaps he will be deceived; then we will prevail over him and take our revenge on him." But the LORD is with me like a mighty warrior; so my persecutors will stumble and not prevail. They will fail and be thoroughly disgraced; their dishonor will never be forgotten. Sing to the LORD! Give praise to the LORD! He rescues the life of the needy from the hands of the wicked.

— JEREMIAH 20:10-11, 13 —

Most of us have something or someone that sometimes terrifies us in our lives. Those of us who had no one we could rely on to act on our behalf in such times probably longed for someone who would come to our rescue and make everything right.

Jeremiah, who was surrounded by enemies, had such a Hero: the strong and mighty Lord, His Deliverer, which is why his persecutors would fall and not win. God is always ready to come to the help of His children. No matter how big or strong your enemy is, He rescues the life of the needy from the hands of the wicked.

What problems do you have to face today? Don't try to solve them in your own strength. Call on the Lord and He will come to your rescue.

Almighty God, please stand alongside me as my strong and mighty hero and save me from my enemies. That is why I sing Your praises.

Amen

Blessed are those who trust the Lord

For the LORD God is a sun and shield; the LORD bestows favor and honor; no good thing does he withhold from those whose walk is blameless. O LORD Almighty, blessed is the man who trusts in you.

— PSALM 84:11-12 —

God will not withhold any of His gifts of grace from those who are obedient to Him. God is compassionate and provides in all our needs.

Often we are envious of other people's good relationships, their bright future prospects or their exorbitant income. We too quickly forget that these things do not necessarily bring happiness. Only a good relationship with God can provide us with eternal joy.

In this song of praise the temple choir sings: *"No good thing does He withhold from those whose walk is blameless."* Things go well for those who trust in the Lord – without a doubt! Then praise the Lord for the blessings that He pours out on His obedient children: grace and protection, favor, honor and joy!

Merciful God, I praise Your holy name for all the undeserved blessings and good things that You give to me.

Amen

You help those who live according to Your ways

For when you did awesome things that we did not expect, you came down, and the mountains trembled before you. Since ancient times no one has heard, no ear has perceived, no eye has seen any God besides you, who acts on behalf of those who wait for him. You come to the help of those who gladly do right, who remember your ways. But when we continued to sin against them, you were angry.

— ISAIAH 64:3-5 —

Have you ever wished that God would reveal Himself to you in all His awesome splendor and majesty? It seems that Isaiah in his unpopular and often lonely task as a prophet of God, longed for some or other revelation of God to confirm His messages so that the Israelites would recommit their love to God.

While Isaiah was meditating on what it would be like if God were to descend from heaven, he also reconfirmed his commitment and dedication to the task God had called him to, no matter what it would cost him. He thought about how, in the past, God had intervened on behalf of the believers, and he proclaimed with conviction: God helps those who live according to His ways.

Take time today to quieten your soul before God. Give yourself, your problems and concerns to Him again. Then wait patiently for His answer.

Holy God, You work miracles on behalf of those who wait on You in faith.

Amen

Save me indeed

Then Jacob prayed, "O God of my father Abraham, God of my father Isaac, O LORD, who said to me, 'Go back to your country and your relatives, and I will make you prosper,' I am unworthy of all the kindness and faithfulness you have shown your servant. I had only my staff when I crossed this Jordan, but now I have become two groups. Save me, I pray, from the hand of my brother Esau, for I am afraid he will come and attack me, and also the mothers with their children."

– GENESIS 32:9-11 –

We might not be in fear for our lives, as Jacob was, but there are times when we do face fears: about our income or for the welfare of our families. In such times we can turn to God and ask Him to watch over us.

Jacob had reason to be afraid of Esau. Jacob had tricked him out of his birthright and the blessing of their father, Isaac. As a result Jacob had to leave their home because Esau wanted to kill him. And now, in obedience to God, Jacob was returning home. He heard that Esau was traveling toward him with an armed force of 400 men. Jacob was convinced that Esau was coming to kill him. He prayed earnestly to God for His protection. His prayer was answered when Esau, instead of being angry, greeted his brother with embraces and tears of joy. That is how God works when we leave our fears in His hands.

Faithful God, watch over my family and me and please take care of those things in my life that cause me to fear.

Amen

My help comes only from the Lord

O LORD, how many are my foes! How many rise up against me! Many are saying of me, "God will not deliver him." But you are a shield around me, O LORD; you bestow glory on me and lift up my head. To the LORD I cry aloud, and he answers me from his holy hill. I lie down and sleep; I wake again, because the LORD sustains me. I will not fear the tens of thousands drawn up against me on every side.

— PSALM 3:1-6 —

It might seem to you that your enemies are pursuing you to your death. Some of them might even say to your face, "God will not deliver you!" Do what David did: call on God, your shield and protection. Then lie down and sleep in peace, because God will watch over you.

When David's son Absalom rebelled against him, he tried to kill David and take the throne of Israel for himself. David fled for his life, and had to hide from Absalom and his mighty army. Some of David's enemies said, "God will not help him or deliver him." In the midst of these serious problems David was able to lie down in peace and sleep because he knew that God was looking after him. He was unafraid because he knew that God was his Protector. That is how God always looks after His children.

Lord, my loving God, I know that You watch over me, because You are my Shield and Protection.

Amen

God is a righteous Judge

God is a righteous judge, a God who expresses his wrath every day. If he does not relent, he will sharpen his sword; he will bend and string his bow.

— PSALM 7:11-12 —

We regularly turn to God when we have difficult situations to handle. David experienced such a situation. It seems that Cush, the Benjaminite, a life-long enemy of David's, found an opportunity to accuse him wrongfully. David did not react to the accusations of Cush.

He rather laid the case before God – the righteous Judge. He trusted God's ability to judge righteously in every situation, and so to defend David's position.

Have you experienced how awful it is to be wrongfully accused? Are there people in your life who hurt you and treat you unfairly? Lay these people and situations before the Lord. He promises that justice will prevail.

Follow David's example in every situation that you cannot handle and where you have been falsely accused.

Righteous God, I trust my life to Your care and know that You will judge righteously.

Amen

In my distress I call on the Lord

The LORD is my rock, my fortress and my deliverer; my God is my rock, in whom I take refuge. He is my shield and the horn of my salvation, my stronghold. I call to the LORD, who is worthy of praise, and I am saved from my enemies. The cords of death entangled me; the torrents of destruction overwhelmed me. The cords of the grave coiled around me; the snares of death confronted me. In my distress I called to the LORD; I cried to my God for help. From his temple he heard my voice; my cry came before him, into his ears.

– PSALM 18:2-6 –

What things give you security in your life? Is it a good retirement plan; a good job; family members and friends? You should rather learn to see that God is your ultimate source of security and protection.

Most of us don't rely on strongholds and forts to protect us, even less a rock or shield! But for David such places were often important for his very existence.

When Saul's armies pursued him, he hid in caves, but still reminded himself that God was his refuge. He used his shield to protect himself from the arrows of his enemies, but he believed that God was his impenetrable shield.

You too should put on the whole armor of God and trust Him for your safety and security.

Almighty God, thank You that You are my strength and my power. I will always call on You when I am in need, and You will always rescue me.

Amen

In You, O Lord, I have taken refuge

In you, O LORD, I have taken refuge; let me never be put to shame. Rescue me and deliver me in your righteousness; turn your ear to me and save me. Be my rock of refuge, to which I can always go; give the command to save me, for you are my rock and my fortress.

– PSALM 71:1-3 –

Life is full of uncertainty, turmoil, and danger. Some of our trials are more psychological or spiritual than physical, but the threat is there none the less. It is good to know in such times that God is your hiding place and refuge.

The Psalmist has known God as his refuge and hiding place. He knew God as a compassionate and righteous God who wants to protect His people. God only has to speak the word and His people are saved! That is why he feels free to call on God to save him.

Spend some time in prayer considering the kinds of "enemies" that are threatening you. Then turn, with the Psalmist, to God, your rock and your stronghold.

Almighty Father God, You have saved me and rescued me from so many dangers in the past. That is why I find shelter in Your compassionate love.

Amen

The eternal God is your refuge

The bolts of your gates will be iron and bronze, and your strength will equal your days. "There is no one like the God of Jeshurun, who rides on the heavens to help you and on the clouds in his majesty. The eternal God is your refuge, and underneath are the everlasting arms. He will drive out your enemy before you, saying, 'Destroy him!' So Israel will live in safety alone; Jacob's spring is secure in a land of grain and new wine, where the heavens drop dew. Blessed are you, O Israel! Who is like you, a people saved by the LORD? He is your shield and helper and your glorious sword. Your enemies will cower before you, and you will trample down their high places."

– DEUTERONOMY 33:25-29 –

At the end of his life Moses stood before the people of Israel and reminded them of all the ways in which God helped them. Then he praised the Lord with the above prayer.

He saw how God parted the heavens to help them and placed His everlasting arms under them, *"Who is like you, a people saved by the Lord?"*

We need to remind ourselves often of the many ways in which God has blessed us. Take time to think back over your life and consider the ways in which God has watched over your family.

Dear Lord, I praise You because You have always been a hiding place for me and Your everlasting arms have always been under me.

Amen

You reign forever, Lord

How great are your works, O Lord, how profound your thoughts! The senseless man does not know, fools do not understand, that though the wicked spring up like grass and all evildoers flourish, they will be forever destroyed. But you, O Lord, are exalted forever. For surely your enemies, O Lord, surely your enemies will perish; all evildoers will be scattered.

— Psalm 92:5-9 —

Eternity gives us an excellent perspective on the present. If we think about God's unlimited power and glory, our earthly problems are seen in context. Even if the wicked flourish, even if all those who do wrong prosper, we know that God will ultimately cause right to triumph, even though we might not see it.

No power on earth, no matter how enormous or immense it might seem, can continually rise up against the Almighty God.

The injustice in the world around us causes us to become frustrated. But remember that God is eternal and righteous.

Praise and thank God for the assurance that He will reward His children and that the wicked will be punished. Pray that this will be your inspiration to live and work in obedience to God.

Almighty and Righteous God, I praise and thank You for Your unshakeable righteousness.

Amen

Do as You have promised

And now, LORD, let the promise you have made concerning your servant and his house be established forever. Do as you promised, so that it will be established and that your name will be great forever. Then men will say, "The LORD Almighty, the God over Israel, is Israel's God!" And the house of your servant David will be established before you.

— 1 CHRONICLES 17:23-24 —

In a world in which almost nothing can be enjoyed "forever", David praises the Lord for the eternal promise that He made to him.

His family would reign on the throne of Israel forever. Imagine David's joy when he realized that this promise would be fulfilled through the Messiah, Jesus Christ. Jesus, the King of kings, was born of the family of David. And at the end of time He will rule over the whole of creation forever.

Centuries after the events referred to in this psalm, we are also moved to prayer when we meditate on the promises of God. May these words of David help us to thank God for His undying promises of eternal salvation and for our eternal inheritance in heaven.

Take time to thank and praise God in prayer for His promises that last for all eternity!

Holy and faithful God, do as You have promised to me. May Your promises of grace last forever. I praise and thank You for this.

Amen

I will always have hope

But as for me, I will always have hope; I will praise you more and more. My mouth will tell of your righteousness, of your salvation all day long, though I know not its measure. I will come and proclaim your mighty acts, O Sovereign LORD; I will proclaim your righteousness, yours alone.

— PSALM 71:14-16 —

What an incredible privilege it is to tell others of the wonderful things that God has done for you. Recall God's protection and guidance in your life, and tell someone how He has helped you in the past.

The Psalmist had trusted God since his childhood and had often proclaimed God's goodness to others. That is why his life was a shining light to others. As he grew older, others plotted against him and he began to feel deserted by God.

That is why he asks God never to leave him and to strengthen him so that he could place all his hope in God. He asks that God will give him the opportunity to declare His saving grace to other people.

May we also have such a passion for souls and may we, too, declare the praise of God as long as we live.

Loving Master, I am overwhelmed at all that You have done and I want to be a witness to Your goodness to everyone I meet.

Amen

You alone are God

And Hezekiah prayed to the LORD: "O LORD, God of Israel, enthroned between the cherubim, you alone are God over all the kingdoms of the earth. You have made heaven and earth. Give ear, O LORD, and hear; open your eyes, O LORD, and see; listen to the words Sennacherib has sent to insult the living God. Now, O LORD our God, deliver us from his hand, so that all kingdoms on earth may know that you alone, O LORD, are God."

– 2 KINGS 19:15-16, 19 –

When King Hezekiah ruled in Jerusalem, the Assyrians were a thorn in the side of all of their neighboring nations. Their king, Sennacherib, mocked the faith that the people of Judah had in God. They scoffed at them with the assertion that their God would be powerless against the approaching Assyrian army – just like the gods of the other nations the Assyrians had defeated.

When Hezekiah asked God for help, he appealed to Him on the grounds of God's "pride." He asked God to defend His honor and to prove Sennacherib wrong.

There are many opportunities when we can ask God to act on our behalf to restore order and to protect His holy name. Don't be afraid to pray to God in such times to uphold His reputation by rescuing you.

Holy God, protect the honor of Your Name and rescue me from the attacks of unbelievers.

Amen

Lead me to a Rock that is higher than I

Hear my cry, O God; listen to my prayer. From the ends of the earth I call to you, I call as my heart grows faint; lead me to the rock that is higher than I. For you have been my refuge, a strong tower against the foe. I long to dwell in your tent forever and take refuge in the shelter of your wings.

– PSALM 61:1-4 –

As commander of the armies of Israel, David was well able to analyze the defense systems of the enemy. Under David's capable leadership, the stronghold of Zion (a fortress in Jerusalem) was captured from the Jebusites. Once it was conquered, David personally oversaw the building of extra fortifications (see 2 Sam. 5:6-10).

But David did not place his confidence in the fortresses that he had erected. He knew that, *"You are my refuge and a strong tower against the foe"*. Only there would he be absolutely safe. There is no safer hiding place than in the refuge of God – the presence of the Almighty God.

Even though we might not realize it, we are all as vulnerable as King David. We need to be led to the safety of the Rock of God. Flee to the Almighty in prayer and trust Him to protect you in safety.

Almighty Father God, lead me to the rock where I will be safe. You alone are my refuge, O God!

Amen

Your love, O Lord, endures forever

*Though I walk in the midst of trouble, you preserve my life; you stretch out
your hand against the anger of my foes, with your right hand you save me. The
LORD will fulfill his purpose for me; your love, O LORD, endures forever – do
not abandon the works of your hands.*

— PSALM 138:7-8 —

You might sometimes feel that God
has abandoned you when you
need Him most. It is a difficult challenge
for most people. But, through faith, we
need to hold fast to what we know is
the truth about God, even though we
cannot see the results. David insists that
God will protect his life *"against the anger
of his foes."*

Although we are inclined to plan our
whole course through life, we can confess, together with David, *"The Lord will
fulfill His purpose for me."* In the time of
his worst trial, David still trusted God
and declared, *"With Your right hand You
save me."* Be assured: the Lord will never
neglect the work of His hands.

In your prayer time today, thank God
for the good plan that He has for your
life. In those dark moments when it
seems He has forsaken you, remember
that God is faithful and you can never
drift away from the sphere of His love.

*Loving God, protect me from the anger of
my enemies. Thank You that there is no end
to Your love.*

Amen

Lord, You bless the righteous

For surely, O LORD, you bless the righteous; you surround them with your favor as with a shield.

– PSALM 5:12 –

Each one of us longs for safety and security. That is why we erect fences and place security systems in our houses. That is why we lock our doors. We need to assure ourselves that no one can harm us.

In his prayer, David delights in the protection of God. He was in charge of armies and fortresses, but he knew it was not enough to keep him safe.

Only God could surround him with the shield of His love when evil people attacked him. Even when he was attacked, David did not fear, because the Lord was his safe hiding place.

It is possible that you are concerned about your future safety. Place yourself unconditionally in God's protection.

Ask Him in prayer to surround you with the shield of His love. Rejoice in the protection of the Lord.

Almighty God of majesty, surround me with the shield of Your love; let things go well for me because I trust in You.

Amen

You are my help and deliverer

May those who seek my life be put to shame and confusion; may all who desire my ruin be turned back in disgrace. Yet I am poor and needy; come quickly to me, O God. You are my help and my deliverer; O LORD, do not delay.

– PSALM 70:2, 5 –

There will be times in your life when you will feel desperate and hopeless and when you will cry out to God in your need. You might remind yourself of God's faithfulness to you – but still become panic-stricken! Remember in such times that you are never alone. Faithful believers in the past experienced that same kind of despair. God will not be deaf to your cry. He will provide everything that you need.

Often, like David, we want to beg God to act quickly. In our prayer today, David asked God to protect him from his enemies. He wants another opportunity to extol God for His deliverance. But then he thinks of his despair once more, and he prays, *"Come quickly to me Lord, do not delay."* In every crisis, remember, God is with you and is always ready to help!

Loving Father God, You are my help and my deliverer. Come swiftly to my help.

Amen

Rescue me from those who pursue me

I cry to you, O LORD; I say, "You are my refuge, my portion in the land of the living." Listen to my cry, for I am in desperate need; rescue me from those who pursue me, for they are too strong for me. Set me free from my prison, that I may praise your name. Then the righteous will gather about me because of your goodness to me.

— PSALM 142:5-7 —

In difficult situations, when it seems that the world is collapsing around you like a house of cards, are you able to sincerely pray, "You are my refuge"? Difficult circumstances have a strange way of revealing what is most important in our lives.

When David took refuge in a cave because Saul was trying to kill him, it seemed that no one had even a passing thought for his situation or cared what happened to him. It was at this low point in his life that David most clearly realized that it was God whom he desired and for whom he longed.

Knowing that God is with us in the midst of our trials, should comfort us and give us the courage to carry on.

Faithful God, You are my refuge and my fortress, my hiding place when I am in danger. Teach me to desire You above all things in life.

Amen

Everything comes from You

Now, our God, we give you thanks, and praise your glorious name. "But who am I, and who are my people, that we should be able to give as generously as this? Everything comes from you, and we have given you only what comes from your hand. We are aliens and strangers in your sight, as were all our forefathers. Our days on earth are like a shadow, without hope. O LORD our God, as for all this abundance that we have provided for building you a temple for your Holy Name, it comes from your hand, and all of it belongs to you."

– 1 CHRONICLES 29:13-16 –

People love to give each other gifts on auspicious occasions to express their love and congratulations. David's prayer helps us to remember that everything that we have comes from the Lord. Sincere offerings express our gratitude to God. We give gifts as a response to God's gifts to us.

Even though God did not allow David to build the temple in Jerusalem, he gathered the materials that Solomon would use to build it. The people contributed generously for the future building. David was touched by their generosity, and showed his gratitude in a concrete way when he prayed to God.

Let us never forget that all that we have comes from God and that we should thank Him for everything in our prayers.

Merciful God, everything that we have comes from You and I give back to You only that which is already Yours.

Amen

MAY

PRAYERS FOR
SPIRITUAL GROWTH

But grow in the grace and knowledge of our Lord and Savior
Jesus Christ. To him be glory both now and forever! Amen.

– 2 PETER 3:18 –

Most of us often become impatient with ourselves about our spiritual growth. Since you gave your heart to Jesus, there has possibly been little progress, and you are dissatisfied with yourself because of that. You know that the Scriptures call you to a life of power and growth that will demonstrate the grace of Jesus Christ. In spite of all your attempts and all your knowledge you feel that your spiritual life is not making any progress along the road that will lead you to a deeper experience with Christ.

Most of us underestimate the power of prayer in our spiritual growth toward maturity. May this month bring the desired changes in your spiritual life as you pray.

Holy God, and in Jesus Christ, I ask that You will protect me from spiritual stagnation: from the danger of remaining a toddler in the faith; from the law of atrophy – that that which is not used will fade and die! Thank You that a fountain of glory flows from Your throne that enables me to grow daily in all the spiritual gifts that You have given me. May this be my lifelong desire and daily process. Let me be a branch that is joined to You, the Vine. Then I will grow and bear fruit according to Your calling in my life. I pray this in Jesus' Name, my Redeemer and Savior. Amen.

Spiritual blessing

Praise be to the God and Father of our Lord Jesus Christ, who has blessed us in the heavenly realms with every spiritual blessing in Christ. For he chose us in him before the creation of the world to be holy and blameless in his sight.

– EPHESIANS 1:3-4 –

We should regularly praise and thank God for all the spiritual blessings that He gives to us: our salvation, our inheritance in heaven, the new body that He has promised us. When you begin to pray today, thank God for the spiritual blessings that you cannot see; such as joy, inner happiness and hope in your heart. Praise and thank our merciful God from whom all our spiritual blessings come.

Paul's letter to the Ephesians was written from jail but was none the less a letter of encouragement. Ephesus was one of the most prominent and strongest congregations that Paul had established on one of his early missionary journeys.

His letter encourages the congregation to praise God for the abundance of His blessings that they enjoyed daily. Paul asks them to look above this world toward heaven so that they will be able to see God's spiritual blessings. Let us, as part of the body of Christ, respond to his age-old request today.

Merciful and loving Lord, I praise Your holy name for all the spiritual blessings in my life.

Amen

The Spirit of wisdom

For this reason, ever since I heard about your faith in the Lord Jesus and your love for all the saints, I have not stopped giving thanks for you, remembering you in my prayers. I keep asking that the God of our Lord Jesus Christ, the glorious Father, may give you the Spirit of wisdom and revelation, so that you may know him better.

– EPHESIANS 1:15-17 –

Do you need to pray for some of your friends and loved ones to receive more insight about who God truly is? Even more, do they know that you pray for them regularly? May Paul's sincere prayer inspire you to pray for your loved ones.

During his stay in Rome, Paul's chains reminded him of his limitations. Although he knew that the new converts in Ephesus needed more guidance, he knew that he could not get there to lead them. That is why Paul chose to show them the pages of his prayer journal.

His prayers had only one theme: that the Ephesians would receive spiritual riches from God.

Like good news that spreads among family members, copies of Paul's prayers were circulated among the members of the congregation of Ephesus. How much potential there is locked up in our prayers!

Lord my God, I earnestly pray for spiritual wisdom for my family and friends and praise You because You hear my prayers.

Amen

Sanctified by the truth

"They are not of the world, even as I am not of it. Sanctify them by the truth; your word is truth. As you sent me into the world, I have sent them into the world. For them I sanctify myself, that they too may be truly sanctified."

— JOHN 17:16-19 —

Jesus prayed these words on the night on which He was arrested. When He was facing His last days on earth, the days on which He would suffer most, His prayer was not for His own well-being, but for the disciples that He would leave behind.

Jesus poured out His heart and prayed for His disciples to maintain purity and holiness in an evil world. He also prayed for us. His desire is that we would be pure and holy in a culture that lusts after sexual immorality, greedy acquisitiveness and avarice, and self-centeredness.

These were among the last words that Jesus spoke to His disciples before He left them. It shows what a high premium Christ placed on purity and holiness in His disciples.

Make Jesus' words your prayer today. Pray that God will purify and cleanse you through teaching you His Word, so that you can glorify Him.

Holy Lord, make me pure and holy through the teaching of Your Word of truth.

Amen

Teach me Your decrees

I have hidden your word in my heart that I might not sin against you. Praise be to you, O LORD; teach me your decrees. With my lips I recount all the laws that come from your mouth. I rejoice in following your statutes as one rejoices in great riches. I meditate on your precepts and consider your ways.

— PSALM 119:11-15 —

Psalm 119 is a long prayer that praises the decrees of God. What would anyone find to celebrate in laws? Most of us find laws limiting because they dictate to us what we may not do. But the Psalmist is praising the laws of God.

He commits himself to memorizing them, and to speaking them aloud. Why is he so eager to learn God's ways? Because he has discovered that there is life in these laws!

Sin separates us from God and the fullness of the life that God offers us. Those who ignore and neglect God's commands are on a road to self-destruction and death. By knowing what God's law is, we are prevented from sinning against Him.

When you approach God in prayer, ask Him to teach you all His commandments and to show you how to apply them to your life.

Merciful Father, help me to keep Your Word in my heart so that I will not sin against You.

Amen

Inner strength!

Now may our God and Father himself and our Lord Jesus clear the way for us to come to you. May the Lord make your love increase and overflow for each other and for everyone else, just as ours does for you. May he strengthen your hearts so that you will be blameless and holy in the presence of our God and Father when our Lord Jesus comes with all his holy ones.

— 1 THESSALONIANS 3:11-13 —

We desperately need each other. God uses other believers to strengthen us and make us holy. While you are asking God in prayer for His strength to empower you, you should expect the answer to come through other believers who worship with you in church on Sundays. At the same time you should earnestly pray that God will use you to strengthen the faith of other believers.

When Paul wrote to the Thessalonians, his love and concern for them was obvious. When he prayed for them He asked God for their love for one another to overflow. He prayed that the church in Thessalonica would be a loving, supporting and concerned community of believers.

No being can live completely isolated from others: we must love and support one another, and above all, pray for one another.

Loving Father, let the work of Your Holy Spirit increase my love so that it will flow over into the lives of other believers.

Amen

Enlighten the eyes of my heart

I pray also that the eyes of your heart may be enlightened in order that you may know the hope to which he has called you, the riches of his glorious inheritance in the saints, and his incomparably great power for us who believe. That power is like the working of his mighty strength.

— EPHESIANS 1:18-19 —

Your prayers should be based on your eternal and glorious inheritance in heaven, just as Paul's were.

Pray that God will help you to understand how immense His strength and power actually are. While the Ephesians were enjoying the luxury of the riches and abundance of a cosmopolitan city Paul was confined to a prison cell in Rome under the constant watch of the Roman guard.

But who could possibly deduce from Paul's prayer that anything was wrong! Paul's faithful description of God's power does not allow a hint of hopelessness or despair to filter through. Instead, he talks of the *"glorious inheritance"* of a future in heaven. His future on earth was in the hands of Caesar, but his eventual hope was not in this world's system: his hope was in heaven and eternity. The eyes of his heart could see clearly.

Are the eyes of your heart open? Pray earnestly to God for this gift of grace.

Wonderful Redeemer, help me, through Your Holy Spirit, to grasp the wonderful future that You have made possible for me.

Amen

He who does these

things will never be shaken

Lord, *who may dwell in your sanctuary? Who may live on your holy hill? He whose walk is blameless and who does what is righteous, who speaks the truth from his heart and has no slander on his tongue, who does his neighbor no wrong and casts no slur on his fellowman, who despises a vile man but honors those who fear the* Lord, *who keeps his oath even when it hurts, who lends his money without usury and does not accept a bribe against the innocent. He who does these things will never be shaken.*

— Psalm 15:1-5 —

Many churches include a time of confession and repentance during their services, so that worshipers can prepare their hearts for hearing the Word. When you enter the presence of God for your own personal time of prayer and worship, sincerely ask the Lord to purify your heart. The people of Israel regularly went up to the temple to celebrate the feasts and to commemorate the acts of God's deliverance.

In this prayer David meditates on the characteristics that should distinguish those who want to worship the Lord in righteousness. Such people should be blameless, they should be people who speak the truth, and should be compassionate and loving.

Let us prepare our hearts through confession before we begin to talk to God about other issues.

Holy Father, purify my heart and my life before I enter Your presence.

Amen

Abound in knowledge and depth of insight

And this is my prayer: that your love may abound more and more in knowledge and depth of insight, so that you may be able to discern what is best and may be pure and blameless until the day of Christ, filled with the fruit of righteousness that comes through Jesus Christ – to the glory and praise of God.

– PHILIPPIANS 1:9-11 –

The defining characteristic of Christians should be love. Like fruit on a tree, it is produced through the life that comes from God and that works continuously in us.

Christ said as much: *"By this all men will know that you are my disciples, if you love one another"* (Jn. 13:35).

Paul earnestly prays for the young believers in Philippi and he lets them know what it is he particularly prays for: that their love for each other will increase and abound – not with a sentimental kind of love, but with true God-inspired love. He well knew that the surest sign that Christ was at work in them would be their loving actions toward one other. This is just as true in our day – if not more so!

Before you begin to pray today, consider what it means to have your love "increase in understanding and depth of insight."

Faithful God, give me that kind of love in my innermost being that will continually flow out to others.

Amen

The Lord is the Victor

The LORD is a warrior; the LORD is his name. Pharaoh's chariots and his army he has hurled into the sea. The best of Pharaoh's officers are drowned in the Red Sea. The deep waters have covered them; they sank to the depths like a stone. Your right hand, O LORD, was majestic in power. Your right hand, O LORD, shattered the enemy.

– EXODUS 15:3-6 –

The miracle that Moses prayed for stands as a symbol of our own deliverance from sin. God is still the God of the helpless. He is unmoved by the might of the arrogant and for this He deserves our heartfelt thanks.

Only after God had sent the ten plagues on the Egyptians, did Pharaoh agree to let the enslaved Israelites go free. But once the Israelites had left, Pharaoh changed his mind and pursued them with chariots and horses. And then God miraculously parted the Red Sea and when the Israelites were safely on the other side, He caused the sea to fall back onto the Egyptians.

God showed Himself to be the ruler of all the nations and the Savior of Israel. This miracle renewed the faith and courage of the Israelites.

Let us remember that God is always ready to help us if we want to grow closer to Him.

Almighty Father God, Your arm is mighty in its works. We glorify Your name because of all the miracles You perform on our behalf.

Amen

I will proclaim Your great deeds

One generation will commend your works to another; they will tell of your mighty acts. They will speak of the glorious splendor of your majesty, and I will meditate on your wonderful works. They will tell of the power of your awesome works, and I will proclaim your great deeds. They will celebrate your abundant goodness and joyfully sing of your righteousness. The LORD is gracious and compassionate, slow to anger and rich in love. The LORD is good to all; he has compassion on all he has made.

– PSALM 145:4-9 –

In the verses quoted above David mentions many attributes of God that deserve our worship and praise: His majesty, His glory, His mighty acts, His greatness, His goodness, and His righteousness. He also praises God's loving-kindness, His faithful love, His grace and compassion.

It is no wonder, then, that David's prayer is full of praise! And that is why he encourages every generation to tell the next generation of God's mighty deeds. He is looking forward to the day when God's mighty deeds will be on every tongue!

Take a few minutes to consider the glory of God and allow the prayer of David to lead you in your own song of praise to the Almighty. Then make a point today of telling someone else about the wonderful things that God has done for you.

Holy God, You are surrounded by majestic glory! Help me to tell others of Your love and grace.

Amen

May you bear fruit in every good work

For this reason, since the day we heard about you, we have not stopped praying for you and asking God to fill you with the knowledge of his will through all spiritual wisdom and understanding. And we pray this in order that you may live a life worthy of the Lord and may please him in every way: bearing fruit in every good work, growing in the knowledge of God.

– Colossians 1:9-10 –

A mother of a newborn baby spends a great deal of her time paying attention to the needs of her baby – and rightly so. She stays near to the child and responds to every sound the baby makes.

Paul treats the Colossians as if he were their parent. Even though he is under house arrest in Rome, his concern for their spiritual well-being is clearly obvious in the tender way in which he appeals to God on their behalf. He prays that God will give them all the spiritual wisdom they need. Spiritual wisdom is a special gift of God's grace.

We, like Paul, ought to ask for spiritual wisdom for ourselves and for all our loved ones.

Let Paul's love for the Colossians inspire us to pray for wisdom and revelation for other believers in every situation in which they might find themselves.

God of grace and wisdom, I pray for this gift in my life and in the lives of all those whom I love.

Amen

Show me Your Ways

To you, O LORD, I lift up my soul; in you I trust, O my God. Do not let me be put to shame, nor let my enemies triumph over me. No one whose hope is in you will ever be put to shame, but they will be put to shame who are treacherous without excuse.

– PSALM 25:1-3 –

One of the greatest fears we have in this life is facing a scandal. We fear the loss of our integrity in the eyes of other people – whether they be friend or foe. As a result of this, one of our innate instincts is to cover up our faults to preserve our reputation.

David understood that his honor was actually in God's hands. God is able to avert scandal from us. He also has the power to raise us up out of scandalous situations in which we might find ourselves. Scandal will follow those who deceive others in order to protect their own reputations.

Instead of being worried about your reputation, your successes or your failures, trust the Lord! Pray for the courage to live honestly and with integrity and God will take care of everything else.

Lord, protect me from scandal, help me to live in such a way that I will have integrity in Your eyes.

Amen

Faithful to those who are faithful

To the faithful you show yourself faithful, to the blameless you show yourself blameless, to the pure you show yourself pure, but to the crooked you show yourself shrewd. You save the humble but bring low those whose eyes are haughty. You, O LORD, keep my lamp burning; my God turns my darkness into light. With your help I can advance against a troop; with my God I can scale a wall.
— PSALM 18:25-29 —

God is indeed the Supreme Judge. Even though it might appear that the wicked are being rewarded for their wickedness, the Lord will, in His time, make all things right. He will cause the wicked to fall and He will raise the upright. On that day all believers will rejoice, because their Protector will come to their rescue.

David wrote this prayer after God had saved him from his enemy, Saul. David had had various opportunities to take Saul's life, but he did not do so. Rather than taking the law into his own hands, David trusted that God would cause right to prosper in His way and in His time.

Waiting for God to cause right to triumph is not always easy, but it is always worthwhile. Pray that God will give you the grace to wait on Him.

Take the opportunity in your prayer time today to praise and thank God for His righteousness.

Holy Judge, teach me to be humble and patient in the assurance that You will cause right to triumph.

Amen

He who calls you is faithful

May God himself, the God of peace, sanctify you through and through. May your whole spirit, soul and body be kept blameless at the coming of our Lord Jesus Christ. The one who calls you is faithful and he will do it.
— 1 THESSALONIANS 5:23-24 —

When we were growing up, our parents taught us how to be independent. They began with small things and built up to larger ones. By the time we were adults, we were inclined to believe that we could do everything on our own.

This kind of attitude spills over into our spiritual lives. The Bible teaches us that we need to live a holy life but we decide that we can become holy through our own efforts. Paul knew that his congregation could not be sanctified through their own efforts. Therefore he prayed: *"May God himself, the God of peace, sanctify you through and through."*

It is impossible for us to become holy in our own strength. But Paul assures the Thessalonians that God will do it, for He is faithful. Strengthen your heart and your faith with Paul's message and pray that God will go ahead with the process of making you holy.

Holy Lord Jesus, keep me pure and holy until that day on which You return.

Amen

My lips will shout for joy when I sing praise to You

I will praise you with the harp for your faithfulness, O my God; I will sing praise to you with the lyre, O Holy One of Israel. My lips will shout for joy when I sing praise to you – I, whom you have redeemed. My tongue will tell of your righteous acts all day long, for those who wanted to harm me have been put to shame and confusion.

– PSALM 71:22-24 –

"My lips will shout for joy when I sing praise to you!" These do not sound like the words of a senior citizen! The writer of this prayer describes himself as old and says that his strength has failed. But after he had examined his life thoughtfully and prayerfully, this "old" person was bubbling over with joy. He sings the praises of God and brings to remembrance everything that God has done for him. The Lord saved him and carried him through all his problems. He promises to testify to God's righteousness and acts of deliverance as long as he lives.

Far too often we find ourselves praying hesitant prayers to God and our songs of praise are rather half-hearted. Let the Psalmist inspire you today to offer your own enthusiastic praise to God and to determine to tell others of His wonderful deeds.

Lord, my God and Father, I will praise You with thanksgiving and singing and tell others of Your wonderful deeds.

Amen

God is my refuge

Your word is a lamp to my feet and a light for my path. I have taken an oath and confirmed it, that I will follow your righteous laws. I have suffered much; preserve my life, O LORD, according to your word. Accept, O LORD, the willing praise of my mouth, and teach me your laws. Though I constantly take my life in my hands, I will not forget your law.

— PSALM 119:105-109 —

In this prayer, the lamp symbolizes the guidance, wisdom and knowledge that we find in the Word. Just as a lamp helps a traveler in the dark, the Word is a light on our path so that we can see where we are going and so that we will not stumble!

This life is like a dark wilderness through which we must find a way. The Word of God shows us the path so that we do not stumble and fall. Like the Psalmist, pray for light and truth from God's Word so that you can stay on the path of life.

Ask God to guide you through the situations that could become stumbling blocks on your spiritual path. Commit yourself anew to God and His Word, as the Psalmist did: *"I have suffered much; preserve my life, O LORD, according to your word."*

Thank You, merciful God, that You light up our dark path with the light of Your Word. Help us to use Your light each day.

Amen

Whom shall I send?

Then I heard the voice of the Lord saying, "Whom shall I send? And who will go for us?" And I said, "Here am I. Send me!" He said, "Go and tell this people: 'Be ever hearing, but never understanding; be ever seeing, but never perceiving.'"

– ISAIAH 6:8-9 –

Are you excited about responding to the call of God? Follow Isaiah's example in prayer and offer your life and your talents to God! "Here am I! Send me!" Isaiah's response to God's call was spontaneous and enthusiastic. After he was purified by a coal of fire from the altar – the symbol in the Old Testament of the Holy Spirit – Isaiah wanted to show his gratefulness to God in a tangible way. When God asked, "Whom can I send?" Isaiah answered with passionate commitment.

Once he had been justified and made righteous in the presence of God, he held nothing back from God. God revealed His need for someone to go to His people as His messenger. Isaiah offered all he had – himself! And God accepted the offer!

Do you know, dear reader, of whom we are speaking here? Pray that God will show you today – and that you will respond with the same obedience as Isaiah did.

Take my life, Lord, let it be consecrated more and more to You so that I will answer when You call.

Amen

I long for Your commands

Your statutes are wonderful; therefore I obey them. The unfolding of your words gives light; it gives understanding to the simple. I open my mouth and pant, longing for your commands. Turn to me and have mercy on me, as you always do to those who love your name. Direct my footsteps according to your word; let no sin rule over me.

— PSALM 119:129-133 —

There are times in life when we long for guidance: we long for someone who clearly knows the road ahead and can help us to avoid the potholes and dead-end streets.

This is the kind of desire that the Psalmist had for the Word of God – that it would lead him every step of the way. He knew that the Word would lead him to true joy. He calls out in prayer: *"Your statutes are wonderful; therefore I obey them!"*

In today's world it often seems easier to desire God's freedom than His commandments. But the Psalmist understood that God's commandments would bring about true joy in his life.

Reconfirm here and now your desire for God's Word to be your guide through life. Pray that God will help you to resist the specific sins that cause you to stumble often.

Lord of the Word, let Your commandments guide me in the right paths.

Amen

I made You known to them

"Righteous Father, though the world does not know you, I know you, and they know that you have sent me. I have made you known to them, and will continue to make you known in order that the love you have for me may be in them and that I myself may be in them."

– JOHN 17:25-26 –

It is a great comfort to know that Jesus included us in this magnificent prayer. *"My prayer is not for them alone. I pray also for those who will believe in me through their message"* (Jn. 17:20).

At the Last Supper Christ prepared His disciples for His approaching death on the cross. He washed their feet and spoke of the coming betrayal. He prophesied Peter's denial and He told them of the Holy Spirit. After that Jesus prayed for them and petitioned God to protect them from the evil one, and He prayed that they would be dedicated to God (see Jn. 17:15, 17).

Even when He was aware that He would be betrayed, denied, crucified, and killed, Jesus was concerned for the welfare of His followers. He did not pray that they would be kept from every trial, but He did pray that they would always remain in the love of God.

Loving Lord Jesus, I praise and thank You for Your personal care for me and that, in Your last hours, You took time to pray for me.

Amen

The earth is full of Your creatures

How many are your works, O LORD! In wisdom you made them all; the earth is full of your creatures.

– PSALM 104:24 –

Famous artists are often admired and remembered for the extent and variety of their works. How much more should we not then worship and admire God for the unbelievable variety and diversity of His creation!

Whether we study biology, archaeology, or astronomy, the great diversity of creation is the first thing that we become aware of. There are oak trees and orchids, mountains and plains, bright stars and black holes.

When we consider the immeasurable variety in creation, we are dumb-struck. God's wonderful creation enthuses and inspires us to praise and worship Him. God finds pleasure in those who appreciate His creation and thank Him for it.

Allow the immeasurable diversity of God's creation to be the starting point for your prayer and meditation today.

O Lord, Your creative ability is awesome. Everything that You made is indescribably beautiful and good.

Amen

Pay tribute to the Awesome God

You are resplendent with light, more majestic than mountains rich with game. You alone are to be feared. Who can stand before you when you are angry? From heaven you pronounced judgment, and the land feared and was quiet – when you, O God, rose up to judge, to save all the afflicted of the land. Make vows to the LORD your God and fulfill them; let all the neighboring lands bring gifts to the One to be feared.

– PSALM 76:4, 7-9, 11 –

Anyone who spends time in the mountains develops an admiration for the powers of nature. We often feel small and insignificant against the massive rock formations. God created these gigantic formations to confirm His power to us. This prayer asks: Who can appear before God when His wrath is displayed? If the whole of creation trembles before God's awesome power, how much more should we approach Him in prayer with admiration and holy fear! We do not want to be counted amongst His enemies when Judgment Day comes!

Praise God today for His breathtaking might and power. Surrender yourself and your possessions to Him afresh today; give to Him the honor and the glory that He deserves. Bring your offerings of time and possessions to your awesome God today.

Awesome God, in Your glory You are mightier than the majestic mountains. I dedicate myself and all that I have anew to You today.

Amen

That Christ will live in you through faith

I pray that out of his glorious riches he may strengthen you with power through his Spirit in your inner being, so that Christ may dwell in your hearts through faith. And I pray that you, being rooted and established in love, may have power, together with all the saints, to grasp how wide and long and high and deep is the love of Christ, and to know this love that surpasses knowledge – that you may be filled to the measure of all the fullness of God.

– EPHESIANS 3:16-19 –

When we intercede for those we love the most, we can ask for nothing better for them than that they would be established in the eternal love of God.

To be admired and loved is one of the most satisfying of human experiences. But precisely because so many people want to be loved, many counterfeits of love are presented to us. The word love has become increasingly cheap and sentimental and commercialized.

But Paul showed through his lifestyle that he loved his converts righteously and unselfishly.

His desire was that they would understand and experience the love of God in their own lives – true love! He knew that their lives had to be founded on something that would stand firm: God's undying love!

Loving God, I pray that those whom I love will experience the love of God through my life.

Amen

Where can I flee from Your Presence?

Where can I go from your Spirit? Where can I flee from your Presence? If I go up to the heavens, you are there; if I make my bed in the depths, you are there. If I rise on the wings of the dawn, if I settle on the far side of the sea, even there your hand will guide me, your right hand will hold me fast.

— PSALM 139:7-10 —

David realized that it was both wonderful and fearful to know that God is everywhere.

One can never escape His presence. But in our human weakness, we attempt to do so. Possibly because of our guilty consciences or because we are reluctant to follow through on something that He has asked of us.

Like Jonah, we try to flee from God. But no one can escape from the omnipresence of God. Even if we should flee to the realms of the dead in Sheol, He would still be there. There is no dark corner in life where the light of God's presence cannot penetrate.

Whatever the consequences of our sins might be, nothing can take us away from the sphere of God's love.

Praise God because He is with you right at this moment. Humbly ask Him to lead you in His paths of righteousness.

Thank You Lord, that there is no place where I can hide where Your love does not surround me. Lead me in Your truth.

Amen

Let Your hand rest on Your people

Return to us, O God Almighty! Look down from heaven and see! Watch over this vine, the root your right hand has planted, the son you have raised up for yourself. Let your hand rest on the man at your right hand, the son of man you have raised up for yourself. Then we will not turn away from you; revive us, and we will call on your name. Restore us, O LORD God Almighty; make your face shine upon us, that we may be saved.

– PSALM 80:14-15, 17-19 –

When we come to the end of our own reserves and find ourselves worn out, there is only one place to which we can flee for refuge. God is our only hope for strength.

Asaph, the Psalmist, addresses this truth in his prayer to God. Why should God rescue us over and over again? Because He created us to live in fellowship with Him. He wants us to call on His name. We are the branches of His vine and we are completely dependent on the One who planted us – God Himself! We cannot grow unless He gives us good ground, pure water, and sunshine. To turn away from our Provider is, in a way, suicide.

In your prayer time today, take the opportunity to thank God for His love that He showers on you. When you feel that you cannot go any further, ask Him once again to renew your strength for the road that you must follow.

Provider God, let Your holy countenance shine down on us in love and provide for our basic needs.

Amen

You crown the year with Your bounty

You care for the land and water it; you enrich it abundantly. The streams of God are filled with water to provide the people with grain, for so you have ordained it. You drench its furrows and level its ridges; you soften it with showers and bless its crops. You crown the year with your bounty, and your carts overflow with abundance.

— PSALM 65:9-11 —

In autumn, the trees lose their leaves; the harvest is gathered and perennial plants subside into winter sleep, awaiting the following spring. It is indeed a time suited to meditation.

We take it for granted that the beauty and growth of plants and trees will be revived each year. We sow seeds in the ground and trust that the rains will come and water the seeds so that they will, in turn, produce a new harvest. But in the long run we know that without the touch of God's hand there can be no new life. God is the Creator of all things, the Giver of life to all: humans, animals, and plants.

We should never take God's gifts of grace for granted. Thank Him for the riches of life that He gives to you. Pray that God will touch your spiritual life and will bring forth new life in you to His glory.

Creator God, thank You that You watch over Your creation. Bring forth in my life spiritual growth that will honor You.

Amen

He is my portion forever

Yet I am always with you; you hold me by my right hand. You guide me with your counsel, and afterward you will take me into glory. Whom have I in heaven but you? And earth has nothing I desire besides you. My flesh and my heart may fail, but God is the strength of my heart and my portion forever. But as for me, it is good to be near God. I have made the Sovereign LORD my refuge; I will tell of all your deeds.

– PSALM 73:23-26, 28 –

Sometimes people are so much "in love" that they often insist that they desire nothing more than to be with each other. How much more then should those who have an intimate and personal relationship with the Lord have everything that they could ever desire.

In this prayer, Asaph meditates on the blessings that he has received since he began walking with God. God was leading him into a glorious inheritance. Asaph could even say that God led him by the hand. The Lord was the most precious thing in Asaph's life – more precious than anything else on earth.

Consider prayerfully, before the face of God, the precious gift of your relationship with Him. Tell Him how and why you love Him and ask Him to always keep you close to Him.

Loving God and Father, I desire intimacy and closeness with You more than anything else on earth.

Amen

Your words are my heart's delight

You understand, O LORD; remember me and care for me. Avenge me on my persecutors. You are long-suffering – do not take me away; think of how I suffer reproach for your sake. When your words came, I ate them; they were my joy and my heart's delight, for I bear your name, O LORD God Almighty. Why is my pain unending and my wound grievous and incurable? Will you be to me like a deceptive brook, like a spring that fails? Therefore this is what the LORD says: "If you repent, I will restore you that you may serve me; if you utter worthy, not worthless, words, you will be my spokesman."

– JEREMIAH 15:15, 16-18, 19 –

In answer to his prayer, God told Jeremiah that he should speak words that have value. Think prayerfully how your words can be used for good rather than evil. Words can be used mightily for either positive or negative ends. We can use words to hurt and humiliate others, but we can also use them to encourage and strengthen them.

In today's prayer, the prophet Jeremiah asked that his persecutors be punished and that they would get what they deserved. And then he said to the Lord, *"Your words were my joy and my heart's delight."* God's encouraging words helped him and supported him greatly during the persecution that he had to endure.

Let your words before God always be positive and let His Word always be a joy in your prayer life.

Lord God Almighty, help me always to speak words that are worthy and that bring glory and honor to You.

Amen

To Him who loved us and freed us from our sins

Grace and peace to you from him who is, and who was, and who is to come, and from the seven spirits before his throne, and from Jesus Christ, who is the faithful witness, the firstborn from the dead, and the ruler of the kings of the earth. To him who loves us and has freed us from our sins by his blood, and has made us to be a kingdom and priests to serve his God and Father – to him be glory and power for ever and ever! Amen.

– REVELATION 1:4-6 –

We are inclined sometimes to wonder if God is really still in control. Trials and tribulations become too much for us and we become discouraged. Our prayers become uncertain and powerless.

In such times we should be encouraged by the vision that John saw when in exile on the Isle of Patmos. The book of his visions – Revelation – is like a kingly coronation ceremony of the Son of God. It sees Him as King of all kings and the final authority over heaven and earth. This prayer glorifies Jesus our Redeemer and Lord. Let us do the same.

Meditate for a while on what it will be like one day to meet this King of all kings face to face. Confess with John that, "To you belong the glory and the power forever!"

Lord, I want to glorify You forever. You have the world and my life securely under Your control.

Amen

He led them by a straight way

Let the redeemed of the LORD say this – those he redeemed from the hand of the foe, those he gathered from the lands, from east and west, from north and south. Some wandered in desert wastelands, finding no way to a city where they could settle. They were hungry and thirsty, and their lives ebbed away. Then they cried out to the LORD in their trouble, and he delivered them from their distress. He led them by a straight way to a city where they could settle.

– PSALM 107:2-7 –

Not many of us have endured the hunger and thirst of those who are starving and thirsty to the point of death, but we do at least know what it means to be hungry and thirsty. In this condition one quickly becomes confused and frustrated. When we finally find someone who can help us, we are flooded by feelings of relief.

In this prayer the Psalmist describes the people of Israel as lost and hungry. They called to God for help and He answered them in a wonderful way, and saved them. The Psalmist declares his thanks through praising God and calls on all of us to do the same.

Has the Lord saved you? Are you excited about it? Then take the words of this psalm to heart. Thank the Lord and tell others what He has done for you.

Loving Master, thank You that You have saved me and quenched my eternal hunger and thirst. Help me to tell others what You have done for me.

Amen

You search the heart

I know, my God, that you test the heart and are pleased with integrity. All these things have I given willingly and with honest intent. And now I have seen with joy how willingly your people who are here have given to you. O LORD, God of our fathers Abraham, Isaac and Israel, keep this desire in the hearts of your people forever, and keep their hearts loyal to you. Then David said to the whole assembly, "Praise the LORD your God." So they all praised the LORD, the God of their fathers; they bowed low and fell prostrate before the LORD and the king.

– 1 CHRONICLES 29:17-18, 20 –

David's prayer came at the peak of his reign as king: the commitment of the nation's talents and gifts for the building of the temple of God.

While the nation was entering a new era in their relationship with God, David prayed that their motives would be pure. He knew that God is more interested in the condition of our hearts than in the silver and gold we bring to Him as an offering. Even with all the authority of his kingship, David could not determine the motives that hid behind their gifts. Only God knows what is in the heart of man. He prayed that God would find integrity and obedience in their hearts, and in his heart.

Follow David's example and pray that God will make you a person of integrity; someone who is willingly obedient.

Father God, examine my heart and help me so that I will always obey You with integrity.

Amen

Praise the Lord, all You nations

And again, "Praise the Lord, all you Gentiles, and sing praises to him, all you peoples." And again, Isaiah says, "The Root of Jesse will spring up, one who will arise to rule over the nations; the Gentiles will hope in him." May the God of hope fill you with all joy and peace as you trust in him, so that you may overflow with hope by the power of the Holy Spirit.

— ROMANS 15:11-13 —

We praise and honor the birth of David's descendant, our Lord and Savior, Jesus Christ. We place all our hope in Him for our salvation. Pray together with your friends and acquaintances that you will find hope and peace in Him. *"May the God of hope fill you with all joy and peace as you trust in him, so that you may overflow with hope by the power of the Holy Spirit!"* What a blessed way for one person to greet another!

Paul wrote this prayer for the Romans when he realized that Christ came to this world to save all people – Jews and Gentiles. That is why Isaiah was able to prophesy that the heathens would place their hope in Christ, the great successor who would sit on the throne of David!

Come let us join together with all believers across the world to honor the Lamb!

Lord Jesus, give hope, peace and joy to all people on earth.

Amen

JUNE

PRAYERS FOR THE COMFORT OF GOD

There are no bearers of crowns in heaven who did not bear crosses on earth.
— CHARLES H. SPURGEON —

If we had even a vague impression of the glories of heaven, then we would not grieve as those who have no hope. The perfect provision that God has prepared for those who love Him and believe in Him is so indescribable that there should be only joy and satisfaction in His presence.

Revelation gives us a few glimpses of this heavenly glory: those who dwell there are raised above all earthly pain and tribulation and are lovingly comforted by Him who sits on the throne. Their hunger is satisfied in green pastures and their thirst is quenched at fountains of living water. God Himself wipes the last tears from their eyes (see Rev. 7:16-17).

With God's comfort in our hearts, we can remain standing even in the face of the greatest sorrows. J. Blinco States, "To believe in God in heaven is not to flee from the reality of life, but to meet life head on."

Heavenly Father, In Your grace and through Your Holy Spirit comfort all those who mourn and strengthen them to face the challenges of each phase of life. Do this through the power that is in our resurrected Savior, Jesus Christ. Amen.

Be still and know that I am God

The LORD said to Job: "Will the one who contends with the Almighty correct him? Let him who accuses God answer him!" Then Job answered the LORD: "I am unworthy – how can I reply to you? I put my hand over my mouth. I spoke once, but I have no answer – twice, but I will say no more." Then the LORD spoke to Job out of the storm: "Brace yourself like a man; I will question you, and you shall answer me."

– JOB 40:1-7 –

Job lost everything. He was left with a few friends who tried to explain his trials and tribulations by blaming him for having acted wrongly. Job and his friends tried to understand everything that had happened to him, but ultimately they did not recognize God's eternal wisdom and absolute sovereignty.

The Almighty does not need to give an explanation to any one of us. His knowledge and might far surpass ours. We might never fully understand His ways, but know enough of His loving nature to be able to trust Him fully. It is not wrong to bring your difficult questions to God. But be careful that your questions do not become an excuse for blaming God for your problems or for turning away from Him. Remind yourself that God is righteous and that His actions and thoughts are far above your understanding. Become quiet before God today – and in one way or another you will hear His voice.

Righteous God, I do not always understand the things that happen, but I am content in the knowledge that You do have the answers.

Amen

Prayer drives away fear

The LORD is my light and my salvation – whom shall I fear? The LORD is the stronghold of my life – of whom shall I be afraid? When evil men advance against me to devour my flesh, when my enemies and my foes attack me, they will stumble and fall. Though an army besiege me, my heart will not fear; though war break out against me, even then will I be confident.

– PSALM 27:1-3 –

In his inaugural address to a nation caught in the grip of fear as the result of the Great Depression, President Franklin D. Roosevelt spoke these uplifting and comforting words, "The only thing we have to fear is fear itself." Fear about an uncertain future can rob the present of its peace and joy. Fear of failure can hold us back from stepping out in faith and doing the wonderful things that God desires for us to do.

In this prayer, David asserts that even if a strong army were to surround and attack him, he would continue to trust in the Lord. His heart would know no fear. David could say this because he knew that God was his light and his salvation.

If fear threatens to paralyze you and to steal your joy, take heart and remember that the Almighty God watches over you. Prayerfully place your trust in God, who delivers you from fear.

Lord, my Light and my Salvation, take all unnecessary fear from my heart and help me to trust in You alone.

Amen

Rest in God's Will

At this, Job got up and tore his robe and shaved his head. Then he fell to the ground in worship and said: "Naked I came from my mother's womb, and naked I will depart. The LORD gave and the LORD has taken away; may the name of the LORD be praised." In all this, Job did not sin by charging God with wrongdoing.

– Job 1:20-22 –

Job went through a time of severe trial, losing his flocks and herds, his servants, and even his children. Yet, in the midst of this agonizing tragedy, Job remembered that everything we have comes from God. Even his children were gifts from God and so he still had reason to praise God.

Faith in God does not lessen the tragedies of this life. Loss is always painful. Our empathy with Job's suffering is simply our empathy with a shared humanity. But what is most astounding is that God allowed His own Son to come into this world and to suffer.

Not only does God give us everything that we have, He gave His Son to free us from our sins. Praise the Name of the Lord!

God of love and grace, You have given me everything that I have, and You gave me Your Son. I praise and honor Your Name.

Amen

Trust in God Alone

We wait in hope for the LORD; he is our help and our shield. In him our hearts rejoice, for we trust in his holy name. May your unfailing love rest upon us, O LORD, even as we put our hope in you.

— PSALM 33:20-22 —

We all need security. When difficult situations threaten or overwhelm us, most of us lean heavily on family and friends for help and support. But this prayer reminds us that, in the long run, only the Almighty God can protect and save us.

It is fitting to admit our dependence on the Lord when we come to Him in prayer. Remember that He is our shield and protector. And while we focus on this wonderful truth, our fear will turn into praise.

Become quiet for a few minutes and think about the ways in which you seek security, in both big and small situations. Then confess to God that you will in future trust fully in Him alone.

Lord Jesus, our Hope and Salvation, surround us with Your unfathomable love and protection.

Amen

Praise for the ways of God

Then my soul will rejoice in the LORD and delight in his salvation. My whole being will exclaim, "Who is like you, O LORD? You rescue the poor from those too strong for them, the poor and needy from those who rob them." May those who delight in my vindication shout for joy and gladness; may they always say, "The Lord be exalted, who delights in the well-being of his servant." My tongue will speak of your righteousness and of your praises all day long.

— PSALM 35:9-10; 27-28 —

In this prayer, David praises God because He has saved him from his enemies. He asks if there is anyone who can be compared with God Himself, He who is so full of love and who saves those too weak to save themselves.

The splendor of all people fades in comparison with the mighty deeds of God. One day all people will bow before God in worship and declare His might and justice with loud cries.

On this day all honor and glory will be given to Him. While we wait for that day, we need to help others recognize the might of God and encourage them to praise and worship Him.

In your prayer time, follow David's example and praise and thank God for the way in which He saved you.

Loving Father God, no one can compare with You in might and compassion. Therefore I will praise You as long as I live.

Amen

Hannah praises God

Then Hannah prayed and said: "My heart rejoices in the LORD; in the LORD my horn is lifted high. My mouth boasts over my enemies, for I delight in your deliverance. "There is no one holy like the LORD; there is no one besides you; there is no Rock like our God."

– 1 SAMUEL 2:1-2 –

In Luke 1:45-55 we read the prayer of thanksgiving Mary prayed when God chose her to bring His Son into this world. Centuries earlier Hannah expressed the same overwhelming gratitude in her prayer.

These two women, centuries apart, were connected by the fact that they both gave birth to special children – the barren Hannah to the boy Samuel, and the virgin Mary to Jesus. Hannah's prayer conveys her awe at the miracle of God that changed her miserable life.

Our prayers should follow Hannah's example, and find ways to express our gratitude for the ways in which God has blessed us. Our praise and gratitude for God's involvement in our lives is also a testimony to others. It bears witness to the fact that God does answer prayers.

Merciful God, You bless me so richly through Your love and grace. My heart delights in You, my God and my Father.

Amen

Stay close to the Shepherd

Even though I walk through the valley of the shadow of death, I will fear no evil, for you are with me; your rod and your staff, they comfort me.

– PSALM 23:4 –

A society that considers success and prestige of prime importance, finds it difficult to talk about the valley of the shadow of death. The Holy Scriptures, however, never try to hide the dark shadows of life – not even death. In this prayer David declares his belief that God is always with him, even in the valleys of the shadow of death. He declares that he will fear no evil, for God is with him.

From time to time we should recall the times in our lives when God was with us in the valley of the shadow of death. And when our earthly life finally comes to an end, another life, filled with joy and excitement, will open before us. Jesus, our Lord, will welcome us into His eternal home.

In your prayers today, thank God for always being near you - and ask yourself if you have always stayed close to Him. Ask Him to be with you through the rest of this year, and through your whole life, and make a commitment to stay close to Him.

Omnipresent God and Father, even when I walk through the valley of the shadow of death, I will not fear, because I know that You are always close to me.

Amen

Joy from the wells of salvation

With joy you will draw water from the wells of salvation. In that day you will say: "Give thanks to the LORD, call on his name; make known among the nations what he has done, and proclaim that his name is exalted. Sing to the LORD, for he has done glorious things; let this be known to all the world."

— ISAIAH 12:3-5 —

These verses are a joyful interlude in an otherwise frightening prophecy from Isaiah the prophet of God, regarding Israel's disobedience. This is the prayer that the Israelites will offer to God when He has saved them from their sins. Isaiah compares their change of heart with the relief that is found when we, with cracked lips and a dry throat, come across a well of life-giving water, and can quench a burning thirst.

It is surprising how the experience of the dire consequences of sin gives us a new appreciation of the joy that is found in obedience to God. The hearts of those new converts overflow with thanksgiving to God for all that He has done.

In your prayer time today, thank God because He has saved and delivered you. Ask Him to refresh and renew your thirsty soul through His Holy Spirit.

Loving and merciful God, I thank and praise You for all the wonderful things that You have done. Praise the Lord, for He is good! There is no end to His love!

Amen

Honor and praise the King of kings

Keep this command without spot or blame until the appearing of our Lord Jesus Christ, which God will bring about in his own time – God, the blessed and only Ruler, the King of kings and Lord of lords, who alone is immortal and who lives in unapproachable light, whom no one has seen or can see. To him be honor and might forever. Amen.

– 1 TIMOTHY 6:14-16 –

The faithful disciples of Christ have a sense of "I can hardly wait until it happens" when they think about the Second Coming of Christ. We longingly wait for Jesus to return in His glory. Just as the ancient Israelites waited for the birth of the Messiah, and just as we eagerly anticipate Christmas each year, we wait for the return of Christ.

Only God knows when that will happen, for He alone knows when the time will be right. But what we can be sure of is that Jesus will come back again – one day. In the meantime we should be as excited as a little child just days before his birthday.

We might not know the exact date, but we do know that He will come. We have the right attitude when we ask the Lord, "Is it time yet for Christ to return?"

Savior and Friend, Lord Jesus, I longingly wait for the time when You will come back to earth from heaven, and we will be with You forever.

Amen

Thankfulness because our God reigns

And the twenty-four elders, who were seated on their thrones before God, fell on their faces and worshiped God, saying: "We give thanks to you, Lord God Almighty, the One who is and who was, because you have taken your great power and have begun to reign. The nations were angry; and your wrath has come. The time has come for judging the dead, and for rewarding your servants the prophets and your saints and those who reverence your name, both small and great – and for destroying those who destroy the earth."

– REVELATION 11:16-18 –

When evil and wickedness go unpunished, we tend to despair of ever finding justice. We might even be tempted to wonder if it is worthwhile to worship God. The Scriptures encourage us to have a broad vision of history.

The twenty-four elders who sit in the throne room of God, paint this picture for us, when they praise the Almighty. They thank the One who is and who was because He controls all the events of earth's history. They praise Him because He ensures that justice is served at the right time and in the right place. God's justice will ultimately triumph, and the servants of God will eventually be declared righteous.

In your prayer time today, picture yourself in the throne room of God at the end of the ages. What praise and prayer of thanksgiving will you personally offer to God?

Sovereign God, I praise and thank You because You will ensure that righteousness will triumph in Your time.

Amen

Plea for assurance

Moses said to the LORD, "You have been telling me, 'Lead these people,' but you have not let me know whom you will send with me. You have said, 'I know you by name and you have found favor with me.' If you are pleased with me, teach me your ways so I may know you and continue to find favor with you. Remember that this nation is your people." The LORD replied, "My Presence will go with you, and I will give you rest." Then Moses said to him, "If your Presence does not go with us, do not send us up from here. How will anyone know that you are pleased with me and with your people unless you go with us? What else will distinguish me and your people from all the other people on the face of the earth?" And the LORD said to Moses, "I will do the very thing you have asked, because I am pleased with you and I know you by name."

– EXODUS 33:12-17 –

God had commanded Moses to lead the Israelites to the Promised Land. But when they disobeyed God by worshiping the golden calf, God refused to go any further with such disobedient and stubborn people. Moses asked God to teach him His ways, so that he could understand God better. God did not rebuke Moses for his hesitation. Moses knew that to go on without God's guidance, presence and strength would be disastrous. That is why he sought the Lord in prayer.

God will answer those who seek Him. Moses asked for assurance and understanding, and God Himself gave these to him. He promised to be with Moses and to guide him every step of the way.

He is willing to do the same for you!

Lord, my God, show me Your ways so that I can do exactly what You have asked of me.

Amen

Expressions of joyful thanks

Then King David went in and sat before the LORD, and he said: "Who am I, O Sovereign LORD, and what is my family, that you have brought me this far? And as if this were not enough in your sight, O Sovereign LORD, you have also spoken about the future of the house of your servant. Is this your usual way of dealing with man, O Sovereign LORD? What more can David say to you? For you know your servant, O Sovereign LORD. For the sake of your word and according to your will, you have done this great thing and made it known to your servant. How great you are, O Sovereign LORD! There is no one like you, and there is no God but you, as we have heard with our own ears."

– 2 SAMUEL 7:18-22 –

"Who am I, O Sovereign Lord, that you have brought me this far?" This was David's response when God revealed to him that his dynasty will never end. God had an awesome plan for David – far greater than David could imagine even in his wildest dreams. Not only would his descendents rule over the people of Israel, but they would remain for all eternity. The eternal King of kings, Jesus Christ, would one day be born of David's line. Nothing David could do would make him worthy of such an honor. Such a wonderful promise is a result of the grace of God alone.

What blessings have you received from the hand of God? Make a list of the ways in which God has blessed you far above your expectations – and thank Him for each one.

Redeemer and Savior, who am I that You have brought me so far, and have blessed me so abundantly? I praise and worship You for Your love and grace.

Amen

Honor our faithful God

"Praise be to the L_{ORD}, who has given rest to his people Israel just as he promised. Not one word has failed of all the good promises he gave through his servant Moses. May the L_{ORD} our God be with us as he was with our fathers; may he never leave us nor forsake us."

– 1 K_{INGS} 8:56-57 –

When King Solomon admired the magnificent temple that God had allowed him to build in Jerusalem, he was moved to consider all the ways in which God had blessed his people. Their forefathers had been nomads in the desert for centuries, but now they had their own land. They had withstood various attacks against their land, and were now enjoying peace. Solomon wisely realized that all of this was because of the grace of God, and praised Him for all these blessings.

How great is our God! Not one of His promises has remained unfulfilled through all generations!

Set aside some time today to meditate on how richly you have been blessed through God's grace. How He has blessed you with food and a home. The many ways in which He has given you peace and rest. Remind yourself of God's promises of eternal peace for those of His children who endure suffering in this world. Then present your thanks to God!

Faithful God, I praise and worship You because You always keep Your promises and I will trust in You my whole life through.

Amen

Wait on the Lord

Give ear to my words, O LORD, consider my sighing. Listen to my cry for help, my King and my God, for to you I pray. In the morning, O LORD, you hear my voice; in the morning I lay my requests before you and wait in expectation.

— PSALM 5:1-3 —

When we have to endure suffering, we often feel that God has abandoned us. But God never hides from us. It is our selfishness that prevents us from seeing and recognizing Him.

If we were, in a moment of clarity, able to understand the complexity of our own predicament, we have the promise of God that he will answer when we call.

When we experience problems in life, it is often extremely difficult to wait on the Lord. The Israelites who were under the yoke of the Roman Empire felt exactly like that. They couldn't wait for the Messiah to come.

After centuries of waiting, their hope was fulfilled in the Baby that was born in Bethlehem. All that they had to do was wait for His perfect timing.

Holy and faithful Father, I bring the desires of my heart to You and faithfully wait for Your answer in Your time.

Amen

Rest in God's Care

I call on you, O God, for you will answer me; give ear to me and hear my prayer. Show the wonder of your great love, you who save by your right hand those who take refuge in you from their foes. Keep me as the apple of your eye; hide me in the shadow of your wings.

— PSALM 17:6-8 —

In this prayer David asks the Lord to protect him as the apple of His eye.

He asks that God would protect him because he believes that God will answer his prayers. He sees God, compassionate and interested, bending down to listen to his prayer.

He believes that God will use His power to protect him. As David looks to God with eyes of expectation, he receives the protection that he has so desperately sought.

Use David's prayer to remind yourself that God is willing and able to protect you lovingly and faithfully. He is the only One who can truly shield and protect you. In prayer, lay your cares at His feet.

I thank You, Almighty God, that You protect me as the apple of Your eye. Hide me in the shadow of Your wings.

Amen

Jesus prays for unity amongst believers

"My prayer is not for them alone. I pray also for those who will believe in me through their message, that all of them may be one, Father, just as you are in me and I am in you. May they also be in us so that the world may believe that you have sent me."

— JOHN 17:20-21 —

We may never forget the purpose of Christ's coming into the world. Just before He was arrested, Jesus prayed that those who believed in Him would be united in their love for God and for each other. This would be the sign to show the world that Jesus was truly sent by God into this world.

Unity amongst Christians does not imply uniformity, with believers becoming carbon copies of one another. Neither is it superficial politeness that attempts to push all important issues aside.

As Jesus prayed, true unity among Christians should be like the unity between the Father and the Son. It is a dynamic unity, a complementary relationship that gives and takes. This is the kind of unity that Jesus prayed His disciples would have.

Jesus' prayer is answered every time we show love to our fellowman in both important and trivial matters. Make this prayer the prayer for your life.

Loving Father, help me to live in unity with other believers, so that the world will believe in You.

Amen

The Lamb is worthy to receive our praise

Then I looked and heard the voice of many angels, numbering thousands upon thousands, and ten thousand times ten thousand. They encircled the throne and the living creatures and the elders. In a loud voice they sang: "Worthy is the Lamb, who was slain, to receive power and wealth and wisdom and strength and honor and glory and praise!" Then I heard every creature in heaven and on earth and under the earth and on the sea, and all that is in them, singing: "To him who sits on the throne and to the Lamb be praise and honor and glory and power, for ever and ever!" The four living creatures said, "Amen," and the elders fell down and worshiped.

— REVELATION 5:11-14 —

The Bible encourages Christians to offer prayers of praise, thanksgiving and commitment to God (see 1 Thes. 5:17-10). Our private devotions are very important, but there is an element that is missing unless we join together with other believers to praise God.

We are fulfilling in our calling as worshipers when we are caught up in the worship the Lord with His children. It is, after all, for worshipers from every place and every age that Christ will receive the worship that He so richly deserves. His disciples will respond to His Second Coming with a united song of praise that magnifies and glorifies the Lord.

I pray that God will help us continuously to be found in the great company of praying people.

Lord Jesus, blessing and honor, glory and power, belong to You. I pray that I will be amongst that joyful, praising throng of believers when You return.

Amen

Longing for God

As the deer pants for streams of water, so my soul pants for you, O God. My soul thirsts for God, for the living God. When can I go and meet with God? Why are you downcast, O my soul? Why so disturbed within me? Put your hope in God, for I will yet praise him, my Savior and my God. My soul is downcast within me; therefore I will remember you from the land of the Jordan, the heights of Hermon – from Mount Mizar. By day the LORD directs his love, at night his song is with me – a prayer to the God of my life.

– PSALM 42:1-2, 5-6, 8 –

Do you sometimes feel that God is far away? The Psalmist, surrounded by his mocking enemies, felt that God was far from him. His enemies express their true thoughts in their mocking question, "Where is your God now?" But their taunts only serve to make him long all the more for God – like a thirsty person desperate for a sip of refreshing water.

He openly admits his discouragement to God, but his despair is not the final word. He soon begins to declare the many ways in which God's love has been poured out on him. And he ends by praising God who preserves his life through His grace.

If you feel that God is far from you, express your longing for Him in your prayers. And then begin to count the many ways that God has shown His care for you.

Lord and Master, sometimes I become discouraged and long desperately for You. I place my hope in You and know that Your grace is sufficient for me.

Amen

Praise of the Gentiles

"Therefore I will praise you among the Gentiles; I will sing hymns to your name." Again, it says, "Rejoice, O Gentiles, with his people." And again, "Praise the Lord, all you Gentiles, and sing praises to him, all you peoples." And again, Isaiah says, "The Root of Jesse will spring up, one who will arise to rule over the nations; the Gentiles will hope in him."

— ROMANS 15:9-12 —

It might have sounded radical to call on the people of Israel as well as the gentiles to praise the Lord, but it wouldn't be so radical today. In Paul's time many of the Jews treated the Gentiles with scorn. But Jesus came to this world to save both the Jews and the Gentiles.

Paul encouraged them to accept one another and even to pray together. He asked them to unite their voices in a song of praise to Jesus, their Redeemer and Savior. Thus the coming of Jesus into this world becomes an inspiration for all people.

Rejoice in the Lord. Make a decision to set aside time today to worship God with other believers and with non-Christians.

Lord, my living Redeemer, today I want to join those who praise Your Name wholeheartedly.

Amen

God is always near

We give thanks to you, O God, we give thanks, for your Name is near; men tell of your wonderful deeds. You say, "I choose the appointed time; it is I who judge uprightly. When the earth and all its people quake, it is I who hold its pillars firm. As for me, I will declare this forever; I will sing praise to the God of Jacob. I will cut off the horns of all the wicked, but the horns of the righteous will be lifted up."

– Psalm 75:1-3, 9-10 –

Don't ever forget that God is near to you! At times He performs mighty miracles to remind us just how close He is. But there are many more times when we are not so consciously aware of His might and His righteousness. This prayer addresses this problem directly.

If we feel tempted to question whether God is even aware of our problems, we should begin to praise Him for His might. We should also remind ourselves that God is close to us and we should think of all the times that we have seen His power at work in the world. God promised to bring justice to this world, but in His own time. While we wait for God to act, we should keep praising Him.

Whatever situation you might find yourself in today, think of one thing God has done for you recently and sincerely thank Him for it. Praise Him because He is always near to you.

Holy and loving God, it comforts me to know that You are always close to me. Thank You for this reassurance.

Amen

Joy in God's presence

How lovely is your dwelling place, O LORD Almighty! My soul yearns, even faints, for the courts of the LORD; my heart and my flesh cry out for the living God. Even the sparrow has found a home, and the swallow a nest for herself, where she may have her young – a place near your altar, O LORD Almighty, my King and my God. Blessed are those who dwell in your house; they are ever praising you.

– PSALM 84:1-4 –

Far too often we envy others because of their healthy relationships, exciting prospects or exorbitant income. We forget too quickly that such things do not determine our joy and that they can never give satisfaction and contentment. Only a healthy relationship with God can ensure that you will have eternal joy.

In this prayer, the temple singers proclaim, *"Blessed are those who dwell in your house; they are ever praising you. As they pass through the Valley of Baca, they make it a place of springs"* (v. 4, 6). They praise God for the blessings that He gives to His faithful children: grace, protection, prosperity, honor, and joy.

God will not withhold any good thing from those who are obedient to Him. He will supply all your needs out of the riches of His grace. Give Him thanks for His goodness and grace.

Lord God, I praise You because You have so generously loaded me with blessings and all good things.

Amen

Praise to my Savior

Teach me your way, O LORD, and I will walk in your truth; give me an undivided heart, that I may fear your name. I will praise you, O Lord my God, with all my heart; I will glorify your name forever. For great is your love toward me; you have delivered me from the depths of the grave.

— PSALM 86:11-13 —

David expressed his deep gratitude to God because He had saved him from death. *"I will praise you with my whole heart!"* But when David came into the presence of God to pray, he was aware that he did not meet the standards that God required of him. Yet he wanted to honor God with his whole life, and so he asks God to give him a pure heart. He wants to stay in unbroken fellowship with God and so asks God to teach him how to serve the Lord with complete commitment.

When we realize the greatness of what God has done for us, we look for ways to express our love for Him. We should remind ourselves when we pray that it is a magnificent privilege to draw close to God in prayer. We were in the deep mire of sin, but God raised us up so that we can stand in His holy presence. Today, ask the Lord to teach you to serve Him with your whole heart so that your life will be a song of praise to Him.

Holy Father, I praise and worship You because You saved me. Help me to walk in Your ways forever.

Amen

Praise God in His glorious majesty

Righteousness and justice are the foundation of your throne; love and faithfulness go before you. Blessed are those who have learned to acclaim you, who walk in the light of your presence, O LORD. They rejoice in your name all day long; they exult in your righteousness. For you are their glory and strength, and by your favor you exalt our horn. Indeed, our shield belongs to the LORD, our king to the Holy One of Israel.

— PSALM 89:14-18 —

This psalm makes use of grand and majestic words to praise God for who He is. They create the picture of the Lord as an impressive King who sits on His throne supported by two pillars: His righteousness and justice. Two servants, love and faithfulness, go before Him to smooth His path.

The Lord's followers serve Him with sheer joy, because He always does what is absolutely right. He alone judges with righteousness and He alone can stand in the truth.

More surprising still, is that this mighty King and righteous Judge, loves His people and allows them to linger in His presence. What undiluted joy there is in simply spending time in the light of the presence of God and praising Him as the King of kings.

King of kings, I respond joyfully to the call to worship and praise You in Your glorious majesty.

Amen

Praise the eternal King

The LORD reigns, he is robed in majesty; the LORD is robed in majesty and is armed with strength. The world is firmly established; it cannot be moved. Your throne was established long ago; you are from all eternity.

— PSALM 93:1-2 —

According to Jewish tradition, this psalm alludes to the coming Messiah who would set God's people free. The opening lines describe the incomparable majesty of the coming King. Christians know that this eternal King is the Lord Jesus Christ. His throne has been established long ago and His existence is eternal. No wonder then that His kingly robes elicit such praise from the Psalmist.

Our image of God directly affects the nature of our prayers. When you spend time in prayer today, let this psalm help you to honor Jesus Christ as the Eternal King, clothed in majesty and girded with strength. Let the image of the Eternal King elicit praise from you today.

Loving Lord Jesus, You are clothed in majesty and girded with strength. I bow before Your throne in thankful worship.

Amen

Meditate on God's Word

Teach me, O LORD, to follow your decrees; then I will keep them to the end. Give me understanding, and I will keep your law and obey it with all my heart. Direct me in the path of your commands, for there I find delight. Turn my heart toward your statutes and not toward selfish gain. Turn my eyes away from worthless things; preserve my life according to your word.

— PSALM 119:33-37 —

Psalm 119 is a long poem that eulogizes the law of God. It is a privilege to learn what God says and to be able to walk the road that leads to eternal life. The writer of this poem knew that he was not always capable of keeping God's law. He knew that he needed someone who could train him in the ways of God and to help him understand what God requires.

But more important still, he had a heart that earnestly sought to do God's will rather than his own. He had experienced how deceitful riches can be, and so prays that God will help him to be eager to live according to His laws.

One of the most important spiritual disciplines is reading and studying the Word of God. Ask the Lord to increase your hunger for His Word, so that you will be able to obey His commands. In them you will find life indeed!

Lord Jesus, Immanuel, thank You for the life that You have given me as I obey Your Word.

Amen

Praise for God's creative power

The seas have lifted up, O LORD, the seas have lifted up their voice; the seas have lifted up their pounding waves. Mightier than the thunder of the great waters, mightier than the breakers of the sea – the LORD on high is mighty. Your statutes stand firm; holiness adorns your house for endless days, O LORD.

– PSALM 93:3-5 –

Through the ages people have marveled at the wonders of God's creation, especially the seas and rivers. The angry waves that break violently against the rocks and crash along the coast fascinate people, because they demonstrate the overwhelming power of water. And yet, as powerful as the water is, the might of the God who created everything, far surpasses all the powers of nature. The energy of surging masses of water, devastating earthquakes and volcanic explosions cannot be compared to the might of God.

If God's power is so much greater than the might of nature, He can undoubtedly handle our problems. Don't allow the din of desperate situations to undermine your trust in God. When you pray today, remember that God is mightier than many waters.

Creator God, we praise and glorify You because You are mightier than any created force in nature, and You put Your power at our disposal.

Amen

Prayer for discernment

Deal with your servant according to your love and teach me your decrees. I am your servant; give me discernment that I may understand your statutes. It is time for you to act, O LORD; your law is being broken. Because I love your commands more than gold, more than pure gold, and because I consider all your precepts right, I hate every wrong path.

— PSALM 119:124-128 —

The trials and tribulations we face in life often cause us to turn to other people for help. Far too often we pour out all the details of our problems to any available ear. The Psalmist knew that he should first turn to God for discernment and wisdom. He asks, *"Teach me your decrees,"* and *"Give me discernment that I may understand your statutes."*

He knew that the way of the Lord would keep him from foolish actions and from the paths that lead to destruction. That is why he has decided to learn the principles found in God's Word and to apply them in his life.

It is possible that you are facing a difficult situation today. God promises to give you wisdom to handle your situation, if you ask Him for it (see Jas. 1:5). Pray that God will give you discernment and ask Him how to apply His wisdom to your specific situation.

Master and Guide, as Your servant I ask that You would give me discernment so that I can live within Your will.

Amen

Honor the Name of God

"Now my heart is troubled, and what shall I say? 'Father, save me from this hour'? No, it was for this very reason I came to this hour. Father, glorify your name!" Then a voice came from heaven, "I have glorified it, and will glorify it again."

– John 12:27-28 –

When we find ourselves in difficult circumstances, we often pray that our problems will disappear. God has saved and redeemed us from all evil and wickedness, and so it is fitting for us to pray as Jesus did. He asked His Father if He could be spared from the torment and suffering of the horrific death on the cross (see Lk. 22:42). But Jesus also understood that enduring this suffering would bring greater honor to His Father. Through Jesus' death on the cross, God gives salvation to all who believe in Him.

When you are uncertain about what lies ahead of you, you can ask our Father to protect you from evil. Following the example of our Lord and Master, we too can ask that God's name would be glorified by the way in which we handle the things we encounter in life.

Heavenly Father, I want to honor Your Name, regardless of the circumstances that I face. May Your Holy Spirit help me in this.

Amen

Jesus prays for His Disciples

"I pray for them. I am not praying for the world, but for those you have given me, for they are yours. All I have is yours, and all you have is mine. And glory has come to me through them. I will remain in the world no longer, but they are still in the world, and I am coming to you. Holy Father, protect them by the power of your name – the name you gave me – so that they may be one as we are one. While I was with them, I protected them and kept them safe by that name you gave me. None has been lost except the one doomed to destruction so that Scripture would be fulfilled."

– John 17:9-12 –

J ust before Jesus was arrested by Roman soldiers, He took time to pray for His disciples. He asked the Father to protect those for whom He would die. Listen to the words of Jesus, *"Holy Father, protect them by the power of your name … that they may be one as we are one."* Jesus' prayer reveals the attitude of His heart. He cares for His disciples and desires for them to live together in unity.

Jesus cares for us, His followers today, just as He cared for His disciples so long ago. Meditate on the wonder of the fact that Jesus cares for you and ask Him to help you to live in peace with your fellow Christians.

Gracious Lord Jesus Christ, You care for me, an unworthy sinner. You look after me day after day. Help me to promote unity amongst Your children.

Amen

Trust in God's Word

I call with all my heart; answer me, O LORD, and I will obey your decrees. I call out to you; save me and I will keep your statutes. I rise before dawn and cry for help; I have put my hope in your word. My eyes stay open through the watches of the night, that I may meditate on your promises.

— PSALM 119:145-148 —

We tend to turn to God only when our backs are against the wall and our world seems to be collapsing in a heap. We might even try to bargain with God and promise to obey Him if He would just deliver us from our difficulties.

The Psalmist does not, however, turn to God as a last resort. For him, God was the *only* answer that he sought. He rose early in the mornings to meditate on God's promises and to ask for His help. If he couldn't sleep at night, he focused his thoughts on all that is holy and true. This kind of commitment to God and His Word helped him over and over again to overcome his problems.

Decide how you can make God's Word a central part of your everyday life. Ask God to help you, through His Spirit, to concentrate on His life-giving words.

Merciful and compassionate Father, I want to get up early in the mornings and meditate on Your words so that I can obey You and can live according to Your Word.

Amen

JULY

PRAYERS FOR ASSISTANCE AND SUPPORT

May God be gracious to us and bless us and make his face shine upon us, that your ways may be known on earth, your salvation among all nations.

– PSALM 67:1-2 –

One of the most powerful concepts, and one that will rid you of your lack of self-confidence, is that God is with you and that He is always ready to help you. One of the most elementary doctrines of Christianity is that God Almighty wants to be your friend and that He will be at your side, helping you and guiding you towards success. There is not a single other idea that is so powerful in building up your self-confidence, than saying to yourself with conviction, "God is my Guide, God helps me, God is my Counselor". Make this your motto for each day and experience its truth.

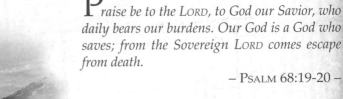

P*raise be to the* LORD, *to God our Savior, who daily bears our burdens. Our God is a God who saves; from the Sovereign* LORD *comes escape from death.*

– PSALM 68:19-20 –

A prayer for restored success

Satisfy us in the morning with your unfailing love, that we may sing for joy and be glad all our days. Make us glad for as many days as you have afflicted us, for as many years as we have seen trouble. May your deeds be shown to your servants, your splendor to their children. May the favor of the LORD our God rest upon us; establish the work of our hands for us — yes, establish the work of our hands.

— PSALM 90:14-17 —

In this prayer, Moses beseeches God to pour out His unfathomable and undying love over His people every day. He prays for his people to see the miracles of God's workmanship in their lives, and he prays for God's blessing on all they do.

Pray to God to assist you and support your efforts and to make them successful. But remember, your requests reveal your definition of success.

Ask God during your prayer time today for His blessing on all your efforts, but first ask yourself whether you really know the meaning of true success.

Lord God, grant that my efforts today will be successful, because I wish to utilize them to glorify You above all else.

Amen

Rejoice in God's omnipotence

You are my lamp, O LORD; the LORD turns my darkness into light. With your help I can advance against a troop; with my God I can scale a wall. As for God, his way is perfect; the word of the LORD is flawless. He is a shield for all who take refuge in him. For who is God besides the LORD? And who is the Rock except our God? It is God who arms me with strength and makes my way perfect. He makes my feet like the feet of a deer; he enables me to stand on the heights. He trains my hands for battle; my arms can bend a bow of bronze. You give me your shield of victory; you stoop down to make me great.

– 2 SAMUEL 22:29-36 –

Regardless of how hard we try to remain true to our promises, at one time or another, we all fall short. However, this is not the case with God. At the end of his reign, David glorifies the Lord with the words, "*As for God, his way is perfect; the word of the LORD is flawless.*"

David describes God as a Rock, a shield, a fortress. And God guides His people onto the heights like fleet-footed deer. All these images imply that dangers and problems still surround God's children. However, God provides security in the midst of all these dangers.

Whether you walk in the sun or the shadows today, reflect on the trustworthiness of our God and praise and glorify Him for that.

Faithful God, You have always proven Yourself to be trustworthy, bringing all Your promises to fruition. I praise and glorify Your Name!

Amen

Rejoice in God's salvation

In that day you will say: "I will praise you, O LORD. Although you were angry with me, your anger has turned away and you have comforted me. Surely God is my salvation; I will trust and not be afraid. The LORD, the LORD, is my strength and my song; he has become my salvation."

– ISAIAH 12:1-2 –

These verses echo Moses' prayer in Exodus 15:2 and comprise the united prayer that will arise from the lips of God's people when Christ will rule the earth forever. God's people will greet Christ with a prayer of praise that will confirm their commitment to Christ.

Even though, at times, God was filled with wrath about the sins of His people, He will forgive and comfort them. He will not come to judge those who remain, but to deliver them. What a privilege and joy it is to know that, although we deserve to be condemned, we need not live in fear of God, because He has redeemed us through Christ.

Today our prayers join those of the faithful who have gone before us, and of all those who will follow us. This praise is the motto of the redeemed – those who realize that God was willing to sacrifice His only Son to heal and deliver them. Join in this glorious prayer of praise and thanksgiving today.

Gracious God and Father, I glorify You in Jesus Christ as my song, my strength, and my salvation!

Amen

God hears our prayers

To you, O LORD, I called; to the LORD I cried for mercy: "What gain is there in my destruction, in my going down into the pit? Will the dust praise you? Will it proclaim your faithfulness? Hear, O LORD, and be merciful to me; O LORD, be my help." You turned my wailing into dancing; you removed my sackcloth and clothed me with joy, that my heart may sing to you and not be silent. O LORD my God, I will give you thanks forever.

– PSALM 30:8-12 –

God undoubtedly knows what is best for us, even before we present our requests to Him.

Why does the omniscient, omnipotent God allow His plans to be executed through our feeble requests? David showed insight into this question. He realized that prayers, which are answered, confirm God's love and grace towards this world.

We often do not even notice the work of God in our lives. But an answered prayer is a clear sign to us that God is at work. God cherishes the heartfelt gratitude and the joyous praise of those who acknowledge His loving hand in their lives.

Therefore, when our prayers are answered, like David, we should not take the miracle for granted.

O, Hearer of Prayers, all flesh must come to You. As our help in times of trouble, we proclaim Your faithfulness.

Amen

In times of trouble, find your strength in God

O LORD, be gracious to us; we long for you. Be our strength every morning, our salvation in time of distress. At the thunder of your voice, the peoples flee; when you rise up, the nations scatter.

— ISAIAH 33:2-3 —

Immediately after praying to God to save Israel, Isaiah describes Israel's distress: The Assyrians have rejected their petition for peace. The entire country finds itself in trouble. The highways are deserted, because no one dares travel. Lebanon has been destroyed and the plains of Sharon are like a wilderness; Bashan and Carmel have been pillaged.

Isaiah's trust in God never faltered. Because he believed God's promises, that He would preserve Israel and deliver His people, Isaiah could pray with confidence: *"Be our strength every morning, our salvation in time of distress."*

Like Isaiah, we can depend on God in times of distress and trouble.

Omnipotent and omniscient God, even though I am weak and find myself in trouble, I steadfastly trust in Your promises. Be my strength and my salvation every day.

Amen

Proclaim the Gospel of Christ

Devote yourselves to prayer, being watchful and thankful. And pray for us, too, that God may open a door for our message, so that we may proclaim the mystery of Christ, for which I am in chains. Pray that I may proclaim it clearly, as I should.

– COLOSSIANS 4:2-4 –

If you find testifying about Christ an un-nerving task, remind yourself that Paul experienced it as a major challenge. That is why Paul asked the Christians of Colosse to pray for him. He wanted to be given the opportunity to preach the Gospel and spread the message of Christ clearly.

Whether he felt that he was lacking in courage, skill or something else, we do not know. But he realized that he needed God's Spirit to work through him – and he knew that God would hear the prayers of the faithful.

Pray for your unbelieving friends and family today. Pray that you will be granted the opportunity to share the message that God has died for their sins, tactfully but clearly.

Lord Jesus, my Lord and Savior, grant me the ability to preach the gospel of salvation as clearly as You expect of me.

Amen

Redemption from shame

Rescue me from the mire, do not let me sink; deliver me from those who hate me, from the deep waters. Do not let the floodwaters engulf me or the depths swallow me up or the pit close its mouth over me. Answer me, O LORD, out of the goodness of your love; in your great mercy turn to me. Do not hide your face from your servant; answer me quickly, for I am in trouble. Come near and rescue me; redeem me because of my foes.

— PSALM 69:14-18 —

David complained to God about the wickedness of those who hated him and spread lies about him. Even his own brothers pretended not to know him.

David complains, *"Those who sit at the gate mock me, and I am the song of the drunkards"* (v. 12). But even though everyone was against him, David did not lose heart. He did not allow the flood of criticism to engulf him. He did not allow his enemies to destroy him. He rather called on God to rescue him from the "mire".

We all feel just like David at some time or another in our lives. When you are the object of ridicule, when lies are being spread about you, when you are humiliated and you feel as though the floodwaters are going to engulf you, respond as David did. Do not quit. Take your shame to God in prayer!

Merciful Lord Jesus, hear my prayer and rescue me from the mire of shame and lies. I glorify You as my refuge and my fortress.

Amen

The prayer of Abraham's servant

Then he prayed, "O LORD, God of my master Abraham, give me success today, and show kindness to my master Abraham. See, I am standing beside this spring, and the daughters of the townspeople are coming out to draw water. May it be that when I say to a girl, 'Please let down your jar that I may have a drink,' and she says, 'Drink, and I'll water your camels too' – let her be the one you have chosen for your servant Isaac. By this I will know that you have shown kindness to my master." Before he had finished praying, Rebekah came out with her jar on her shoulder. She was the daughter of Bethuel son of Milcah, who was the wife of Abraham's brother Nahor.

– GENESIS 24:12-15 –

When believers need to make important decisions, they yearn to do so in line with God's will and purpose.

Abraham asked his servant to find the right wife for his son, Isaac. The servant realized the extent of the responsibility resting upon him, therefore he laid the matter before God without delay, rather than depending on his own wisdom. He asked God for a sign and God granted his request at once. Before he had finished praying, Rebecca appeared and offered water to both him and his camels. What a special answer to a prayer!

It is good to seek God's guidance and direction in prayer, as Abraham's servant did.

Gracious God, help me to trust in You completely as I seek to do Your will.

Amen

Seek shelter with God

But my eyes are fixed on you, O Sovereign Lord; in you I take refuge – do not give me over to death. Keep me from the snares they have laid for me, from the traps set by evildoers. Let the wicked fall into their own nets, while I pass by in safety.

— Psalm 141:8-10 —

A newspaper carried a report about a hiker who got lost, and walked through a blinding snow storm for hours, without seeing any sign of life. Exhausted, hungry and almost freezing to death, he was ready to give up hope, when he spotted a cabin between the trees. Even though it was not luxurious, the deserted cabin offered warmth and shelter to the young man, until rescue workers could save him.

How welcoming the sight of that cabin must have seemed to the hiker – his refuge and his safe fortress. It quite literally saved his life. Similarly, in this psalm, David describes the Lord as a refuge against the dangers surrounding him.

It is comforting to know that, when we are surrounded by enemies, we can call on God to deliver us. Cast all your cares and concerns on God – He is your refuge and your safe fortress.

Savior and Redeemer, today I look to You for help. Please open Your hand and provide in all my needs.

Amen

Thanksgiving for God's goodness

Give thanks to the LORD, for he is good; his love endures forever. Cry out, "Save us, O God our Savior; gather us and deliver us from the nations, that we may give thanks to your holy name, that we may glory in your praise." Praise be to the LORD, the God of Israel, from everlasting to everlasting. Then all the people said "Amen" and "Praise the LORD."

– 1 CHRONICLES 16:34-36 –

King David had just brought the ark of God into Jerusalem. The entire community gathered there to experience this milestone in the history of Israel. God had established them in their country and conquered their enemies.

David prayed, *"Save us, O God our Savior; gather us and deliver us from the nations, that we may give thanks to your holy name, that we may glory in your praise."*

Gratitude flows from our hearts when we think about the good things God has done for us. He establishes us and graciously provides all that we need. Think of all the ways in which He shows kindness to you and your family, and thank and praise Him for His infinite goodness. His love is everlasting.

Gracious and Loving Lord and Savior, I wish to thank You for being so good to me. Thank You for Your everlasting love.

Amen

A prayer to do God's will

Going a little farther, he fell with his face to the ground and prayed, "My Father, if it is possible, may this cup be taken from me. Yet not as I will, but as you will."

— MATTHEW 26:39 —

To surrender to the will of God for our lives, could be a formidable challenge. At times our dreams and aspirations are in conflict with God's will for us. Jesus wrestled in prayer over this issue in the Garden of Gethsemane. God's plan to ensure the redemption of mankind was at stake.

God's plan involved suffering and crucifixion. Jesus saw the difficult road ahead and spent a night of torment in prayer about it. The courage and strength that He found in prayer that night helped Him to face the suffering that He had to endure the next day.

The choices we have to make are of far lesser importance than those Jesus had to make, but they could result in intense anguish that forces us to our knees before the Father.

As His will becomes clear to us, may God enable us to yield to His perfect will, following the example set by our Lord and Master.

Gracious Father, the sincere prayer from my heart is that Your will be done!

Amen

Proclaiming God as our only hope

Do not withhold your mercy from me, O LORD; may your love and your truth always protect me. For troubles without number surround me; my sins have overtaken me, and I cannot see. They are more than the hairs of my head, and my heart fails within me. Be pleased, O LORD, to save me; O LORD, come quickly to help me. Yet I am poor and needy; may the LORD think of me. You are my help and my deliverer; O my God, do not delay.

— PSALM 40:11-13, 17 —

As king of Israel, David had a wealth of treasures: jewelry, gold, money, and a host of servants to carry out his every wish. And yet, David reached a time in his life when he declared that God was his only hope. We do not know the particular circumstances in which this prayer was written, but we can appreciate the fact that it was a landmark in David's life.

What would it take for you to proclaim God as your "help and deliverer"? What would it take for you to look towards God alone for the solution to your problems?

When you find yourself in a difficult situation, approach His throne of grace in prayer. Declare boldly to God that you trust in Him alone to deliver you.

Holy God, my only hope is in Your unfailing love. Do not withhold Your mercy from me, Lord.

Amen

An urgent prayer for help

Hear, O Lord, and answer me, for I am poor and needy. Guard my life, for I am devoted to you. You are my God; save your servant who trusts in you. Have mercy on me, O Lord, for I call to you all day long. Bring joy to your servant, for to you, O Lord, I lift up my soul. You are forgiving and good, O Lord, abounding in love to all who call to you. Hear my prayer, O Lord; listen to my cry for mercy.

– Psalm 86:1-6 –

In his deepest distress, David cries out, *"Have mercy on me, O Lord, for I call to you all day long."* David does not cry out to God because he expects to be repaid for all he has done. *"You are forgiving and good, O Lord, abounding in love to all who call to you."* The Lord is truly a gracious God and He wants to deliver those who are facing troubled times.

Like David, we must take refuge in the Lord – not only in times of trouble, but at all times. We must approach God with humility, trusting in His unfailing character. Yet, we can pray with confidence, because God answers the prayers of His loyal servants.

Faithful Lord of my life, my entire existence is dependent upon Your mercy and I know that You will hear my prayer of distress.

Amen

Glory be to the Lord who answers

Not to us, O LORD, not to us but to your name be the glory, because of your love and faithfulness. Why do the nations say, "Where is their God?" Our God is in heaven; he does whatever pleases him. But their idols are silver and gold, made by the hands of men. They have mouths, but cannot speak, eyes, but they cannot see; they have ears, but cannot hear, noses, but they cannot smell.

– PSALM 115:1-6 –

Children can easily tell which adults will pay attention to them and which will ignore them. When they find someone who pays attention to them, they are keen to interact with that person.

This prayer portrays God as someone who does exactly that. Like a caring father, He descends to our level, to assure us that He hears us and cares for us and that He appreciates us.

Like a discerning child, we must persevere to reach God in prayer because He has proven Himself to be faithful. Not only does He hear us, but He also answers us in His perfect time and according to His wisdom.

The Lord deserves our worship and trust! May our Lord grant you the eyes to notice the faithfulness of His character and to persevere in prayer with Him.

Dear Lord Jesus, I thank You because You bend down and listen to my prayers, and because You answer them in Your time and according to Your wisdom.

Amen

Praise God's glorious deeds

Sing to the Lord, all the earth; proclaim his salvation day after day. Declare his glory among the nations, his marvelous deeds among all peoples. For great is the Lord and most worthy of praise; he is to be feared above all gods.

— 1 Chronicles 16:23-25 —

A t times, on an indescribably glorious spring day when the splendor of renewal is all around us, we want to express our praise as part of something that is far greater than ourselves.

This prayer of David reflects that selfsame sentiment: *"Sing to the Lord, all the earth!"* To David, each day was an opportunity to declare the good news of salvation and the amazing deeds of God.

This prayer was written for a very special celebration: When David brought the ark of God into the tent that he had specially prepared for it. It is especially fitting, on such occasions, to passionately proclaim the glory of God.

Imagine for a moment, that all the faithful for miles around joined together to praise God and pray to Him. How would that sound? What words would you use to praise and glorify your God?

Almighty God, I want to glorify You and stand before You in wonder and worship.

Amen

A prayer for strength from the Lord

Then Samson prayed to the LORD, "O Sovereign LORD, remember me. O God, please strengthen me just once more, and let me with one blow get revenge on the Philistines for my two eyes." Then Samson reached toward the two central pillars on which the temple stood. Bracing himself against them, his right hand on the one and his left hand on the other, Samson said, "Let me die with the Philistines!" Then he pushed with all his might, and down came the temple on the rulers and all the people in it. Thus he killed many more when he died than while he lived.

– JUDGES 16:28-30 –

Before the birth of Samson, an angel of the Lord told his mother that she would give birth to a son. His hair was never to be shaved and he was to be dedicated to the Lord. He was destined to free Israel from the hands of the Philistines. He became a big, strong man. He served the Lord for years but then he strayed from the Lord.

Now we find him in a Philistine jail, blind, weak, and far from God. And yet he remembers that his strength once came from God. He prays, asking God to help him one last time. The Lord heard his prayer and he achieved a major victory over the Philistines.

Should it seem as though you have strayed from God, always remember the Source of your strength. Pray that God will strengthen you to be victorious in the battle to which He has called you.

Gracious God, strengthen me and help me to trust in You rather than in my own strength.

Amen

A Redeemer from God

For our offenses are many in your sight, and our sins testify against us. Our offenses are ever with us, and we acknowledge our iniquities: rebellion and treachery against the LORD, turning our backs on our God, fomenting oppression and revolt, uttering lies our hearts have conceived. "The Redeemer will come to Zion, to those in Jacob who repent of their sins," declares the LORD.

— ISAIAH 59:12-13, 20 —

When too many things pile up – whether in the office or dishes in the sink – we feel guilty because we have not paid attention to our responsibilities sooner. However, Isaiah prays about something of a far more serious nature. He describes the sins of Israel as "many". God is grieved by these sins which deserve His punishment. Israel was powerless to rid themselves of these sins but God could.

Although the Israelites rebelled against God, although they turned their back on the Almighty, God promised to send them a Redeemer. Only He could free them from the bondage of sin. This Redeemer was Jesus.

Let us thank God anew today that He has sent Jesus as Redeemer to this world torn apart by sin.

Lord Jesus, I confess that my offences are "many". Thank You for redeeming me from sin and disobedience.

Amen

Security with God

So I said: "Do not take me away, O my God, in the midst of my days; your years go on through all generations. In the beginning you laid the foundations of the earth, and the heavens are the work of your hands. They will perish, but you remain; they will all wear out like a garment. Like clothing you will change them and they will be discarded. But you remain the same, and your years will never end."

— PSALM 102:25-29 —

This anonymous prayer reflects the sad tidings of someone who is going through great affliction and misery. These words could have been a journal entry in the life of anyone overwhelmed by problems. And yet, this tortured soul, after pouring out his distress to the Lord, sees a ray of hope in his desperate situation: he remembers that he is a child of the Eternal God and Father. This God rises above all our problems, as well as above time and space.

He is willing and able to keep His children safe and to let them live in His holy presence forever.

Should you find yourself in distress today, because of the problems of life, then make this prayer your own.

Let God know of your anxieties and then thank Him for providing stability in your ever-changing world.

O God, my refuge and my fortress, thank You for the security which You have brought into my life.

Amen

A prayer for courage in times of affliction

"Sovereign Lord," they said, "you made the heaven and the earth and the sea, and everything in them. Indeed Herod and Pontius Pilate met together with the Gentiles and the people of Israel in this city to conspire against your holy servant Jesus, whom you anointed. They did what your power and will had decided beforehand should happen. Now, Lord, consider their threats and enable your servants to speak your word with great boldness. Stretch out your hand to heal and perform miraculous signs and wonders through the name of your holy servant Jesus."

– ACTS 4:24, 27-30 –

Before His ascension, Jesus said to His followers: *"You will receive power when the Holy Spirit comes on you"* (Acts 1:8). They received that strength on the day of Pentecost, but they still faced fierce opposition – such as threats from the Sanhedrin who forbade them to preach the Gospel of Jesus Christ. Therefore, the faithful gathered to pray.

We can learn from their prayer today. They did not ask for the destruction of the opposition, but for courage, and for God to demonstrate His omnipotence through them. They mentioned the threats they had received to God, and reminded themselves of how the religious leaders opposed Jesus, their Savior.

Ask Jesus to grant you the courage and strength to preach the Good News to all who cross your path today. The Holy Spirit will help you in this.

Lord Jesus, my Power and my Strength, grant me courage to be a steadfast witness for You.

Amen

An appeal to God to listen

I said to the LORD, "You are my LORD; apart from you I have no good thing." LORD, you have assigned me my portion and my cup; you have made my lot secure. The boundary lines have fallen for me in pleasant places; surely I have a delightful inheritance.

– PSALM 16:2, 5-6 –

We have all heard of families who were torn apart forever because of conflict over an inheritance. Sometimes brothers and sisters who used to love one another spend the rest of their lives in a greedy effort to hold onto what they have inherited from their parents. Others might go to their graves filled with hatred and resentment towards family members who have received more than they have.

How refreshing is it therefore, to hear David telling the Lord in prayer, *"The boundary lines have fallen for me in pleasant places; surely I have a delightful inheritance."*

Are we satisfied with what the Lord has granted us, regardless of how great or small? Can you honestly and sincerely say, "I have You Lord, and that is sufficient for me!"

Make a list of all the things that God has given to you and rejoice in your inheritance – in all the good that God has done for you.

Gracious Provider of every good gift, You are my most precious inheritance. All that I am and have are from You. I kneel in grateful adoration before You.

Amen

Mercy from our unchanging God

You, O Lord, reign forever; your throne endures from generation to generation. Why do you always forget us? Why do you forsake us so long? Restore us to yourself, O Lord, that we may return; renew our days as of old unless you have utterly rejected us and are angry with us beyond measure.

— LAMENTATIONS 5:19-22 —

Jeremiah holds an unshakeable conviction: God does not change! Our loyalty and our feelings are as transitory as a breath of air, but God always remains the same. We stray, and God brings us back. We lose our joy, and God restores it.

Although Jeremiah is praying for his people, his words help us to put our own lives in perspective. The eternal God is in control and He has the power to lift us up when we have fallen.

In prayer, acknowledge your complete dependency on God. This is one of the first steps that we should take in prayer. We should always approach God with humility with our requests.

God remains the same for all eternity, it is we who have strayed from Him. When you pray today, find the time to thank God for His constancy.

Eternal God, bring me back to You from the distant land of sin. Thank You that we cannot drift beyond the sphere of Your love.

Amen

A prayer for God's grace and favor

Blessed are those who dwell in your house; they are ever praising you. Look upon our shield, O God; look with favor on your anointed one. Better is one day in your courts than a thousand elsewhere; I would rather be a doorkeeper in the house of my God than dwell in the tents of the wicked.

— PSALM 84:4, 9-10 —

When talking about the "good life", we do not normally start by mentioning strength in the Lord. The Psalmist, however does exactly that when he says, *"They go from strength to strength"* (v. 7). We tend to describe our happy families, cozy homes, world travels, or a satisfying career. It is not wrong to desire these things, but if your thoughts about the good life exclude God, then they are wrong indeed.

In this prayer, the Psalmist reminds himself that to worship God is far better than to have a good life in the company of men. He understands that God fully knows what the good life is and that He will surely grant it to His obedient children.

What a wonderful God we worship! He showers us with blessings and rewards those who follow Him faithfully. Thank God today for the blessings that you receive from His hand.

Great and gracious God, look down on us in goodwill and help us to remain obedient and faithful.

Amen

A prayer for victory

May the LORD answer you when you are in distress; may the name of the God of Jacob protect you. May he send you help from the sanctuary and grant you support from Zion. May he remember all your sacrifices and accept your burnt offerings. May he give you the desire of your heart and make all your plans succeed. We will shout for joy when you are victorious and will lift up our banners in the name of our God. May the LORD grant all your requests.

— PSALM 20:1-5 —

Imagine the shining, sharp points of weapons gleaming in the morning sun, while God's children, armed for battle, encourage their king through their prayers. While they gather to advance on the enemies of Israel, they are led in this prayer by David's director of music.

Who knows what battles your loved ones have to fight today? When you think of your family and friends, do you see in your mind's eye how they prepare for battle? How they prepare for the new school year, for the issues they will face at work, worrying about what they have to achieve that day?

Pray therefore that God will make them victorious in that which they have to do.

Pray that their achievements will glorify God, and then ask God for the same for yourself. God will grant us victory if we are sincere in our prayers!

God of grace, grant victory today to all those who ask You for it with sincerity.

Amen

Call on God with expectation

But I call to God, and the LORD saves me. Evening, morning and noon I cry out in distress, and he hears my voice. He ransoms me unharmed from the battle waged against me, even though many oppose me. God, who is enthroned forever, will hear them and afflict them – men who never change their ways and have no fear of God.

– PSALM 55:16-19 –

Regardless of where you find yourself, or of when it happens, when you hear a distress call for help, you know that immediate and decisive action is required. The person in distress may be at the end of his tether, completely lost unless someone intervenes.

Believers can turn with any problem to God Himself. He always listens and He has the power to come to our rescue. David knew this. In times of trial and tribulation, David knew for certain: *"But I call to God, and the LORD saves me."*

The more desperate your situation, the more sense it makes to present your complaint audibly to God. As David experienced, you will discover that He responds to your call of distress.

God our Father, life has taught me that I can take refuge in You in every situation of distress. I know that You will come to my rescue, time and again. I thank You from the bottom of my heart for that.

Amen

Hezekiah's prayer for purification

But Hezekiah prayed for them, saying, "May the Lord, who is good, pardon everyone who sets his heart on seeking God – the Lord, the God of his fathers – even if he is not clean according to the rules of the sanctuary." And the Lord heard Hezekiah and healed the people.

– 2 Chronicles 30:18-20 –

King Hezekiah's prayer demonstrates the timeless truth that, in the final instance, we are purified by God, and not by our good works. The people of Israel and Judah had been separated for many years, but Hezekiah was courageous enough to invite everyone from Israel and Judah to celebrate the Passover festival at the temple in Jerusalem.

The majority of the Israelites turned down the invitation, but some men humbled themselves, repented and went to Jerusalem. Hezekiah prayed for these unpurified Israelites, because forgiveness is part of God's nature – and God forgave them.

Even though we should never take the goodness and kindness of God for granted, we may rest assured in the knowledge that He will purify us. We must humble ourselves and go to Him repenting, deeply aware of the fact that we cannot justify ourselves.

God of grace and love, thank You for forgiving us, even before we decided to follow You, and for cleansing us from all sin.

Amen

Glorify and thank God for hope

For you have been my hope, O Sovereign LORD, my confidence since my youth. From birth I have relied on you; you brought me forth from my mother's womb. I will ever praise you. I have become like a portent to many, but you are my strong refuge. My mouth is filled with your praise, declaring your splendor all day long.

– PSALM 71:5-8 –

This prayer is probably that of an elderly King David, looking back over his life, and praising God for His constant presence throughout his life. He gives thanks to God for comfort and shelter during his youth, when virtually all had forsaken him.

He also gives thanks to God for sheltering him in old age. The essence of David's experience with God is hope. God gave him hope when all else went wrong.

How would you describe the role of God in your life so far? As the One who delivers? Who strengthens? Who comforts? Through prayer we can reaffirm our hope in God daily, as well as declare our love for Him.

Dear Lord, in You alone I place my hope. As I have trusted in You in my youth, in old age, my only hope is in You.

Amen

Trust God to provide for your needs

Your kingdom is an everlasting kingdom, and your dominion endures through all generations. The LORD is faithful to all his promises and loving toward all he has made. The LORD upholds all those who fall and lifts up all who are bowed down. The eyes of all look to you, and you give them their food at the proper time. You open your hand and satisfy the desires of every living thing.

– PSALM 145:13-16 –

Life exposes us to many conflicting demands: children requiring attention, employers requiring productivity and performance, or marriage partners requiring support at home.

While we make an effort to pay attention to all these responsibilities, we may feel that we deserve more attention. We may even start wondering whether God can truly provide for all our needs. He promised to help carry our heavy burdens when they cause us to stumble and fall. What a comforting thought to know that the Lord will provide in all our needs.

Jesus, the Living Christ, commanded us not to worry, because God will take care of us. Therefore, cast all your troubles upon Him in prayer, and trust in Him to provide for you.

Holy and Loving God and Father, I look to You for help in providing for my needs. Open Your hand and provide according to Your will and wisdom.

Amen

A cry for God to take action

O God, do not keep silent; be not quiet, O God, be not still. See how your enemies are astir, how your foes rear their heads. Cover their faces with shame so that men will seek your name, O Lord. May they ever be ashamed and dismayed; may they perish in disgrace. Let them know that you, whose name is the Lord – that you alone are the Most High over all the earth.

– Psalm 83:1-2, 16-18 –

The people of Israel were being attacked. At least ten nations formed an alliance against them. Prospects looked grim. However, the Israelites had found themselves in similar situations before. God destroyed their enemies in the past and He was sure to do so again.

This is what the Psalmist prays. He beseeches God, not so much for Israel's survival, as for God's glory and respect amongst the nations. The plans of Israel's enemies were, after all, plans against God.

Although God's people are no longer represented by a single nation, there are still many evil rulers who are working against God's plans.

Christians should pray that these leaders will come to acknowledge God as the Sovereign Ruler over all of creation.

Omnipotent and omnipresent God, You will not look on passively. Let Your enemies come to realize and acknowledge that You are the "Lord", the Most High over the entire earth.

Amen

Glory be to God for deliverance

Then my enemies will turn back when I call for help. By this I will know that God is for me. In God, whose word I praise, in the LORD, whose word I praise – in God I trust; I will not be afraid. What can man do to me? I am under vows to you, O God; I will present my thank offerings to you. For you have delivered me from death and my feet from stumbling, that I may walk before God in the light of life.

– PSALM 56:9-13 –

Desperate people do desperate things, but eventually it is God who delivers them. When David fled to the Philistine city of Gath in order to escape the wrath of King Saul, he very quickly realized that his life was in danger. He was an Israelite soldier who, in all probability, had killed many Philistines.

David then pretended to be deranged and the king of Gath allowed him to leave the place unchallenged. He soon found a safer home in the cave of Adullam. It was probably there that David found the opportunity to write this prayer in which he praises the Lord for delivering him.

Perhaps you are facing a difficult situation at present. Faithfully trust in God to deliver you. If you place your trust in the Almighty, you have no reason to fear.

Faithful God our Father, I will not fear and get panic-stricken, as long as I trust in Your omnipotence. Praise the Lord because He is good! His love knows no bounds!

Amen

Glory be to God for power and strength

Let them praise the name of the Lord, for his name alone is exalted; his splendor is above the earth and the heavens. He has raised up for his people a horn, the praise of all his saints, of Israel, the people close to his heart. Praise the Lord.
— Psalm 148:13-14 —

This prayer calls on the creation in its entirety to glorify God for His power, strength and splendor. Even though we, as human beings, live with weaknesses and limitations, this prayer reminds us of God's supernatural powers.

The entire creation glorifies the Lord, for *"his name alone is exalted"*. Our wealth, possessions, even our friends and family, cannot deliver us from our troubles. God alone has a *"splendor (that) is above the earth"*. He gives us strength to endure our troubles and to conquer our temptations. No prayer is devoid of power, because prayer connects us with the mighty God of all creation.

When you approach God in prayer today, repeat the words of this psalm as a testimony of His power and strength.

Omnipotent and omniscient God, thank You for not only possessing power and strength but that You also made me strong and powerful.

Amen

Thirst for God

O God, you are my God, earnestly I seek you; my soul thirsts for you, my body longs for you, in a dry and weary land where there is no water. I have seen you in the sanctuary and beheld your power and your glory. Because your love is better than life, my lips will glorify you.

– PSALM 63:1-3 –

Anyone who has been lost in the desert without water for a long period of time, knows what it means to be thirsty. Your mouth becomes bone-dry, your lips crack, your throat aches and soon you start imagining that there is a large glass of water, sparkling in the sun in front of you. It looks so good! You can almost taste it!

David experienced this kind of thirst during his sojourn in *"a dry and weary land"* in the wilderness of Judea. In this prayer, he compares that thirst to his yearning for God. He seeks the Lord with all his might. His soul thirsts and his body yearns for God.

When last have you yearned for the Lord to such an extent? During your prayer time, you have the opportunity to satisfy your thirsty yearning for God.

Lord my God, I thirst for You like a deer panting for water. Thank You for always quenching that thirst through Your grace.

Amen

AUGUST

GLORY BE TO GOD FOR HIS LOVE!

But God demonstrates his own love for us in this: While we were still sinners, Christ died for us.

– ROMANS 5:8 –

God's love for His chosen people does not date from yesterday: it also does not start with their love for Him. We love Him because He first loved us. It was in His heart long before man was delivered from the power of darkness and was saved for His kingdom through our Savior and Redeemer, Jesus Christ, the Son of love. It does not start in time, but was born out of eternity. Over time, His chosen people were called from the darkness into His wondrous light. Before the world came into existence, God loved us. He chose Christ as the embodiment of His eternal love for this world. God proved His love on the cross: when Christ was hanging there, bleeding and dying, God was actually saying to the world, "I love you!"

Dear friends ... love comes from God. Everyone who loves has been born of God and knows God. Whoever does not love does not know God, because God is love. This is how God showed his love among us: He sent His one and only Son into the world that we might live through Him. This is love: not that we loved God, but that he loved us and sent his Son as an atoning sacrifice for our sins.

– 1 JOHN 4:7-10 –

Hear, O Lord

Hear my voice when I call, O LORD; be merciful to me and answer me. My heart says of you, "Seek his face!" Your face, LORD, I will seek. Do not hide your face from me, do not turn your servant away in anger; you have been my helper. Do not reject me or forsake me, O God my Savior. Though my father and mother forsake me, the LORD will receive me.

— PSALM 27:7-10 —

David experienced times when he felt forsaken by God. In this prayer, David beseeches God to hear his prayer and answer him. We also go through nights when our soul seems lost in darkness, when it feels as though there is a wall between God and us and that He is far away. We too will call on Him, our hearts filled with anguish, *"Hear my voice when I call, O LORD and answer me!"*

Even before David had received an answer, and while he was wrestling the storm of doubt, he prayed, *"Though my father and mother forsake me, the LORD will receive me."* He assures his troubled soul that God is always near, no matter how he feels.

During those times when it feels to us as though God is far away, we must remind ourselves that God is near to those who call on Him in their distress.

Listen to my plea, O God. I know that even though my mother and father may forsake me, You will hold me close to Your heart.

Amen

Manoah prays for God's teachings

Then Manoah prayed to the Lord: "O Lord, I beg you, let the man of God you sent to us come again to teach us how to bring up the boy who is to be born." God heard Manoah, and the angel of God came again to the woman while she was out in the field; but her husband Manoah was not with her.

– Judges 13:8-9 –

Manoah and his wife were surprised by the news that they would become the parents of a very special boy. For this barren couple, the possibility of parenthood was unexpected and seemed impossible. However, God had even greater plans.

Manoah wisely realized that he would have to receive more instruction on how to raise this special boy. Manoah simply prayed, "Let the man of God you sent to us come again to teach us how to bring up the boy who is to be born." God answered by sending an angel.

Unexpected developments often expose our shortcomings. When this happens, our spiritual maturity will be measured against our willingness to ask God for wisdom. Listen to what James says, *"If any of you lacks wisdom, he should ask God, who gives generously to all without finding fault; and it will be given to him"* (Jas. 1:5).

Holy Teacher and Lord, teach me how to handle the crises in my life in such a way that I will glorify You.

Amen

Praise the Lord in the morning and in the evening

It is good to praise the LORD and make music to your name, O Most High, to proclaim your love in the morning and your faithfulness at night, to the music of the ten-stringed lyre and the melody of the harp. For you make me glad by your deeds, O LORD; I sing for joy at the works of your hands. How great are your works, O LORD, how profound your thoughts!

– PSALM 92:1-5 –

What a positive way to start every day! This psalm was one of the first prayers to be said by the priests on the Sabbath day, *"For you make me glad by your deeds, O LORD!"*

Before reading the morning paper, before walking out of the door, before starting your numerous tasks of the day, how about deciding to start the day by glorifying God, by praying, *"For you make me very glad by your deeds, O Lord!"*

Right now, you have the opportunity for a fresh start, a new day awaits you. Why not start off in the right way, with praises to the Creator, instead of your familiar, everyday routine?

Declare your undying love in prayer this morning and before going to bed tonight, praise God again for His faithfulness.

Holy and loving God and Father, I praise You for Your undying love in the morning and in the evening, for You gladden my heart!

Amen

Give thanks for Christ's victory

But thanks be to God, who always leads us in triumphal procession in Christ and through us spreads everywhere the fragrance of the knowledge of him. For we are to God the aroma of Christ among those who are being saved and those who are perishing. To the one we are the smell of death; to the other, the fragrance of life. And who is equal to such a task?

— 2 CORINTHIANS 2:14-16 —

When the Roman generals of old victoriously returned to Rome from the battlefields, they paraded through the city with the loot that they had captured as well as numerous warriors taken captive.

In this prayer of thanksgiving, Paul uses the image of a victory parade to thank God for victory over the forces of evil of this world.

It is interesting that Paul describes the faithful in Christ as prisoners. There was a time when we formed part of Satan's armies, but then Jesus took us captive. However, unlike the prisoners of the Roman conquerors, Christ set us free from our old master and we are no longer destined to be sold into bondage and humiliation. Indeed, we have become brothers and sisters of Jesus.

Thank God in your prayer time today that you are part of His victory parade and His family!

I praise and thank You, victorious Lord Jesus, that I am part of Your victory parade.

Amen

Praise and glory to God the Creator

When I consider your heavens, the work of your fingers, the moon and the stars, which you have set in place, what is man that you are mindful of him, the son of man that you care for him? You made him a little lower than the heavenly beings and crowned him with glory and honor. You made him ruler over the works of your hands; you put everything under his feet: O LORD, our Lord, how majestic is your name in all the earth!

– Psalm 8:3-5, 9 –

After meditating on the beauty and immensity of only *one* aspect of God's creation – the stars in the nocturnal skies – David is moved to ask; *"What is man that you are mindful of him?"* We are merely specks in this vast universe that we inhabit. And yet God has made us just a little lower than Himself! He bestowed a great honor on us by first creating us as the crowning glory of the creation and later, after we had sinned, by sending His Son to redeem us.

When you are touched by the majesty or complexity of something that God has created in this physical world you should also remember that God who created this amazing world, has also bestowed on us His immeasurable love.

When praying today, try putting into words just how great your awe and gratitude are towards God the Creator.

My Heavenly Father and Creator God, through Jesus Christ I thank You for the grace shown to me and for crowning me with glory and honor.

Amen

Thank God for His glorious grace

Yet this I call to mind and therefore I have hope: Because of the LORD's great love we are not consumed, for his compassions never fail. They are new every morning; great is your faithfulness. I say to myself, "The LORD is my portion; therefore I will wait for him." The LORD is good to those whose hope is in him, to the one who seeks him; it is good to wait quietly for the salvation of the LORD.

– LAMENTATIONS 3:21-26 –

In Lamentations, the prophet Jeremiah expresses his anguish over the fall of Jerusalem – the culmination of God's judgment that he had personally predicted over a period of several years.

Nevertheless, even through his tears over his spurned people, Jeremiah praises God. He still trusts in God's unfailing love for His people. He calls God's faithfulness and grace to mind. God personally freed His people from bondage, and established them in a prosperous land. God Himself was the reason that Judah and Israel were not completely destroyed.

The memories of what God in His unfathomable grace has done for us, causes hope to rise in our hearts. Once our hope has been restored, we find ourselves able, even willing, to quietly wait upon His deliverance that will surely come.

Gracious God, You are inconceivably good to those who are willing to wait on You and to ask that Your will be done.

Amen

Praise for God's grandeur

Among the gods there is none like you, O LORD; no deeds can compare with yours. All the nations you have made will come and worship before you, O LORD; they will bring glory to your name. For you are great and do marvelous deeds; you alone are God.

— PSALM 86:8-10 —

Sometimes our prayers are so intertwined with the word, "Help", so focused on danger and affliction, that we forget to whom we are praying. David avoided this mistake. He realized that his God was greater than all the pagan gods, and that his God had already demonstrated His miraculous power in many ways and on many occasions.

David looks forward to the day when all the nations, and not only the Israelites, will acknowledge the sovereignty of the Almighty God. He alone is God!

Let us lift our eyes above the surrounding problems, and let us look to the Eternal and Triumphant King. Cast the problems that are causing you to worry upon your miraculous God.

Glory be to You, O greatest God! You perform miracles, even in my life. Let me take note of them and glorify Your name for them. You alone are God!

Amen

Moses extols the grandeur of God

Who among the gods is like you, O LORD? Who is like you – majestic in holiness, awesome in glory, working wonders? You stretched out your right hand and the earth swallowed them. In your unfailing love you will lead the people you have redeemed. In your strength you will guide them to your holy dwelling.

– EXODUS 15:11-13 –

Free at last! Precious freedom! For many centuries, the Israelites were slaves in Egypt, but now they witnessed a miracle: God parted the Red Sea so that they could walk through it on dry ground, escaping from their enemies. They were free from bondage and the Promised Land awaited them! Moses led the Israelites in a hymn of praise to the Victor – God.

He reminds the Israelites that they have been liberated to do as they please. They were free to worship God as His holy people. Moses asks God to lead the people to the Promised Land.

Set aside time today to praise and thank God for your freedom in Christ Jesus. Remember that you were liberated from sin to serve God as His child.

Loving Lord, let me not stray from Your path. Lead me, in Your holiness and omnipotence, into the Promised Land, so that I can be in Your presence for all eternity.

Amen

Let all creation glorify God

Say among the nations, "The LORD reigns." The world is firmly established, it cannot be moved; he will judge the peoples with equity. Let the heavens rejoice, let the earth be glad; let the sea resound, and all that is in it; let the fields be jubilant, and everything in them. Then all the trees of the forest will sing for joy; they will sing before the LORD, for he comes, he comes to judge the earth. He will judge the world in righteousness and the peoples in his truth.

— PSALM 96:10-13 —

Sometimes our hearts are slow to realize what a privilege it is to draw near to the Eternal God in prayer. Too often, we rush into God's presence with a hasty word of thanks or with all our requests.

In contrast, the writer of this psalm takes time to reflect on who it is that he prays to. He is so overwhelmed by God's grandeur that he calls on the heavens and the earth to sing God's praises. The trees in the forest, the fields and everything in them, the sea and all that is in it, must unite in a powerful chorus to the glory of God the Creator.

In your prayer today, express your appreciation for the world that God has created and rejoice in the fact that He is God, your Creator.

Gracious God, You are the source of all life. Together with all Your creatures, I want to glorify Your Name and praise You for Your powerful deeds!

Amen

Praise and gratitude for God's great deeds

Lord, you establish peace for us; all that we have accomplished you have done for us. O Lord, our God, other lords besides you have ruled over us, but your name alone do we honor. They are now dead, they live no more; those departed spirits do not rise. You punished them and brought them to ruin; you wiped out all memory of them. You have enlarged the nation, O Lord; you have enlarged the nation. You have gained glory for yourself; you have extended all the borders of the land.

— Isaiah 26:12-15 —

Whether it means scoring a goal, or running faster than your opponent, the fact remains that competitors do not necessarily win. Some successful athletes claim the credit for all their achievements and declare that their success is solely because of their commitment and perseverance.

Today's prayer embraces a different attitude about where credit is due. Isaiah prophesies that God's people will be victorious one day, but only by virtue of what God will do for them. Instead of honoring the people for their victory, Isaiah glorifies the Lord, *"Lord, you establish peace for us; all that we have accomplished you have done for us."*

What have you achieved recently? Gratefully acknowledge today that it is God who enables you to achieve your objectives, and praise and thank Him for what He has done for you.

Gracious God, all that I have achieved in life is solely by virtue of Your grace and the strength that You give me. I praise and thank You for it.

Amen

A plea that God would hear

To you I call, O LORD my Rock; do not turn a deaf ear to me. For if you remain silent, I will be like those who have gone down to the pit. Hear my cry for mercy as I call to you for help, as I lift up my hands toward your Most Holy Place. Praise be to the LORD, for he has heard my cry for mercy.

— PSALM 28:1-2, 6 —

There are times when it seems that God is far away from us. We pray … and pray … and pray … and there is no answer. Where is God? Does He really hear us? In this psalm David expresses his frustration over seemingly unanswered prayers. He called to the Lord for help and all he heard was silence.

But David, instead of turning away from God, turned to God and renewed his pleas that God would hear him. He refused to throw in the towel with God because he knew that God was the only One able to deliver him.

The good news is that David was not disappointed. The second half of David's prayer describes how God answered his prayer.

Today, rejoice in the knowledge that God is willing to hear and answer your prayers.

Loving Hearer of Prayers, hear my petition when I call to You for help.

Amen

Thank God for His unfailing love

Within your temple, O God, we meditate on your unfailing love. Like your name, O God, your praise reaches to the ends of the earth; your right hand is filled with righteousness.

— PSALM 48:9-10 —

The characteristics of power and love seem to be opposites. We often picture a powerful ruler as a tyrant or dictator, someone abusing his power to suppress others. We often imagine a loving person to be soft and tender. However, this prayer describes God both as powerful and loving. He uses His power in a loving way: He protects His people, but He punishes them when they sin.

God must be revered and glorified, because He will triumph over His enemies. In the meantime, we have the privilege of adding our voice to that hymn of praise, regardless of our circumstances.

Reflect on God's unfailing love for you today and tell someone what He, in His great love, has done for you.

God of love, embrace me with Your omnipotence and Your unfailing love.

Amen

Glory be to God who keeps His promises

Praise the LORD. Praise the LORD, O my soul. I will praise the LORD all my life; I will sing praise to my God as long as I live. Do not put your trust in princes, in mortal men, who cannot save. When their spirit departs, they return to the ground; on that very day their plans come to nothing. Blessed is he whose help is the God of Jacob, whose hope is in the LORD his God, the Maker of heaven and earth, the sea, and everything in them – the LORD, who remains faithful forever.

– PSALM 146:1-6 –

All of us have been left in the lurch by someone at one time or another. A friend or family member broke an important promise. A prominent church leader succumbed to sin. Through these experiences we learn not to trust completely in people, because they do not always keep their promises.

The writer of this prayer calls on all people to put their faith in God and not in other people, because the Lord remains faithful for ever. The heavens above us, and the ground beneath are signs of His unfailing love for His people. God maintains His creation day after day and He will also faithfully provide for His children.

Put time aside today to praise and thank God for keeping His promises forever and for being personally faithful to you in His love.

Dear Lord, from personal experience we know that You are the One who always keeps His promises. We thank and praise You for that.

Amen

Glory be to God for His great deeds

Sing to the LORD a new song; sing to the LORD, all the earth. Sing to the LORD, praise his name; proclaim his salvation day after day. Declare his glory among the nations, his marvelous deeds among all peoples. For great is the LORD and most worthy of praise; he is to be feared above all gods.

— PSALM 96:1-4 —

Every morning, in almost every household, people are greeted by newspapers presenting the often depressing daily news. If only we were greeted instead by the Good News that Jesus Christ has come to save the world from its distress.

The Psalmist commits himself to proclaim the great deeds of God that take place around the world every day. As God's people, we should hear about His saving grace each day and proclaim it to the world around us.

Resolve to start every morning by calling to mind something that God has done for you. How He has created a brand new day for you to enjoy, how He has given you food and clothing, how He has saved you through Christ. Then tell others of God's great deeds.

Father God, I will joyfully proclaim Your deeds of love to the world and, in so doing, bear testimony to Your grace and peace.

Amen

Give thanks to God for His loving guidance

Do good to your servant, and I will live; I will obey your word. Open my eyes that I may see wonderful things in your law. I am a stranger on earth; do not hide your commands from me. My soul is consumed with longing for your laws at all times. Your statutes are my delight; they are my counselors.

– PSALM 119:17-20, 24 –

As August draws to a close, we begin to notice the changing of the seasons and begin to prepare for all the demands and activities of the new season. More than ever, we should consult the Word of God for guidance on how to conduct our lives. The author of this psalm regards himself as a stranger here on earth – someone who has lived on this earth with a higher purpose than merely completing the monotonous task of getting through each day. He lives to please God and to obey His commands. In those things he finds his guidance and counsel. He prays that God will increasingly reveal to him His wonderful deeds and truths from His Word.

When you put time aside to pray to God, first study the Scriptures. Ask God to enlighten your mind so that you may understand His Word and apply it to your life.

Holy God and God of goodness, open my eyes to the truths of Your Word. I treasure Your Word in my heart so that I may not sin against You.

Amen

God's light of love

You, O Lord, keep my lamp burning; my God turns my darkness into light. With your help I can advance against a troop; with my God I can scale a wall. As for God, his way is perfect; the word of the Lord is flawless. He is a shield for all who take refuge in him. For who is God besides the Lord? And who is the Rock except our God? It is God who arms me with strength and makes my way perfect.

– Psalm 18:28-32 –

There are few of us who have not yet experienced times when everything in our lives turned dark; when it seemed futile to hope and when we felt all alone.

David knew just how dark life could become at times. When he wrote this prayer, he was filled with memories of his terror-stricken flight from the murderous Saul. Yet, he focuses on God as the light of his life!

The Light that expelled the darkness and shed light on confusion. In this light, David saw that God's ways were perfect, even though they led him through dark valleys and dangerous depths. God would always keep watch over him and remain true to His promises.

If your road is dark, remember how God guided David through the darkness. Use David's prayer to assure yourself that God is the light of your life.

I worship You as the Light of the world. Thank You for casting light on the dark patches on my road through life.

Amen

Wait on God's faithful love

Answer me quickly, O LORD; my spirit fails. Do not hide your face from me or I will be like those who go down to the pit. Let the morning bring me word of your unfailing love, for I have put my trust in you. Show me the way I should go, for to you I lift up my soul. Rescue me from my enemies, O LORD, for I hide myself in you. Teach me to do your will, for you are my God; may your good Spirit lead me on level ground.

– PSALM 143:7-10 –

At this time of year, there is a slight sharpness in the air. Morning breaks with effervescent, life-giving strength and it is glorious to walk along the beach. On such mornings it is easy to become aware of God's presence. It might have been on such a morning when David prayed, *"Let the morning bring me word of your unfailing love; for I have put my trust in you. Show me the way I should go."*

David longed for God's fellowship in the early morning. He wanted God's Spirit to lead him on level ground.

Resolve to start every morning in God's presence. Then ask God to determine your every step through the day, and ask Him to walk with you.

Father God, let the morning remind me of Your unfailing love. Show me the way that I should walk today.

Amen

God's smile of love

"The LORD bless you and keep you; the LORD make his face shine upon you, and be gracious to you; the LORD turn his face toward you and give you peace. So they will put my name on the Israelites, and I will bless them."

– Numbers 6:24-27 –

The power of a sincere smile is a very real thing. It shows love and affection, as well as approval and support. God personally provided Moses and the Levites with this benediction to pray for His favor and salvation.

The Levites would bestow the benediction on the Israelites, and God would carry into effect that which the Levites had prayed for. In other words, God teaches Moses and the Levites that He will smile upon His people.

What a picture of the living God! He teaches us to pray for Him to come to our rescue. He wants us to ask Him to protect us, to save us and to bless us.

Take the words of this age-old God-given prayer, and use it to pray for someone whom you know and love.

Loving God and Father, smile upon my life and come to my rescue when I find myself in a crisis. Do the same for my family and friends.

Amen

Our lives are in God's loving hands

Come and see what God has done, how awesome his works in man's behalf! He turned the sea into dry land, they passed through the waters on foot – come, let us rejoice in him. He rules forever by his power, his eyes watch the nations – let not the rebellious rise up against him. Praise our God, O peoples, let the sound of his praise be heard; he has preserved our lives and kept our feet from slipping.

– PSALM 66:5-9 –

Some of the prayers contained in the psalms are proclamations from the place of worship, meant for all the faithful to hear. The author of this prayer invites us all to glorify God for caring for His people. He wants them hear about, *"His awesome works on man's behalf"*.

Through His omnipotence, He reigns for all eternity. When the time is right, all the world will proclaim God's glory, because He holds us all in His loving hands. He keeps our feet from slipping. God is especially worthy of our praise.

Let us join our voices with those faithful people of old and let us praise Him for who He is and for what He does. Let us trust Him completely. Let us give thanks to Him for keeping our feet from slipping.

Eternal and Holy God, I give thanks to You because You hold my life in Your loving hands and that You keep my feet from slipping.

Amen

Praise God who knows and loves us

O LORD, you have searched me and you know me. You know when I sit and when I rise; you perceive my thoughts from afar. You discern my going out and my lying down; you are familiar with all my ways. Before a word is on my tongue you know it completely, O LORD. You hem me in – behind and before; you have laid your hand upon me.

– PSALM 139:1-6 –

One of man's greatest needs is intimacy: to know and to be known. Our relationship with God is unique because He alone knows us completely. It is an act of worship and submission to acknowledge that God knows everything about us. Regardless of where we may find ourselves, God knows our every thought, He shows us the way to go, where to rest and He gives us peace.

Unfathomable as it may seem to our limited human understanding, God's knowledge is not limited to the past and the present. To use the words of David, *"Before a word is on my tongue you know it completely, O LORD."* That is how intimately He knows and loves you and me.

Glorify God in your prayer today as the One who knows you absolutely and still loves you.

Lord my God, I glorify You that You know all about me and still love me.

Amen

Give thanks for God's loving salvation

A glorious throne, exalted from the beginning, is the place of our sanctuary. O Lord, the hope of Israel, all who forsake you will be put to shame. Those who turn away from you will be written in the dust because they have forsaken the Lord, the spring of living water. Heal me, O Lord, and I will be healed; save me and I will be saved, for you are the one I praise.

— Jeremiah 17:12-14 —

Jeremiah had the difficult and dangerous task of warning God's rebellious people that there would be serious consequences as a result of their sinful lives. After announcing God's judgment of the people, Jeremiah turned to God because that was his only hope.

He turned away from all the evil surrounding him and reflected on God's throne, *"A glorious throne, exalted from the beginning"*. He repeats the truths that he has already proclaimed: that those who turn away from the Lord will be humiliated and will face death, because they have forsaken *"the spring of living water"* and refused to listen to God.

On the other hand, Jeremiah confirms his dependency on God. After reminding himself of these timeless truths, he glorifies the Lord God.

We must also remember that it is God who saved and healed us. We should praise and thank Him for that.

Almighty Father, You alone can save, You alone can heal! Praise the Lord, because He is good! His love knows no bounds!

Amen

Children praise God's love

O LORD, our Lord, how majestic is your name in all the earth! You have set your glory above the heavens. From the lips of children and infants you have ordained praise because of your enemies, to silence the foe and the avenger.
— PSALM 8:1-2 —

If we tried to determine the extent of God's glory, we would find that the universe cannot contain it. And yet God ordains praise from children and infants. What an astounding thought!

The simple prayers of thanksgiving coming from the lips of children often put adults to shame. With their sincere faith in God, they are not distracted by all the complicated issues that cause adults to experience conflict in their praise.

Perhaps that is why Jesus says, *"Unless you change and become like little children, you will never enter the kingdom of heaven"* (Mt. 18:3). Furthermore, the praise of children can silence His enemies. How can anyone scorn the simple, yet sincere prayer from the lips of a little child?

Make an attempt this week to listen to children praying. Let their simple prayers inspire you to confirm your childlike faith in God as well.

Almighty God, the majesty of Your Name fills the universe. Grant me the grace to have the faith of a little child and, in so doing, glorify You with sincerity.

Amen

The glory of God

He says, "I will declare your name to my brothers; in the presence of the congregation I will sing your praises."

— HEBREWS 2:12 —

After staring for hours on end at television, film, and computer screens, it is just possible that we may lose our sense of awe at the beauty of nature. Even more disturbing is that we allow these things to divert our attention from the miracles that God performs in our lives.

One of the reasons why Jesus came to dwell on this earth, was to proclaim the miracles of God. His prayer was that He would proclaim to the world the miracle of God's Name. Through His life, death and triumphant resurrection, Jesus did precisely that. He inspired His followers to praise and glorify God for His wonderful and loving deeds.

Make a decision to tell someone this week about the miraculous things that God has done for you and your family.

Miraculous and loving God, I want to proclaim the miracle of Your Name to all my brothers and sisters. Help me to present a sincere testimony.

Amen

God's love declares our innocence

Answer me when I call to you, O my righteous God. Give me relief from my distress; be merciful to me and hear my prayer.

— PSALM 4:1 —

Gossip and slander ruin relationships and destroy people's trust in one another. Often we are tempted to respond to slander with disparaging words of our own. However, David offers a better solution. In this psalm he responds to false accusations by calling on God's love to declare his innocence.

We can look to God when we are being defamed and slandered too, because He is the One who declares us guilty or innocent. We need not fear the accusations of others, nor those of the great "accuser" (that is what "Satan" means), because the Lord declares His redeemed innocent through the death of His Son, the Living Christ!

Give thanks to God in prayer today because He has declared you innocent. But first ensure that you have confessed your intentional and unintentional sins to Him and have received His forgiveness.

Dear Savior and Redeemer, thank You for declaring me innocent because I have confessed my sins and shortcomings to You and have been granted forgiveness.

Amen

Take note of God's deeds of love

Others went out on the sea in ships; they were merchants on the mighty waters. They saw the works of the LORD, his wonderful deeds in the deep. For he spoke and stirred up a tempest that lifted high the waves. They mounted up to the heavens and went down to the depths; in their peril their courage melted away. They reeled and staggered like drunken men; they were at their wits' end. Then they cried out to the LORD in their trouble, and he brought them out of their distress. He stilled the storm to a whisper; the waves of the sea were hushed. They were glad when it grew calm, and he guided them to their desired haven.

– PSALM 107:23-30 –

When we have come through a very dramatic and life-threatening experience, the whole world seems fresh and new to us. We have a new appreciation for the gift of health and life.

That is the Psalmist's point of view in this psalm. When some of the exiles were aboard a ship that was tossed to and fro by strong winds and merciless waves, God stilled the wind and the sea in answer to their distress call. We can just imagine how these exiles rejoiced when they sailed into a safe harbor.

Think about all the times God has worked in your life in miraculous ways. Glorify Him for allowing you to go through trials and for using them to strengthen your faith in His love.

Thank You Lord, for Your omnipotence and love. Praise the Lord!

Amen

Jesus prays for our protection

"I am coming to you now, but I say these things while I am still in the world, so that they may have the full measure of my joy within them. I have given them your word and the world has hated them, for they are not of the world any more than I am of the world. My prayer is not that you take them out of the world but that you protect them from the evil one."

— John 17:13-15 —

After the Last Supper, Jesus was in the upper room with His disciples. Jesus knew that His time on earth was short. Therefore, He prayed for His disciples and asked God the Father to preserve and protect them against the attacks of Satan. Jesus also prayed for those who would come to Him through the testimony of the disciples. This includes us.

In the last moments before His crucifixion, Jesus prayed for the protection of His disciples, as well as for ours! This should indeed be of great comfort to us and should free us from anxiety, worries and uncertainty.

If God is for us who then can be against us?

Pray that God will preserve you from those who plot against you and ask Him to deliver you from evil. You can rest assured that He will answer your prayer.

Thank You, Lord Jesus, that I do not belong to the world, but to You. Deliver me from evil for Your Name's sake.

Amen

Thank God for friendship

Grace to you and peace from God our Father and the Lord Jesus Christ. I always thank my God as I remember you in my prayers, because I hear about your faith in the Lord Jesus and your love for all the saints. Your love has given me great joy and encouragement, because you, brother, have refreshed the hearts of the saints.

– PHILEMON 1:3-5, 7 –

We are often forced onto our knees by tragedies or difficult circumstances in our lives. We tell God everything about our problems and ask for His help. There is nothing wrong with that. Paul found himself, without doubt, in difficult circumstances when he wrote this letter to Philemon.

He was in Rome under house arrest, and was awaiting trial before the Roman Emperor. That he had a lot to pray for, is certain. But in his letter, his attention is focused on someone else. Paul did not forget to tell Philemon that he was praying for him, that he thanked God constantly for him.

Have you been comforted by other Christians? Have you told them how highly you regard them and how much you appreciate them, and that you pray for them? Resolve to tell them – and God in prayer – how deeply you appreciate them.

God of love and grace, thank You for the many brothers and sisters in You who support me and pray for me. I also thank You for Your love.

Amen

God's love is near

I will praise the LORD, who counsels me; even at night my heart instructs me. I have set the LORD always before me. Because he is at my right hand, I will not be shaken.

– PSALM 16:7-8 –

Sometimes we do all we can to handle the storms in our lives single-handedly. We think if we only stay strong and persevere we could overcome the problem.

However, David realized that he could not make it on his own. In the past, he had found help in the Lord his God. In this prayer David once again looks to the Lord for protection, "*Because he is at my right hand, I will not be shaken.*" He rejoices in the guidance and support of the Lord. Although his enemies tried to conquer him, David stood firm because God was with him.

During your prayer time today, realize that God is with you to preserve and to guide you. Give thanks to Him because He is with you to help you and will never leave you or forsake you.

I thank and praise You, O God of love, that You are here with me now to protect me and sustain me so that I will not be shaken.

Amen

Glory be to the loving King of kings

No one is like you, O LORD; you are great, and your name is mighty in power. Who should not revere you, O King of the nations? This is your due. Among all the wise men of the nations and in all their kingdoms, there is no one like you.

— JEREMIAH 10:6-7 —

Through the ages, cruel, egotistical dictators had often gained power over nations across the world. These tyrants would live in luxury and plenitude, while their subjects were suffering in poverty. Tyrants always live and act as though they are gods and they rule people with an iron fist.

However, the Bible informs us that there is but one true King, and Jeremiah states that only God is worthy of love, worship and praise. *"Who should not revere you, O King of the nations? This is your due."*

Let us glorify and extol the Name of our God who is the only King of all the world, but who allows other rulers to prosper or causes them to fall. Glorify and worship God who is without equal.

Almighty Father, there is no one like You in all the world. You are King of all the nations and also King of my heart and life.

Amen

Celebrate the Father's love

You prepare a table before me in the presence of my enemies. You anoint my head with oil; my cup overflows. Surely goodness and love will follow me all the days of my life, and I will dwell in the house of the LORD forever.

— PSALM 23:5-6 —

Although lions and wolves may roam the countryside, a faithful shepherd will always protect his flock. He will lead them to the very best pastures and to fresh streams of water. He will protect them against predators and at the end of the day lead them back to a safe shelter.

David regarded God as his Faithful Shepherd who provides for him and protects him. And yet God does more for His children than a shepherd does for his sheep. Not only does He provide food, He prepares a feast for David in the presence of his enemies. He treats David as His guest. Not only does He give him gifts: His cup overflows with blessings.

Remember all the ways in which the Lord has provided for you – more than you could ever deserve – and thank Him for His grace.

Faithful Lord, You let my cup overflow with blessings. I dearly want to abide in Your house forever.

Amen

Prayer of praise for God's constant love

O God, whom I praise, do not remain silent, for wicked and deceitful men have opened their mouths against me; they have spoken against me with lying tongues. With words of hatred they surround me; they attack me without cause. With my mouth I will greatly extol the LORD; in the great throng I will praise him. For he stands at the right hand of the needy one, to save his life from those who condemn him.

– PSALM 109:1-3, 30-31 –

In good times and bad, when we are excited about success or depressed about failure, we must praise God. As believers, we know that our circumstances should not influence our faith in God.

In this prayer, David admits that he was in deep trouble. The wicked people slandered him and told lies about him. They returned evil for good and hate for love. His enemies tried to destroy him, even while he was praying for them. And yet, in the midst of this predicament, David says, *"With my mouth I will greatly extol the Lord."*

Regardless of your circumstances today, give thanks to God and glorify Him, because He is the One who sustains you and loves you.

God of love and grace, regardless of the circumstances in which I may find myself, I will persevere in glorifying and giving thanks to Your Name.

Amen

SEPTEMBER

SUPPLICATION

Going a little farther, he fell with his face to the ground and prayed, "My Father, if it is possible, may this cup be taken from me. Yet not as I will, but as you will."

– MATTHEW 26:39 –

In our supplication we must above all guard against placing limitations on God. We can do so by doubting, but also by imagining that we know better than God Himself what He should do. Expect the unexpected from God. *"Now to him who is able to do immeasurably more than all we ask or imagine, according to his power that is at work within us, to him be glory"* (Eph. 3:20-21). Every time we pray we must become still before God and reflect on and worship His holiness, omnipotence, and glory. Think about that which He wants to and can do for you and how He loves having His children talk to Him. Think about your position with God, and of the special privileges He has granted you for the sake of His Son, Jesus Christ, and then expect great things of God. He listens to His children's prayers.

Cleanse me with hyssop, and I will be clean; wash me, and I will be whiter than snow. Let me hear joy and gladness; let the bones you have crushed rejoice. Hide your face from my sins and blot out all my iniquity. Create in me a pure heart, O God, and renew a steadfast spirit within me. Do not cast me from your presence or take your Holy Spirit from me. Restore to me the joy of your salvation and grant me a willing spirit, to sustain me.

– PSALM 51:7-12 –

Prayer in a crisis

Then Jehoshaphat stood up in the assembly of Judah and Jerusalem at the temple of the LORD in the front of the new courtyard and said: "O LORD, God of our fathers, are you not the God who is in heaven? You rule over all the kingdoms of the nations. Power and might are in your hand, and no one can withstand you. O our God, did you not drive out the inhabitants of this land before your people Israel and give it forever to the descendants of Abraham your friend? They have lived in it and have built in it a sanctuary for your Name, saying, 'If calamity comes upon us, whether the sword of judgment, or plague or famine, we will stand in your presence before this temple that bears your Name and will cry out to you in our distress, and you will hear us and save us.'"

— 2 CHRONICLES 20:5-9 —

King Jehoshaphat was surrounded by hostile forces when he prayed this prayer. He knew that his God is like a Mountain Stronghold that can withstand all the attacks of the enemy. Even though their situation seemed to be hopeless, Jehoshaphat listed the ways in which God faithfully delivered His people in the past. Then he asked for help for the situation they faced. His faith was abundantly rewarded, because the next day God caused Judah's enemies to turn against each other.

When you face impossible situations, take time to remind yourself of the ways in which God has come to your rescue in the past. You may be powerless but, through your supplication, you have access to the omnipotence of God!

Almighty God, I am helpless and broken, therefore I plead for Your help. As You have done in the past, do so again now, Father.

Amen

When God feels far away

My God, my God, why have you forsaken me? Why are you so far from saving me, so far from the words of my groaning? O my God, I cry out by day, but you do not answer, by night, and am not silent. Yet you are enthroned as the Holy One; you are the praise of Israel. In you our fathers put their trust; they trusted and you delivered them. They cried to you and were saved; in you they trusted and were not disappointed.

– PSALM 22:1-5 –

Trust is built up over time but can so quickly be destroyed. When dark and hopeless circumstances surround us, we can start feeling as though God has forsaken us and then we lose faith in Him. However, it may be a comforting thought to know that we are not the only ones to feel this way. *"Why have you forsaken me?"* David, the man after God's own heart, called out, and his words have been echoed by none other than Jesus on the cross.

However, such a significant question requires an intimate relationship of trust between the seeker and God. And David waited hopefully upon God, because he knew that God always responds to the heartfelt call of His children.

Do you feel alone and far away from God – forsaken by God? Remind yourself of some of the ways in which God has worked in your life. God never leaves His children in the lurch.

Omnipresent God, even though I feel alone and unwanted at the moment, I trust in You, knowing that You hear my call.

Amen

A prayer in times of discouragement

I am laid low in the dust; preserve my life according to your word. I recounted my ways and you answered me; teach me your decrees. Let me understand the teaching of your precepts; then I will meditate on your wonders. My soul is weary with sorrow; strengthen me according to your word. Keep me from deceitful ways; be gracious to me through your law.

— Psalm 119:25-29 —

To whom do you turn when you feel completely disheartened? The Psalmist turns to the Word of God and His commandments. There he finds renewal, although circumstances have laid him low in the dust. He wants to know more about God and truly wants to understand God's ways. He reflects on all God's glorious miracles and reminds himself of the privilege of knowing God's decrees.

In the long run, it was God's decrees *"that kept me from deceitful ways"*. They set him free from the quicksand of self-deceit and placed him firmly on the solid ground of God's commands.

In the secular and self-assured world we live in, despair is fairly common. Even when you feel most discouraged, seek God's help to enable you to comprehend this truth: God knows about our discouragement and despair and He will handle the situation.

God of Comfort, I weep from sorrow and despair. Encourage me through Your Word.

Amen

A prayer in times of sickness

Hezekiah turned his face to the wall and prayed to the Lord, "Remember, O Lord, how I have walked before you faithfully and with wholehearted devotion and have done what is good in your eyes." And Hezekiah wept bitterly. Before Isaiah had left the middle court, the word of the Lord came to him: "Go back and tell Hezekiah, the leader of my people, 'This is what the Lord, the God of your father David, says: I have heard your prayer and seen your tears; I will heal you. On the third day from now you will go up to the temple of the Lord'."

– 2 Kings 20:2-5 –

Hezekiah was on his deathbed. He was, however, aware of God's compassion and His power over disease. Therefore he called upon God in his anguish. When God answered Hezekiah's prayer, He did so in a dramatic way. Within three days the king was able to go to the temple.

God does not always answer our prayers for healing in such a dramatic way. We know that God is capable of doing so and in some cases He does dramatically heal a sick person!

In sickness and in health, God's wisdom is far above ours. Even though we may never understand why things happen in life, we can always rest assured that God loves us and cares about us.

Regardless of how hopeless your condition may be, trust in God's love for you and know that He will listen to your call for help.

Gracious God and Father, in my anguish and sickness I call upon You. Thank You for always being faithful and loving.

Amen

Abraham pleads for mercy

Then Abraham approached him and said: "Will you sweep away the righteous with the wicked? What if there are fifty righteous people in the city? Will you really sweep it away and not spare the place for the sake of the fifty righteous people in it? Far be it from you to do such a thing – to kill the righteous with the wicked, treating the righteous and the wicked alike. Far be it from you! Will not the Judge of all the earth do right?"

– Genesis 18:23-25 –

In the days before their fiery judgment, the residents of Sodom and Gomorrah probably did not have the slightest idea that their neighbor, Abraham, was wrestling with God for their sake.

Abraham realized the necessity for justice, but he also prayed for God to have mercy on them. He asked God to spare the cities for the sake of a few righteous people, and God agreed.

Moreover, God sent His angel to protect Lot and his innocent family and to deliver them from judgment. However, as the destruction of Sodom and Gomorrah has proven, God's grace is infinite, but He will not let sin go unpunished forever.

Just as God listened to the righteous Abraham so many years ago, God will also listen to your cry of anguish for righteousness and your plea for mercy. God will do what is right.

Righteous Judge, have mercy upon me, a poor sinner!

Amen

The prayer of Jesus

After Jesus said this, he looked toward heaven and prayed: "Father, the time has come. Glorify your Son, that your Son may glorify you. For you granted him authority over all people that he might give eternal life to all those you have given him. Now this is eternal life: that they may know you, the only true God, and Jesus Christ, whom you have sent."

– JOHN 17:1-3 –

At the Last Supper, Jesus prayed this prayer. In preparation for the suffering that He would have to endure in the days ahead, He prayed for God to be glorified in His body.

We often think that the road to glory is paved with success. However, Jesus' road to glory was paved with suffering and an apparent defeat in the form of a terrible death on the cross. How could this "defeat" bring glory to God? Jesus explains in His prayer that God is glorified through the obedience of the Son.

We seldom feel that our suffering and defeat could be to God's glory. We often do not have God's perspective on our situation. God's glory is reflected in our deeds of obedience, love and loyalty in this life. Follow Jesus' example today by praying that God will be glorified in your life and by your obedience.

Loving Father, help me to contribute to the glory of Your Name by doing everything in obedience to Your will and by completing that which You have requested me to do.

Amen

Jesus pleads with His Father

About the ninth hour Jesus cried out in a loud voice, "Eloi, Eloi, lama sabach-thani?" – which means, "My God, my God, why have you forsaken me?"
– MATTHEW 27:46 –

D id God truly forsake Christ on the cross, so that He alone had to bear the suffering and sins of all people through all the ages? Perhaps the best way to approach this unusual prayer is to place it within a biblical context. Jesus' prayer is a quote from Psalm 22:1: a psalm that deals with God's salvation. Perhaps Jesus had the entire psalm in mind, including verse 24, *"For he has not despised or disdained the suffering of the afflicted one; he had not hidden his face from him but has listened to his cry for help."*

Jesus knew that His suffering on the cross was not a final rejection by God. As the author of Hebrews rightly states, *"For the joy set before him [he] endured the cross, scorning its shame, and sat down at the right hand of the throne of God"* (Heb. 12:2).

Even though we may never suffer as our remarkable Savior did, we will experience affliction. When this happens, we must look past our suffering towards our triumph in God, our loving Father.

Gracious and merciful God, when I feel alone, help me to remember that You promised never to forsake me.

Amen

A prayer for equipping

May the God of peace, who through the blood of the eternal covenant brought back from the dead our Lord Jesus, that great Shepherd of the sheep, equip you with everything good for doing his will, and may he work in us what is pleasing to him, through Jesus Christ, to whom be glory for ever and ever. Amen.

– HEBREWS 13:20-21 –

The Bible often refers to the children of God as sheep that are totally dependent on the Shepherd for food and protection. Although the majority of us now live in a society where individual performance is highly regarded, we should never think that we can be everything that Christ expects from us in our own strength.

We have been brought into a covenant with our Lord Jesus and with one another – through the sacrificial blood of Christ. That is why the writer wrote this letter to the Hebrews. He wanted all Christian believers to join forces with him and pray for the motivation to do the work of God together.

Pray that God will equip you, as well as the believers in your community and local congregation, to join forces in doing God's work.

Lord Jesus, our Good Shepherd, equip Your children so that they will want to do Your work in unity.

Amen

Take refuge in God in your distress

But I will sing of your strength, in the morning I will sing of your love; for you are my fortress, my refuge in times of trouble. O my Strength, I sing praise to you; you, O God, are my fortress, my loving God.

– PSALM 59:16-17 –

Human love can be a source of great joy or of great pain at the same time – especially if someone's love is fickle and inconstant. In contrast, God's love is infallible! David wrote one of his great songs of worship on this theme. He sings the praises of God's might, as well as of His love. Because of who He is, God is a *"refuge in times of trouble"*.

David's day of distress in the psalm was the day when Saul sent soldiers to kill him. On that day, David called upon God and realized that God was his strength. He once again glorified the Lord for the infallible love shown to him.

When you experience your own times of trouble, find your power, strength and your refuge in the infallible love of God.

Holy God, You are my refuge and my fortress in times of trouble. Let me experience Your infallible love.

Amen

Moses prays to see the Promised Land

At that time I pleaded with the LORD: "O Sovereign LORD, you have begun to show to your servant your greatness and your strong hand. For what god is there in heaven or on earth who can do the deeds and mighty works you do? Let me go over and see the good land beyond the Jordan – that fine hill country and Lebanon."

— DEUTERONOMY 3:23-25 —

One can detect a trace of longing in Moses' prayer. He dearly wanted to enter the Promised Land: the land overflowing with milk and honey, which God had promised to His people. Unfortunately, Moses allowed his anger to influence his obedience to God and therefore the Lord had forbidden him to enter the land.

Although Moses had received a divine "No!" to his prayer, he knew that God had a good plan with his life and he submitted to it. When God says "No", there is always a good reason for it. He always has our best interests at heart.

It is never wrong to express our desires to God. When you draw near to God in prayer, lay the desires of your heart before Him. Then ask Him to prepare you for His good plan with your life. The Heavenly Land to which God took Moses, was far better than the terrestrial Promised Land.

Sovereign King, help me to accept Your good plan for my life. I know that You love me and only want the best for me.

Amen

Hannah prays for a child

In bitterness of soul Hannah wept much and prayed to the LORD. And she made a vow, saying, "O LORD Almighty, if you will only look upon your servant's misery and remember me, and not forget your servant but give her a son, then I will give him to the LORD for all the days of his life, and no razor will ever be used on his head."

– 1 SAMUEL 1:10-11 –

Hannah, who was childless, lived at a time when it was regarded as a disgrace for women to be unable to bear children. Peninnah, the other wife of her husband, Eli, was Hannah's rival. She boasted in Hannah's presence about her own children. When the whole family went to Jerusalem for the festival, Hannah found it impossible to join in the festivities. Instead, she went to the tabernacle where she expressed her deepest longing and grief to God.

She knew whom to turn to in her extreme anguish. She realized that the Almighty was the only one who could help her. She did not arrogantly demand God to grant her a son. Instead, she declared herself willing to return her gift to God.

What is the prayer of your heart today? Have you poured out your heart to the Lord? Are you willing to give the answer to your prayer back to Him?

Lord, God Almighty, look upon my misery and grief and hear my prayer.

Amen

Waiting on God

How long will the enemy mock you, O God? Will the foe revile your name forever? Why do you hold back your hand, your right hand? Take it from the folds of your garment and destroy them! Rise up, O God, and defend your cause; remember how fools mock you all day long. Do not ignore the clamor of your adversaries, the uproar of your enemies, which rises continually.

– PSALM 74:10-11, 22-23 –

God has to listen endlessly to our impatient prayers! Nothing reveals our lack of faith more than our impatient "why?" and "how long?" questions. And yet God allowed such prayers to be recorded in the Bible.

In this prayer, the Psalmist calls on God to defend His Holy Name against those who mock and revile it. He wants God to unleash sudden revenge on these people. Even though the Lord does not always tell us when He will act, we may rest assured in the knowledge that He will do that which has to be done at the right time.

God wants us to express our feelings and urgent requests. Pray with conviction against the enemies of the faith, but also trust God for the future. The final outcome will always be in His competent hands.

Almighty God, why do You hold back Your powerful hand? Appear in Majesty and defend the faith in Your own time and way.

Amen

A shepherd faces persecution

They keep saying to me, "Where is the word of the LORD? Let it now be fulfilled!" I have not run away from being your shepherd; you know I have not desired the day of despair. What passes my lips is open before you. Do not be a terror to me; you are my refuge in the day of disaster. Let my persecutors be put to shame, but keep me from shame; let them be terrified, but keep me from terror. Bring on them the day of disaster; destroy them with double destruction.

– JEREMIAH 17:15-18 –

Jeremiah knew that he was faithful to his calling when he called on God's people to show remorse – a message that they did not want to hear. They persecuted Jeremiah. The prophet could have defended himself, but he did not want to. He simply obeyed God and waited upon Him to take action in His time.

This is the kind conduct of which Paul spoke of when he said, *"Do not take revenge, my friends, but leave room for God's wrath, for it is written: 'It is mine to avenge; I will repay,' says the Lord"* (Rom. 12:19).

When you are doing what God has called you to do and people oppose you for it, do not take matters into your own hands. Simply persevere in faithfulness to God and trust in Him to handle matters as He sees fit.

Dear Father God, help me to glorify You and to trust in You at all times.

Amen

Supplicatory prayer of the despised

You know how I am scorned, disgraced and shamed; all my enemies are before you. Scorn has broken my heart and has left me helpless; I looked for sympathy, but there was none, for comforters, but I found none. I am in pain and distress; may your salvation, O God, protect me. I will praise God's name in song and glorify him with thanksgiving.

– PSALM 69:19-20, 29-30 –

There is an old Negro spiritual that captures the feelings expressed in this psalm extremely well: Nobody knows the trouble I've seen, nobody knows but Jesus.

This lament reflects David's state of mind. He feels that all are against him. He is being scorned and shamed and it is clear that he is hurting inside. He wishes that even one person would take pity on him and offer him comfort. But, amidst all his pain and loneliness, he perseveres in praying to God. He trusts that, regardless of how severe his suffering is, God will still save him.

In your times of trial and tribulation, it might feel as though all around you have rejected you. But remember that God will never forsake you (see Heb. 13:5).

He will answer when you call and He knows what is best for you.

Omnipresent God, You alone know the depth of my suffering. Let Your saving grace intervene on my behalf. I glorify and give thanks to Your holy Name.

Amen

Samson pleads for water

Because he was very thirsty, he cried out to the LORD, "You have given your servant this great victory. Must I now die of thirst and fall into the hands of the uncircumcised?" Then God opened up the hollow place in Lehi, and water came out of it. When Samson drank, his strength returned and he revived. So the spring was called En Hakkore, and it is still there in Lehi.

— JUDGES 15:18-19 —

No Israelite had the courage to stand up against their oppressors, the Philistines. Then God raised up Samson and did mighty deeds through him. He caused such pandemonium amongst the Philistines that they sent an entire army to take him captive. But Samson killed a thousand of them with the jawbone of a donkey!

After this staggering achievement, he realized that he was very thirsty. Like a sulking child he asked God for water, "Must I now die of thirst?" And God, who is able to provide in all His children's needs, answered Samson's prayer by creating a spring right where he stood.

When we ask God to fulfil our needs we should, unlike Samson, do so humbly and respond gratefully for the things God grants us.

Merciful Lord, provide in my daily needs as You have promised to do. I know that I will lack nothing and I thank You for that.

Amen

Abram's frustration

But Abram said, "O Sovereign LORD, what can you give me since I remain childless and the one who will inherit my estate is Eliezer of Damascus?" And Abram said, "You have given me no children; so a servant in my household will be my heir." Then the word of the LORD came to him: "This man will not be your heir, but a son coming from your own body will be your heir."

– GENESIS 15:2-4 –

Abram's intimate relationship with God is clearly illustrated by this prayer. He exposes his soul to God. He tells God what life looks like from his perspective and exactly how he feels about this. He is even presumptuous enough to complain that his blessings from God were not sufficient!

Many of us would have felt uncomfortable if we were to present our case to God in this way. However, God did not reprimand Abram for his impudence. Instead, He explained His promise to Abram – that his own son would be his heir.

Do you have long-term desires that have not been fulfilled? Abram's example should comfort you and encourage you to talk to God about them. Do not hesitate to place your deepest desires before God. Simply trust in Him: He will answer. Sometimes He answers in ways that we find amazing and that we could not have conjured up in our wildest dreams.

Sovereign God, I expose my soul to You and place my frustrations before Your throne of grace. Please listen to my prayer.

Amen

Trust in the midst of problems

Listen to my prayer, O God, do not ignore my plea; hear me and answer me. My thoughts trouble me and I am distraught at the voice of the enemy, at the stares of the wicked; for they bring down suffering upon me and revile me in their anger. I said, "Oh, that I had the wings of a dove! I would fly away and be at rest – I would flee far away and stay in the desert; I would hurry to my place of shelter, far from the tempest and storm."

– PSALM 55:2-4, 7-9 –

Most of us have occasionally wished that we had the wings of a bird so that we could fly away from our troubles and problems.

David also had such a desire. He was completely overwhelmed by his problems. His enemies were hunting him down, threatening him with loud threats. His world was falling apart, and David feared that death would descend on him. He longed for the wings of a dove so that he could fly away from his problems to a place of peace and quiet. Yet, in the midst of his most severe troubles, David calls upon God for help.

When you are overwhelmed by problems, just cast your troubles upon the Lord and trust the Lord to come to your rescue.

Loving Lord, I am overwhelmed by my problems. Listen to my anguished cry for help and rescue me soon.

Amen

The prayer of the helpless

Arise, Lord! Lift up your hand, O God. Do not forget the helpless. But you, O God, do see trouble and grief; you consider it to take it in hand. The victim commits himself to you; you are the helper of the fatherless. You hear, O Lord, the desire of the afflicted; you encourage them, and you listen to their cry,

– Psalm 10:12, 14, 17 –

David saw a lot of injustice in his lifetime, but he never got used to it. In this prayer David is furious about someone who is unfair and callous, *"He lies in wait like a lion in cover; he lies in wait to catch the helpless"* (v. 9).

His heart was filled with compassion for the oppressed, the poor, the weak and the innocent. He sees how unjustly they are treated and he pleads with God to come to their rescue.

Do you remain uninvolved or does the injustice of this world infuriate you? Has your heart become cold and callous? Ask God to grant you a heart filled with compassion. Pray today that God will allow justice to triumph in our world.

Righteous Judge of the universe, please do not forget the helpless in their anguish.

Amen

A plea for help

Then Asa called to the LORD his God and said, "LORD, there is no one like you to help the powerless against the mighty. Help us, O LORD our God, for we rely on you, and in your name we have come against this vast army. O LORD, you are our God; do not let man prevail against you."

– 2 CHRONICLES 14:11 –

Asa was one of the few kings in Judah who feared the Lord and who prohibited and banned images of idols amongst God's people. God rewarded him with a decade of peace even though his peaceful kingdom was often threatened by unrest. When the Cushite, Zerah, king of Ethiopia, gathered a large army against him, Asa realized he needed to place his trust in God.

Because he understood that this was God's battle and not his, he asked God for help and then acted in God's Name and placed his full trust in the Lord. God had proven Himself to be trustworthy in so many crises in Asa's life in the past.

Perhaps you are facing overwhelming situations in life today. Entrust every situation to the Lord and pray that He will use it to demonstrate His omnipotence and to glorify His Name.

Help me, Lord my God, in every crisis in my life. I trust completely in You, my Savior and my Redeemer.

Amen

Hear my prayer, O Lord!

Hear my prayer, O LORD; let my cry for help come to you. Do not hide your face from me when I am in distress. Turn your ear to me; when I call, answer me quickly. For my days vanish like smoke; my bones burn like glowing embers. But you, O LORD, sit enthroned forever; your renown endures through all generations.

— PSALM 102:1-3, 12 —

Like a page torn from a journal, this prayer offers us insight into the prayer life of someone who finds himself in great distress and anguish. Many people think that these are the thoughts written down by an Israelite who was in exile in the evil city of Babylon. The heartbeat of this prayer is simple: *"Hear my prayer when I am in distress."* The supplicant asks God, *"Let my cry for help come to you"* There is no pretence. No effort to sound brave. The author of this prayer is despondent, therefore he calls on God and beseeches Him to hear his prayer.

Go to your Father with your every need today. Ask Him to hear your cry and to reach out His hand to deliver and comfort you. Express your concerns and anxiety to Him.

Dear Lord, hear my supplication and answer me, so that I may once again experience joy.

Amen

Prayer for direction

But I, by your great mercy, will come into your house; in reverence will I bow down toward your holy temple. Lead me, O LORD, in your righteousness because of my enemies – make straight your way before me.

– PSALM 5:7-8 –

David writes these words in the midst of controversy and confusion. His enemies often attempted to harass him with false rumors and blatant lies.

In those difficult and disturbing times, David immediately turned to God for advice and direction. Surrounded by lies, David searched for the truth. Confronted by choices, he chose to follow the right path.

During your prayer time today, express your desire for God to guide you and give you direction, especially if life offers you confusing choices. Ask God for clarity and discernment.

Counselor and Guide, indicate to me very clearly, through Your Holy Spirit, what is the right thing to do. Show me the direction I must take in order to glorify Your Name.

Amen

A prayer to our only true Helper

Save me, O God, by your name; vindicate me by your might. Hear my prayer, O God; listen to the words of my mouth. Strangers are attacking me; ruthless men seek my life – men without regard for God. Surely God is my help; the LORD is the one who sustains me.

— PSALM 54:1-4 —

David had served King Saul for many years and led his armies to victory against the enemies of Israel. Nevertheless, Saul suddenly turned against David and tried to kill him. As a fugitive, David was often betrayed, first by Doeg the Edomite and then by the residents of Keilah, and also by the Ziphites (see 1 Sam. 22-23.)

It was during this time, when it seemed as though all were against him, that David wrote this prayer. He prays for God to come to his defense quickly. He acknowledges God as the only One who can keep him alive – and God did this for him: *"The LORD is the one who sustains me."* Eventually, God saw to it that he ascended to the throne of Israel.

The same God who protected and preserved David, is still willing to come to our rescue today. You can confidently lay all your problems at His feet today.

Almighty God, come in Your majesty and glory today and deliver me.

Amen

Prayer for guidance

Show me your ways, O LORD, teach me your paths; guide me in your truth and teach me, for you are God my Savior, and my hope is in you all day long. Remember, O LORD, your great mercy and love, for they are from of old.

— PSALM 25:4-6 —

Sometimes we come face to face with various options and we do not know which course to take. In this psalm, David asks God for guidance. Perhaps he remembers how, as a young shepherd, he had to show the wandering sheep the way. Just as he knew which path would lead to safety for his sheep, God knows the path leading to eternal life.

Just as the sheep looked to him for direction so that they were led along the path of least danger, so David knew that he had to look to God for direction and guidance.

God still guides us in His truth today. His Word and His Spirit enable us to understand His guidance. If you are unsure about which course to take, pray as David prayed. Read what God has already said in His Word. It is, after all, the manifestation of God's will. He will indicate to you the path to life.

Loving Father, let me hear Your voice behind me, indicating to me the path to life. Thank You for Your Word and Your Spirit that give me guidance.

Amen

Jehoshaphat's prayer for help

When the chariot commanders saw Jehoshaphat, they thought, "This is the king of Israel." So they turned to attack him, but Jehoshaphat cried out, and the LORD helped him. God drew them away from him.

– 2 CHRONICLES 18:31 –

During the battle, the evil King Ahab disguised himself as an ordinary soldier. This cowardly conduct made his ally, King Jehoshaphat, dressed in brightly colored robes, an easy target for the enemy, the Aramean army.

Although God had warned Jehoshaphat not to enter an alliance with Ahab, when Ahab asked him to fight against the Arameans, he agreed. In spite of his mistake, Jehoshaphat knew he could turn to God when he found himself in trouble.

This story should soften our pride, especially when we want to cling to our own wrong decisions. When our wrong decisions land us in trouble, our prayer must simply be, "Lord, deliver me!"

When we turn to God in prayer, we never hear, "I told you so." Call on God for help and He will deliver you, even though you do not deserve it.

Gracious and merciful God, forgive me my sinful pride. Please come and rescue me, although I do not deserve it.

Amen

Elijah pleads for the life of a child

Then he stretched himself out on the boy three times and cried to the LORD, "O LORD my God, let this boy's life return to him!" The LORD heard Elijah's cry, and the boy's life returned to him, and he lived. Elijah picked up the child and carried him down from the room into the house. He gave him to his mother and said, "Look, your son is alive!" Then the woman said to Elijah, "Now I know that you are a man of God and that the word of the LORD from your mouth is the truth."

– 1 KINGS 17:21-24 –

The widow of Zarephath opened her house to Elijah during a time of severe famine even though she did not even have enough food for her young son and herself. She trusted that God would provide. And God did provide! Sometime later, the woman's child became ill and died. Elijah immediately turned to the Lord and pleaded for the child's life. God heard Elijah's plea and raised him from the dead. This shows us how precious each individual is in the eyes of God.

Make time today to pray fervently for someone who is experiencing sorrow or tragedy in his or her life.

Pray for God to use His life-giving power in their situation. We may pray for anyone, no matter what their status in life is. God cares for every person.

God of life and death, You have allowed tragedy and sorrow to come into my life, but You also pour the balm of Gilead into my wounds and give me comfort.

Amen

Jabez's prayer for God's blessing

Jabez cried out to the God of Israel, "Oh, that you would bless me and enlarge my territory! Let your hand be with me, and keep me from harm so that I will be free from pain." And God granted his request.

– 1 CHRONICLES 4:10 –

Amongst all the names in the long family tree that is quoted in 1 Chronicles, one name in particular stands out: that of Jabez. His mother called him that because of the pain she suffered during his birth. Jabez means *pain*.

However, this is not what he was best known for. Jabez became known for his prayer. His prayer for blessing was common enough: who does not yearn for prosperity and the absence of problems! Jabez trusted sufficiently in God to ask for these things. The Bible records that God granted him these things. Jabez told anyone who was prepared to listen how God had answered his prayer.

Follow the example of Jabez. Confidently ask for God's blessing. Simply ask Him in faith to be by your side, whatever you do or wherever you may find yourself.

Hearer of prayers, grant me Your rich blessing and keep me from harm.

Amen

Prayer that God would reveal Himself

At the time of sacrifice, the prophet Elijah stepped forward and prayed: "O LORD, God of Abraham, Isaac and Israel, let it be known today that you are God in Israel and that I am your servant and have done all these things at your command. Answer me, O LORD, answer me, so these people will know that you, O LORD, are God, and that you are turning their hearts back again."

– 1 KINGS 18:36-37 –

When Elijah prayed this prayer, the worship of Baal was rampant in Israel. Elijah challenged the prophets of Baal to see whether Baal or the true God would be able to set the sacrifice on fire. The prophets of Baal called upon their god and even slashed themselves, but there was no reaction.

Then it was Elijah's turn. After pouring water over the sacrifice, he prayed to God to set his offering on fire, so that the Israelites would mend their ways and return to God. God answered Elijah's prayer by sending fire from heaven that consumed the sacrifice completely.

We may never find ourselves in the same situation as Elijah, but there are times when we would like God to reveal Himself. Humbly ask God to reveal Himself by answering your prayer convincingly and tangibly.

Almighty God and Father, come and reveal Yourself so that people may know that You alone are God.

Amen

Prayer for healing

When he had gone indoors, the blind men came to him, and he asked them, "Do you believe that I am able to do this?" "Yes, Lord," they replied. Then he touched their eyes and said, "According to your faith will it be done to you."

— MATTHEW 9:28-29 —

Have mercy on us, Son of David!" Although the two blind men could not see what was taking place around them, they could very well see that Jesus could help them. They pleaded for one thing: mercy.

By calling Jesus the "Son of David" they revealed that they believed that Jesus was the Messiah. They called out to Jesus as He passed by, but did not give up hope when He did not stop.

They followed Him into the house where He was staying. They were obviously more focused on receiving mercy from the Master than being concerned about what others might think of them. They knew that He alone held the answer to their suffering and needs.

May our own prayers be filled with as much faith and trust as those of the blind men: they asked for mercy and received mercy from God!

Son of David, have mercy on me and provide for my needs according to the abundance of Your mercy and the measure of my faith.

Amen

Trust in God who answers prayers

"When my life was ebbing away, I remembered you, LORD, and my prayer rose to you, to your holy temple. Those who cling to worthless idols forfeit the grace that could be theirs. But I, with a song of thanksgiving, will sacrifice to you. What I have vowed I will make good. Salvation comes from the LORD."

– JONAH 2:7-9 –

This amazing prayer was prayed by the prophet Jonah, from inside a large fish. In the depths of his heart, Jonah probably realized that he could not escape God's calling.

On a ship going in the opposite direction from which God had sent him, he was caught in a fierce storm. He knew that he was the cause of this impending disaster. He asked to be thrown overboard so that the rest of the people onboard could be saved.

Instead of destroying him, God sent a large fish to swallow him. Jonah wasted no time, from the insides of the fish he prayed to God. He knew that his salvation could come from none other than God.

As Jonah did, focus your thoughts on God. In times of trouble, affirm your dependence on God and trust Him for salvation and deliverance.

Redeeming God, I focus my thoughts on You, because salvation comes from You alone.

Amen

Prayer in sorrow

How long, O LORD? Will you forget me forever? How long will you hide your face from me? How long must I wrestle with my thoughts and every day have sorrow in my heart? How long will my enemy triumph over me? Look on me and answer, O LORD my God. Give light to my eyes, or I will sleep in death; but I trust in your unfailing love; my heart rejoices in your salvation. I will sing to the LORD, for he has been good to me.

– PSALM 13:1-3, 5-6 –

Do you sometimes feel as though God has forgotten about you? You pray and pray and yet seem to get no response. Even though David had an intimate relationship with God, he felt like this on more than one occasion. But he did not wallow in self-pity and helplessness. He took his feelings of rejection straight to God. He expressed his impatience with the Lord honestly, *"How long, O LORD? Will you forget me for ever?"* As he opens his heart in this way, a change starts taking place within him. He remembers how faithful God has been in the past. His anguished calls of despair change into a song of praise to the glory of the Lord.

When you enter the presence of God with your complaints, you will undergo a similar change. Instead of feeling forgotten, you will experience the greatness of God's faithfulness and love for you.

Omniscient God, You know how often I have to wrestle with torment in my soul because I do not understand Your ways. But I trust in Your unfailing love.

Amen

OCTOBER

PRAYERS FOR SALVATION AND REDEMPTION

Salvation is found in no one else, for there is no other name under heaven given to men by which we must be saved.

– ACTS 4:12 –

Salvation is so deceptively simple that we could easily underestimate its necessity, and yet so amazing that we will never understand it fully. There is no concept so soul-destroying as the idea that sinners can redeem themselves. This false idea leads to many people believing that they can simply sin and confess their sins when it suits them.

It is a Scriptural truth that an unsaved person can not bring about his own salvation. Such a person must be led to the conviction of this truth. This conviction is the work of the Holy Spirit. When this happens that person will look for help from the only Source of salvation. *"For it is by grace you have been saved, through faith – and this not from yourselves, it is the gift of God"* (Eph. 2:8).

Out of the depths I cry to you, O LORD; O LORD, hear my voice. Let your ears be attentive to my cry for mercy. If you, O LORD, kept a record of sins, O LORD, who could stand? But with you there is forgiveness; therefore you are feared. O Israel, put your hope in the LORD, for with the LORD is unfailing love and with him is full redemption. He himself will redeem Israel from all their sins.

– PSALM 130:1-4, 7-8 –

Seeking God

The path of the righteous is level; O upright One, you make the way of the righteous smooth. Yes, LORD, walking in the way of your laws, we wait for you; your name and renown are the desire of our hearts. My soul yearns for you in the night; in the morning my spirit longs for you. When your judgments come upon the earth, the people of the world learn righteousness.

— ISAIAH 26:7-9 —

We need God in every situation in life. Isaiah was intimately and personally aware of this. He wanted God to level the path before him. The path might be steep and treacherous, but for those who follow God, it is not be impassable.

Isaiah's world seems to be crumbling, but he waited on the Lord for salvation and deliverance. He knew that the strength to handle every situation comes only from God. The author of Revelation has a similar longing for God. He ends his revelation of the coming judgment with the cry, "*Amen. Come, Lord Jesus*" (Rev. 22:20).

We need to develop a similar sense of longing for God, desiring that He would cleanse the sin from our hearts and protect us from the sin surrounding us. He is our only and final hope.

Lord, my Savior and Redeemer, through the darkness of this world, I seek You, for You are my only true help and salvation.

Amen

A prayer for deliverance and salvation

The arrogant are attacking me, O God; a band of ruthless men seeks my life –
men without regard for you. But you, O LORD, are a compassionate and gra-
cious God, slow to anger, abounding in love and faithfulness. Turn to me and
have mercy on me; grant your strength to your servant and save the son of
your maidservant.

– PSALM 86:14-16 –

Which of your life experiences has most clearly exposed your vulnerability and weakness? When did you need God's strength and help the most?

In this prayer, David tells God about the crisis in which he finds himself. Arrogant people had risen against him and some even wanted to kill him. He was overwhelmed by the forces arrayed against him and he frankly admits his fear to God. Nevertheless, David uses two simple little words to turn his prayer around, *"You Lord!"* This turned his thoughts away from his overwhelming problems and focused them on his almighty God.

Once you have made a list of your problems and laid them before God, follow David's example and confess that, regardless of how critical your circumstances may be, God is greater than they are. He is the Source of your strength and salvation – today and forever!

Almighty God and Father, You have always
been my refuge in danger. Please come to me
in this present crisis and deliver me.

Amen

A prayer for the whole world

That your ways may be known on earth, your salvation among all nations. May the peoples praise you, O God; may all the peoples praise you.

– PSALM 67:2-3 –

God's salvation is not only meant for His chosen people, Israel, but also for all people on earth. This prayer firstly asks God to be gracious to Israel, but the Psalmist continues to plead for God's plans and His redeeming salvation to be *"known on earth"*, so that God may be glorified by all nations.

The birth, death and resurrection of His Son, Jesus Christ, is God's answer to this prayer. Before Jesus ascended to heaven, He said to His disciples, *"This is what is written: The Christ will suffer and rise from the dead on the third day, and repentance and forgiveness will be preached in his name to all nations, beginning at Jerusalem"* (Lk. 24:46-47).

May God help us, as followers of Jesus Christ, to understand His will, so that we may also pray for the salvation of all nations.

Father God, may Your holy Name be glorified amongst all the nations of the world. Use me as Your humble instrument in making Your Name known. I glorify Your great Name!

Amen

A prayer for God's discipline

I know, O LORD, that a man's life is not his own; it is not for man to direct his steps. Correct me, LORD, but only with justice – not in your anger, lest you reduce me to nothing.

– JEREMIAH 10:23-24 –

We so often become impatient while waiting for God to show us what He want us to do, and then we move forward in our own strength, following our own plans. When this happens we lose perspective and we need someone to get us back on track.

It is not always easy to accept a reprimand, but it is necessary. Jeremiah must have realized that he was making his own plans and following his own path, and therefore he asks God, "*I know, O LORD, that … it is not for man to direct his steps. Correct me, LORD, but only with justice – not in your anger, lest you reduce me to nothing.*"

The Lord has a plan for each one of us, a path that He wants us to follow. When we lose our way, then it is good to pray like Jeremiah prayed, and to ask the Lord to direct our paths.

Merciful Father, show me Your way by Your grace and lead me on the right path so that I will not follow my own way.

Amen

Place your trust in God

My heart is steadfast, O God, my heart is steadfast; I will sing and make music. Awake, my soul! Awake, harp and lyre! I will awaken the dawn. I will praise you, O LORD, among the nations; I will sing of you among the peoples. For great is your love, reaching to the heavens; your faithfulness reaches to the skies. Be exalted, O God, above the heavens; let your glory be over all the earth.

– PSALM 57:7-11 –

David prayed this prayer while fleeing for his life. We would expect a fugitive to be focused on what his enemies were doing and how he could escape their traps. But after David has placed his predicament before the Lord, He focuses on the omnipotence of God.

His prayer is soon transformed into a resounding, clear hymn of praise, *"I will awaken the dawn. I will praise you, O LORD, among the nations"*.

Why is David moved to displaying such gratitude while he is fleeing for his life? Because he knows that God's unfailing love is greater than any of his problems. His prayer puts his worldly troubles in an eternal perspective.

How can God's eternal perspective help you to handle your problems in life? Place your trust fully in the Lord and believe in His omnipotence in every situation. He is your Savior and your God.

Almighty God, I place my trust fully in You and know that You will come to my rescue at the right time.

Amen

Trust in God's protection and deliverance

I cry out to God Most High, to God, who fulfills his purpose for me. He sends from heaven and saves me, rebuking those who hotly pursue me; God sends his love and his faithfulness. I am in the midst of lions; I lie among ravenous beasts – men whose teeth are spears and arrows, whose tongues are sharp swords.

– PSALM 57:2-4 –

David was hiding from the wrath of Saul, who had pursued David into a cave in the wilderness. But David knew that his hope did not depend on how fast he could run or how creatively he could hide.

His protection came from God. The darkness of a cave could not protect him as effectively as the shadow of God's wings. David trusted in God alone for his safety.

What have the fierce storms of life taught you about God's faithfulness? Can you say, along with David, *"God sends his love and his faithfulness"*? Find peace in God's protection, and trust that He will lead you along the right path, away from your adversaries. God will deliver you if you trust in Him.

Living God and God of deliverance, help me to trust unfailingly that You will fulfil Your purpose for me.

Amen

Comfort and strength are found in God alone

May our Lord Jesus Christ himself and God our Father, who loved us and by his grace gave us eternal encouragement and good hope, encourage your hearts and strengthen you in every good deed and word.

– 2 THESSALONIANS 2:16-17 –

In Paul's letter to the young congregation in Thessalonica, he expressed concern about persecution and false teachers who would inevitably cross their path. Paul never watered down true Christian discipleship.

He wanted Christians to be willing to endure affliction for Christ's sake. This prayer reveals a sincere fatherly concern for the Thessalonians because he was not able to be with them. He prays for God to comfort them personally and to give them strength when confronting false teachers.

These special promises are true for all God's children. We can also draw near to God with confidence and ask Him to comfort us and give us strength. He is our Faithful Deliverer.

Merciful Lord Jesus Christ, comfort our hearts and give us the strength to do and say only that which is right.

Amen

A prayer for deliverance from evil forces

You are always righteous, O LORD, when I bring a case before you. Yet I would speak with you about your justice: Why does the way of the wicked prosper? Why do all the faithless live at ease? You have planted them, and they have taken root; they grow and bear fruit. You are always on their lips but far from their hearts. Yet you know me, O LORD; you see me and test my thoughts about you. Drag them off like sheep to be butchered! Set them apart for the day of slaughter!

– JEREMIAH 12:1-3 –

Often, it seems as though the people who do not fear the Lord, prosper abundantly. This causes some people to question God's righteousness. Jeremiah did so!

The prophet of the Lord found it difficult to understand why wicked people prosper and are so happy. After all, he had devoted his life to telling God's people that true happiness and security are only to be found through our obedience to God.

Although Jeremiah questioned God about this, he knew that evil will ultimately be destroyed. He also knew that God sees right through the false piety of the wicked.

Ask God to reveal the true condition of your heart to you. Can you, like Jeremiah, declare that your thoughts are pure? If not, pray that God will cleanse you of every evil thought, otherwise they will cause you great harm.

Gracious Father, preserve me from envying the wicked and cleanse my heart and mind of every evil thought and deed.

Amen

A prayer for healing

Then the king said to the man of God, "Intercede with the Lord your God and pray for me that my hand may be restored." So the man of God interceded with the Lord, and the king's hand was restored and became as it was before. The king said to the man of God, "Come home with me and have something to eat, and I will give you a gift."

— 1 Kings 13:6-7 —

When a prophet confronted King Jeroboam about the evil practices of worship that he had introduced at Bethel, he arrogantly commanded his soldiers to arrest the prophet. As he stretched out his hand toward the prophet, it shriveled up.

Jeroboam had clearly challenged God. He realized how sinful his behavior was and asked the prophet to pray for him. The prophet prayed and God answered. What a gracious God we serve! He was under no obligation to listen to any prayer. But He heard and He answered.

We may not have committed the atrocities Jeroboam did, but we are still sinful. God does not punish us simply to pay us back for our wrongful deeds, but He wants to bring us to repentance. He wants to heal us, but first He wants us to repent of our sins.

Righteous God and faithful Father, I acknowledge my sins with remorse and pray for Your gracious forgiveness and for healing. I praise and thank You for it.

Amen

Trust in God's unfailing love

"Here now is the man who did not make God his stronghold but trusted in his great wealth and grew strong by destroying others!" But I am like an olive tree flourishing in the house of God; I trust in God's unfailing love for ever and ever. I will praise you forever for what you have done; in your name I will hope, for your name is good. I will praise you in the presence of your saints.

— PSALM 52:7-9 —

Where you place your trust is of utmost importance. We all hope that everything we undertake will succeed, that our friends will support us, or that our wealth will provide us with security.

But all these things will eventually vanish. Our plans are easily thwarted, our friends might leave us in the lurch, our wealth might be lost.

In the end, God is the only one who can offer us real security. Those who put their trust in Him will not be disappointed and they will receive an inheritance that can never be destroyed. God will never fail them.

When you draw near to God in prayer today, tell Him that you trust Him completely. Ask Him to reveal to you His good plan for your life, and then live in obedience to His plan of love.

Loving Lord Jesus, I fully trust in Your unfailing love that lasts for all eternity.

Amen

Our time is short

"Show me, O LORD, my life's end and the number of my days; let me know how fleeting is my life. You have made my days a mere handbreadth; the span of my years is as nothing before you. Each man's life is but a breath. Man is a mere phantom as he goes to and from: He bustles about, but only in vain; he heaps up wealth, not knowing who will get it. But now, LORD, what do I look for? My hope is in you."

– PSALM 39:4-7 –

We all know people who seem to be more wedded to their work than to their marriage partner. They take work home that keeps them busy for hours on end and their bosses undoubtedly reward them for it. They accumulate a large bank balance, but their obsession with work leaves them emotionally and spiritually bankrupt.

This prayer portrays how foolish it is to waste your energy on accumulating material wealth that will soon be worthless. David realizes that his time on earth is short, *"You have made my days a mere handbreadth ... Man is a mere phantom as he goes to and fro: He bustles about, but only in vain ..."* What should we then do? In who or what must we place our hope? David provides an answer to this question: *"My hope is in you."*

Always place your hope in God. Abandon yourself to Him totally.

Lord my God, You are my Deliverer and I place my hope fully in You. Have mercy on me and help me to view life from Your holy perspective.

Amen

Commit your cause to God

But, O LORD Almighty, you who judge righteously and test the heart and mind, let me see your vengeance upon them, for to you I have committed my cause.

— JEREMIAH 11:20 —

These days, everyone has a "cause" that they want to promote. We are bombarded with mail and telephone calls from organizations that ask us for money and time to support their cause.

The prophet, Jeremiah, also had a cause: to convey God's message and call the people of Israel to repent and return to God.

However, Jeremiah's enemies were plotting to kill him. They wanted to silence him and his message. He asked the Lord to intervene and to take revenge on his enemies. He reminded God that he committed his cause to God a long time ago.

If the cause you support glorifies God, and you have committed it to Him, you may rest assured that He will bless all you do. In prayer today, ask God to make clear to you that you are supporting His cause, and then ask His blessing upon it.

Omniscient God, You know my deepest thoughts. I commit my cause to You and pray for Your blessing upon it, for it is to Your greater glory alone.

Amen

Seek God's approval

Gideon said to God, "If you will save Israel by my hand as you have prom-
ised – look, I will place a wool fleece on the threshing floor. If there is dew only on
the fleece and all the ground is dry, then I will know that you will save Israel by
my hand, as you said." And that is what happened. Gideon rose early the next
day; he squeezed the fleece and wrung out the dew – a bowlful of water.

– JUDGES 6:36-38 –

There are times when we can scarcely believe what God is asking us to do. That was the case with Gideon. God told Gideon to save Israel from the Midianites, but Gideon could not believe this. He asked God for a sign to confirm that this was really a call from Him.

When God gave him the sign, Gideon asked for yet another sign, and once again God answered him. Gideon was finally convinced, and he obeyed God's call. He led an army of Israelites against the Midianites and God granted him a miraculous victory over the enemy – just as He had promised.

God graciously answered Gideon's request for a sign. He is equally gracious regarding our requests. However, if we already know what God's will is, especially if He has declared it in His Word, we must not hesitate to obey it.

Ask God's approval for that which you have to do in His Name and then go out in faith and do it.

Counselor and God, show me what You
want me to do and let my conduct always
be acceptable to You.

Amen

Cast your problems upon God

O LORD, the God who saves me, day and night I cry out before you. May my prayer come before you; turn your ear to my cry. For my soul is full of trouble and my life draws near the grave. I am counted among those who go down to the pit; I am like a man without strength. I am set apart with the dead, like the slain who lie in the grave, whom you remember no more, who are cut off from your care.

– PSALM 88:1-5 –

Difficulties, affliction and problems can be harrowing. For the majority of us, life is filled with them.

Heman, the author of this prayer, was no stranger to suffering. Night and day, he called on God to help him in his trouble. Heman was not afraid to admit his predicament, to describe his suffering, and to call on God for help. Even though God had not yet delivered Heman, he persevered in prayer and cast his problems upon God.

When we are surrounded by problems and difficulties, we need to follow Heman's example and persevere in reminding God of our affliction, because God will give us an answer in His perfect time.

Oh Hearer of prayers, listen to my urgent call and answer me. I am surrounded by darkness, send Your light and Your deliverance.

Amen

An appeal for God's deliverance

Send forth your light and your truth, let them guide me; let them bring me to your holy mountain, to the place where you dwell. Then will I go to the altar of God, to God, my joy and my delight. I will praise you with the harp, O God, my God.

— PSALM 43:3-5 —

To be lost in darkness can be a frightening experience. And even more so if you are being pursued by people who are intent on killing you!

This was the Psalmist's predicament. He realized that the only One who could help him was God. He called on God to show him the way and to lead him into the truth till he enters the presence of God.

Ask God in prayer to guide your footsteps. Focus on your final destination – the dwelling place of God. Comfort yourself with the prospect of living joyously in the dwelling of the Lord for all eternity.

Dear Lord, my Counselor and my Guide, in Your light and Your truth, lead me to my final destination – the house of the Father!

Amen

Trust in God's deliverance

Be merciful to me, O LORD, for I am in distress; my eyes grow weak with sorrow, my soul and my body with grief. My life is consumed by anguish and my years by groaning; my strength fails because of my affliction, and my bones grow weak.

– PSALM 31:9-10, 15-16 –

Suffering and pain are unavoidable in this life. Tense relationships, financial obligations and demands and pressures at work could drain your strength and leave you with little to offer others.

In this prayer David tells God about his affliction and suffering. His sorrow and grief have made him weak and caused him to say, *"My strength fails because of my affliction, and my bones grow weak."*

Nevertheless, even in this bitter struggle, David finds strength in the Lord by placing his future in His hands. We too can trust God regarding our plans for the future.

Perhaps you are facing a situation that is causing you pain and sorrow. While spending time in prayer, cast your burdens on God and place your future in His competent and loving hands.

Loving and Gracious God, I place my future in Your hands with confidence and know that in You alone salvation and redemption are to be found.

Amen

Find strength in God

How great is your goodness, which you have stored up for those who fear you, which you bestow in the sight of men on those who take refuge in you. In the shelter of your presence you hide them from the intrigues of men; in your dwelling you keep them safe from accusing tongues. Love the LORD, all his saints! The LORD preserves the faithful, but the proud he pays back in full. Be strong and take heart, all you who hope in the LORD.

— PSALM 31:19-20, 23-24 —

In this prayer, David portrays God as a place of refuge in which he is protected against the dangers of the world: his enemies, harmful lies and conspiracies.

As king of Israel, David would have had the might of a kingdom behind him. At the same time, he would have been the target of all sorts of attacks.

Therefore, he wisely looks to God for protection. He knows that God preserves and blesses those who turn to Him for safety. He takes heart in the knowledge that God will protect him from any danger that could possibly cross his path.

In your prayer today, ask God to preserve you and your family by His omnipotent presence. Pray for His protection and the courage to complete the task He has given you, so that He will be glorified.

Merciful God, in Your presence I want to take refuge. Help me to take heart in the knowledge that You are my Deliverer and Protector.

Amen

Humble yourself before God

Then Job replied to the LORD: "I know that you can do all things; no plan of yours can be thwarted. You asked, 'Who is this that obscures my counsel without knowledge?' Surely I spoke of things I did not understand, things too wonderful for me to know. You said, 'Listen now, and I will speak; I will question you, and you shall answer me.' My ears had heard of you but now my eyes have seen you. Therefore I despise myself and repent in dust and ashes."

— JOB 42:1-6 —

Sometimes we complain to God without thinking about what we say, and then we have to take back our words. Even though Job had much time to think, he had to repent of his lack of humbleness. The Lord listened to Job's complaints, criticism and questions and then He reprimanded him. Job criticized God's actions, and yet he could not answer God's questions. When Job realized what he had said he was remorseful and immediately asked the Lord for forgiveness.

We might not openly challenge God as Job did, but sometimes we question the way in which God cares for us. In such times, God wants us to come to Him, believing that He has the answers, for He is good, righteous and filled with love. Pray for faith to overcome your doubt. Trust in God and cast your burdens on Him.

Loving God and Father, I know that nothing is impossible for You and that nothing can prevent You from providing for all my needs – You have saved me and bestowed Your blessings on me.

Amen

Call out to God for deliverance

I cry aloud to the LORD; I lift up my voice to the LORD for mercy. I pour out my complaint before him; before him I tell my trouble. When my spirit grows faint within me, it is you who know my way. In the path where I walk men have hidden a snare for me. Look to my right and see; no one is concerned for me. I have no refuge; no one cares for my life. I cry to you, O LORD; I say, "You are my refuge, my portion in the land of the living."

— PSALM 142:1-5 —

No doubt you have been overwhelmed by difficulties at times, and were unsure of where to turn for help and support. Wherever David went, his enemies set traps for him. He looked for someone to help him, but no one gave him a second thought. No one was concerned for him or cared in the least what became of him.

Perhaps this sounds familiar to you. Sometimes we need to give vent to our frustrations about a difficult situation with no apparent solution. Our lament is, "No one is concerned about me. All are against me; no one appreciates me; no one cares what becomes of me."

If you feel discouraged and it seems as if the tide is against you, seek the Lord. Pour out your complaints to Him and tell Him about all your problems. God is great and will handle your problems and He will show you the way to go.

Gracious God, You know how overwhelmed and discouraged I am feeling at this moment. Please show me the way.

Amen

Moses prays for the salvation of his people

Surely it is you who love the people; all the holy ones are in your hand. At your feet they all bow down, and from you receive instruction.
— DEUTERONOMY 33:3 —

Shortly before Moses' death, he brought all the people of Israel together to bestow a special blessing on each tribe. But the salient theme of all his prayers can be found in his introduction.

He starts by giving them all the assurance, *"Surely it is you (Lord) who love the people."* The people of Israel needed to respond to the Lord's love by accepting His teachings in His Word and following where He led them.

Moses' prayer also holds a lesson for us. The Lord loves all His people and keeps them safely in His omnipotent hands. It is our responsibility to accept His teachings through His Word and follow in His footsteps.

Thank the Lord that He loves you and holds you in His hands. Ask Him for the strength to walk in His footsteps.

Merciful Heavenly Father, thank You that You keep me safe in Your loving hand. Help me to live according to the decrees of Your Word.

Amen

Moses intercedes on behalf of his people

So Moses went back to the LORD and said, "Oh, what a great sin these people have committed! They have made themselves gods of gold. But now, please forgive their sin – but if not, then blot me out of the book you have written."

– EXODUS 32:31-32 –

Moses had every reason to be dismayed and angry with the people of Israel. While he was receiving the Ten Commandments from God on Mount Sinai, the people made a golden calf and worshiped it.

By doing so, they not only broke their covenant to worship God and God alone, but they were also rejecting Moses' spiritual leadership.

Moses could easily have asked God to annihilate them on the spot, but instead he pleaded for God's mercy towards them. Moses shows how much he loved the Israelites even though they rebelled against his authority.

Are you concerned about the welfare of others: your friends, family, colleagues and acquaintances? Go to God and ask Him to show His mercy to those who least deserve it.

Holy God, teach me to love others like Moses loved his people. Teach me to look past their sins and to see Your grace instead.

Amen

Prayer for harmony in the church of Christ

May the God who gives endurance and encouragement give you a spirit of unity among yourselves as you follow Christ Jesus, so that with one heart and mouth you may glorify the God and Father of our Lord Jesus Christ.

– ROMANS 15:5-6 –

It is wonderful to worship in a congregation that is excited about God's work. Jesus said to His disciples, "*All men will know that you are my disciples, if you love one another*" (Jn. 13:35). In his letter to the Romans, Paul prays that the faithful in Rome will have "*a spirit of unity among (them)selves.*" Only when believers live like that, will they, "*with one heart and mouth … glorify the God and Father of our Lord Jesus Christ.*"

Think about the impact that it could have on this cynical world if all Christians were to live in harmony as the Bible teaches us. Pray for that kind of harmony in your church community.

Eternal Father of grace, help me to live in harmony with my fellow-believers so that Your Name may be glorified through it.

Amen

A plea for the Savior to remember

Blessed are they who maintain justice, who constantly do what is right. Remember me, O LORD, when you show favor to your people, come to my aid when you save them, that I may enjoy the prosperity of your chosen ones, that I may share in the joy of your nation and join your inheritance in giving praise.

— PSALM 106:3-5 —

To feel forgotten is one of the worst things a person can experience, especially if the people who have forgotten about you are your only hope. That is probably how Samson felt when he wasted away in captivity: blind, weak and alone. He called out to God, "*O Sovereign Lord, remember me*" (Judg. 16:28).

Likewise, Job pleaded with God after experiencing numerous personal crises, "*If only you would set me a time and then remember me!*" (Job 14:13). Even the criminal on the cross beseeched Jesus, "*Jesus, remember me when you come into your kingdom*" (Lk. 23: 42).

Like the Psalmist in this prayer, all these people realized that their lives depended on God's grace and the way in which He lovingly cared for them.

Remember that God never forgets His children – even when they foolishly drift away from Him. If you feel alone and unwanted, call out to God and remember that He lovingly watches over you.

Loving Father, I want to rejoice with all Your children and glorify and praise Your Name.

Amen

Jesus prays for the church

"I have revealed you to those whom you gave me out of the world. They were yours; you gave them to me and they have obeyed your word. Now they know that everything you have given me comes from you. For I gave them the words you gave me and they accepted them. They knew with certainty that I came from you, and they believed that you sent me."

– JOHN 17:6-8 –

In His last hours before the Crucifixion, Jesus prayed to the Father for the protection of His disciples. In this part of His prayer, Jesus explains that He has clearly and lucidly conveyed the word of His father to His disciples, as the Father had required.

Jesus' task was complete. Now it was the turn of the disciples to share God's message with others. We, as followers of Jesus Christ, have a legacy so rich that it defies description.

The actual words of God that were entrusted to the disciples, were also conveyed to us. It is a precious treasure that was given to us.

Do we regard God's words with the reverence which they deserve, and do we fervently convey the message of redemption and salvation to others? Thank God today for His everlasting Word.

Eternal Word, thank You that Jesus became the Incarnate Word to convey to us Your message of redemption and salvation.

Amen

Solomon's prayer

And when a prayer or plea is made by any of your people Israel — each one aware of his afflictions and pains, and spreading out his hands toward this temple — then hear from heaven, your dwelling place. Forgive, and deal with each man according to all he does, since you know his heart (for you alone know the hearts of men), so that they will fear you and walk in your ways all the time they live in the land you gave our fathers.

— 2 CHRONICLES 6:29-31 —

After the building of the temple of the Lord had been completed, Solomon gathered the people to dedicate it to God and to pray for the people. Although peace reigned in his kingdom, and although there was material prosperity, Solomon knew that God was the origin of all those blessings.

Solomon prays that when the people strayed from God He would still look down on them with grace and would hear their prayers. God answered Solomon's prayer. Time and again He came to the rescue of His people when they called to Him in distress.

God still finds pleasure in answering the prayers of His people today.

Do not hesitate to seek help from God. Ask Him to hear your prayers and grant you forgiveness.

Heavenly Father, listen to my anguished cry with grace and forgive me when I have knowingly or unknowingly sinned against Your will.

Amen

Prayer for vindication

Vindicate me, O LORD, for I have led a blameless life; I have trusted in the LORD without wavering. Test me, O LORD, and try me, examine my heart and my mind; for your love is ever before me, and I walk continually in your truth.

— PSALM 26:1-3 —

There are few people who like being put to the test, and even fewer who enjoy clashing with the law. No one likes their every deed and action to be cross-examined by lawyers.

But David prays that God would examine him, so that the accusations of his enemies would be silenced forever. Because he tried to walk conscientiously in the ways of God, David was confident that the Lord would protect him against all the false accusations.

If we live carefully and walk according to God's will, we may rest assured in the knowledge that God will vindicate us.

Dedicate your life and conduct to the Lord in prayer today. Ask Him to examine you and to help you change those aspects of your life that are not in accordance with His will and decrees.

Omniscient and loving Father, put my motives and deeds to the test. Help me to live every day in accordance with Your standards of truth and love.

Amen

Prayer in the midst of a storm

Instead, the men did their best to row back to land. But they could not, for the sea grew even wilder than before. Then they cried to the Lord, "O LORD, please do not let us die for taking this man's life. Do not hold us accountable for killing an innocent man, for you, O LORD, have done as you pleased." Then they took Jonah and threw him overboard, and the raging sea grew calm. At this the men greatly feared the LORD, and they offered a sacrifice to the LORD and made vows to him.

– JONAH 1:13-16 –

The sailors were desperate. As the wind grew strong and the waves became bigger, they feared for their lives. They tried everything and even prayed to their gods. But nothing worked, until Jonah confessed that he was fleeing from God.

This was an unusual way to witness to non-believers. It was these pagan sailors who encouraged Jonah to obey the living God, and not the other way round! Nevertheless, God brought Jonah back to Him and also demonstrated His omnipotence to those unbelieving sailors. They subjected themselves to God's will, prayed for Him to save their lives, and dedicated themselves to following Him.

Like these sailors, we must realize that, even in the most difficult and dangerous circumstances God is implementing His will.

Gracious God of deliverance, You allow storms to come into our lives for Your own good reasons. Please protect me so that I can continue to do Your work.

Amen

David seeks God's will

In the course of time, David inquired of the LORD. "Shall I go up to one of the towns of Judah?" he asked. The LORD said, "Go up." David asked, "Where shall I go?" "To Hebron," the LORD answered.

– 2 SAMUEL 2:1 –

When we have to make important decisions, we are often quick to seek the advice of trusted friends or, to look for signs in the midst of our circumstances. We often go to God in prayer first.

In today's prayer, David wanted to know where he should start his reign as king.

Rather than conducting an opinion poll or discussing the matter with others, David sought the will of the Lord. God quickly answered him. He delights in answering our prayers and often reveals His will through circumstances or through the advice of other people. He often also speaks to us through His Word.

Thank the Lord in your prayer today for leading you thus far. Then ask Him to reveal to you His will for your future and listen sensitively to His reply.

Loving Lord and Counselor, hold my hand and lead me safely in Your ways. Reveal Your will for my life and help me to obey Your commands.

Amen

An anguished cry for God's deliverance

Rescue me, O LORD, from evil men; protect me from men of violence, who devise evil plans in their hearts and stir up war every day. Let slanderers not be established in the land; may disaster hunt down men of violence. I know that the LORD secures justice for the poor and upholds the cause of the needy. Surely the righteous will praise your name and the upright will live before you.
PSALM 140:2-3, 12-14 –

Every day we hear about innocent people who suffer or become the victims of thugs. Sadly it is often children who suffer abuse and cruelty. The transgressors are often unscrupulous adults who show no remorse for their deeds. When we hear about these inhumane and merciless deeds, many of us become furious. We may ask, "O God, where is justice?"

David was concerned about the injustice that the poor, the helpless and the innocent were suffering. He asked the Lord to help those who being persecuted, to uphold the rights of the poor and to destroy those who committed these violent crimes.

Take a little time in your prayer today to intercede for innocent people who suffer in our world today. Ask God to deliver those who suffer.

Almighty and Righteous Father, uphold the rights of the poor and the innocent. Deliver them from evil people and replace their suffering with Your justice.

Amen

Trust in God to deliver you

My heart is steadfast, O God; I will sing and make music with all my soul. Awake, harp and lyre! I will awaken the dawn. I will praise you, O LORD, among the nations; I will sing of you among the peoples. For great is your love, higher than the heavens; your faithfulness reaches to the skies. Be exalted, O God, above the heavens, and let your glory be over all the earth. Save us and help us with your right hand, that those you love may be delivered.

– PSALM 108:1-6 –

The difference between victory and defeat for a team is often only the measure of trust that team mates have in one another.

In this prayer, David fully places his trust in God. He knows that he cannot save himself – only God can save him! He reminds himself that God's love is higher than the heavens and that His glory covers the earth. No wonder that he calls out, "*My heart is steadfast, O God!*" It is easy for us to forget the extent of God's omnipotence and love. We fret about our problems of the moment, instead of focusing on God who is our deliverer.

In your prayer today, think of all the ways in which God has delivered His people in the past. Use the words of David and praise and thank Him for His omnipotence and love.

Almighty God, Your unfathomable love is higher than the heavens. I once again put my trust fully in You.

Amen

Prayer for deliverance from suffering

O LORD, see how my enemies persecute me! Have mercy and lift me up from the gates of death, that I may declare your praises in the gates of the Daughter of Zion and there rejoice in your salvation. Arise, O LORD, let not man triumph; let the nations be judged in your presence. Strike them with terror, O LORD; let the nations know they are but men.

– PSALM 9:13-14, 19-20 –

Life is difficult enough without people constantly attacking you in different ways. David soon realized this when he became king. The more power and responsibility that is entrusted to you, the more enemies will rise up against you.

When enemies attack us, we instinctively fight back. But this prayer teaches us that your first reaction against opposition should be to turn to God. Instead of devising ways to destroy his enemy, David considers how God can be honored and praised through his circumstances.

Perhaps you are facing a difficult situation at present. Place your anxieties in prayer before God and ask for His deliverance so that you may rejoice in Him.

Savior and Redeemer, You know about my anxieties and how I am suffering the wrath of my enemies. Teach me to glorify You in my situation.

Amen

NOVEMBER

PRAYERS OF
THANKSGIVING

Sing to the LORD with thanksgiving; make music to our God on the harp.

–PSALM 147:7 –

Gratitude is the praise we give to God: for His unfailing love, for His Son who redeemed us, for the Holy Spirit who comforts and guides us, for our family and the prosperity we experience, for friends who support us, for teachers who instruct us, for all who have contributed to our growth and success, for books, sermons, conversations and prayers.

For all of these and for so many other things that come to us so undeservedly from God's hand of love, things that we are aware of and unaware of, that are visible or invisible, that are remembered and that have been forgotten – praise the Lord for He is good! His love endures forever!

Shout for joy to the LORD, all the earth. Worship the LORD with gladness; come before him with joyful songs. Know that the LORD is God. It is he who made us, and we are his; we are his people, the sheep of his pasture. Enter his gates with thanksgiving and his courts with praise; give thanks to him and praise his name. For the LORD is good and his love endures forever; his faithfulness continues through all generations.

– PSALM 100:1-5 –

Gratitude for God's grace and favor

I will exalt you, O Lord, for you lifted me out of the depths and did not let my enemies gloat over me. O Lord my God, I called to you for help and you healed me. O Lord, you brought me up from the grave; you spared me from going down into the pit. Sing to the Lord, you saints of his; praise his holy name. For his anger lasts only a moment, but his favor lasts a lifetime; weeping may remain for a night, but rejoicing comes in the morning.

PSALM 30:1-5 –

Even though God prevented David from building the temple in Jerusalem, this psalm was sung when the temple was dedicated. It reflects the experiences of someone who has survived God's wrath and who gratefully rejoices in the grace of God. Even a single moment of God's wrath results in a night of weeping for David. But the darkness and sorrow of the night of weeping is followed by the dawning of a joyful day: David's relationship with the Lord was restored.

David realized that God's wrath was not provoked without reason and the right response to God's anger was remorse and confession.

In your darkest nights of painful waiting, you must remember that God will undoubtedly bring forth a morning of untold joy. You can even now rejoice with gratitude in your heart, when you think of the day when He will dry every tear from your eyes.

Holy Father, I confess my transgressions with sadness and remorse, but I thank You for Your grace and deliverance.

Amen

Joy in God's love

Your love, O LORD, reaches to the heavens, your faithfulness to the skies. Your righteousness is like the mighty mountains, your justice like the great deep. O LORD, you preserve both man and beast. How priceless is your unfailing love! Both high and low among men find refuge in the shadow of your wings. They feast on the abundance of your house; you give them drink from your river of delights. For with you is the fountain of life; in your light we see light.

– PSALM 36:5-9 –

David, in this prayer, uses images of things that he can see: the sky, the mountains, the oceans. Through these visible things he illustrated those things that he could not see: the Lord's unfailing love, His faithfulness to His people, His righteousness and His commitment to mercy.

The fact that God sustains His creation on a daily basis, and that He feeds His people, clearly demonstrates the depth of His love for everything that He has made. God finds pleasure when His people *"drink from [His] river of delights."*

Make time today to look at the world round about you and look at the beauties of nature from David's perspective.

Our God is great and His signature is visible all around us. Let us bow before Him in admiration and worship.

Creator God, how precious is Your unfailing love. O God, open my eyes and my heart so that I may see the wonders of Your love and care.

Amen

Holy reverence for God

The works of his hands are faithful and just; all his precepts are trustworthy. They are steadfast for ever and ever, done in faithfulness and uprightness. He provided redemption for his people; he ordained his covenant forever – holy and awesome is his name. The fear of the LORD is the beginning of wisdom; all who follow his precepts have good understanding. To him belongs eternal praise.

– PSALM 111:7-10 –

A large section of modern-day society no longer has any regard or respect for authority. In fact it seems that many people admire insolence. These people cynically suggest that there is nothing that is holy. This kind of attitude does not mean that less reverence is due to God now than in the days when the Psalmist wrote this prayer. God must be revered, for all that He says and does is righteous and good.

We must not approach God in a frivolous and demanding manner, but rather with respect, humility and reverence. True wisdom is to realize that God should be thanked for all we have and all we are. And there are tangible rewards for those who conform their lives to this truth.

During your prayer time today, consider the foundation of your faith and the fountain of all your wisdom. Kneel in grateful worship before the Lord God and pay Him all the honor that He deserves.

Most Holy and Almighty God, all that You do is righteous and good. I honor and worship You with my entire being.

Amen

Rejoice in the presence of God

Therefore my heart is glad and my tongue rejoices; my body also will rest secure, because you will not abandon me to the grave, nor will you let your Holy One see decay. You have made known to me the path of life; you will fill me with joy in your presence, with eternal pleasures at your right hand.

— PSALM 16:9-11 —

Often our prayers reflect our problems, fears and all sorts of anxieties, which all focus on ourselves.

In this psalm, David describes what happened to him when he entered the presence of God. He was then not concerned about protecting or defending himself, for his loving God is his protector.

When he draws near to God in prayer, he is set free from self-absorbtion and his own problems. He focuses on his King and his prayer time becomes a joyful celebration. In prayer, David meets Someone who is awesome, and yet comforts him. He no longer focuses on himself, but on his Creator.

The joy of entering God's presence should give us perspective on our lives and provide us with the strength to serve the Lord every day. Ask God to fill your life with His holy and loving presence.

Loving God, grant me the joy of Your holy presence every day.

Amen

Glory be to God!

I will exalt you, my God the King; I will praise your name for ever and ever. Every day I will praise you and extol your name for ever and ever. Great is the LORD and most worthy of praise; his greatness no one can fathom. One generation will commend your works to another; they will tell of your mighty acts. They will speak of the glorious splendor of your majesty, and I will meditate on your wonderful works. They will tell of the power of your awesome works, and I will proclaim your great deeds.

– PSALM 145:1-6 –

We have many reasons to praise God. Not only did He create us and give us life, but He also provides in our daily needs and brings us into fellowship with other believers, among whom we can become the person God has intended us to be.

Above all, He reconciled us with Himself through Jesus Christ. But David was not thinking of any of these things. Instead, he glorified the Lord God simply because He is his great King. God's position alone makes Him worthy of all praise! Moreover, David not only glorifies the Lord, but blesses Him! What an overwhelming thought! A small measure of praise and blessing is bestowed upon God when we communicate with Him in prayer and worship.

Reflect for a few moments on how God reigns over the great universe. Then glorify Him and bless the great King of all kings!

My God and King, I glorify and bless You, for You alone are worthy of all praise. Thank You that I can draw near to You.

Amen

Welcome the mighty King

Lift up your heads, O you gates; be lifted up, you ancient doors, that the King of glory may come in. Who is this King of glory? The Lord strong and mighty, the Lord mighty in battle. Lift up your heads, O you gates; lift them up, you ancient doors, that the King of glory may come in. Who is he, this King of glory? The Lord Almighty – he is the King of glory.

– Psalm 24:7-10 –

When the president of a country goes on a journey, it is a newsworthy event. He is accompanied by a horde of advisors and members of the secret service. When they come to a gate, the president never gets out of his car to identify himself, nor to open the gate. The guards simply know that it is the president.

During David's time, the gates of cities were locked with wooden beams while the king was away on warfare. But when he returned victorious, the gates would be opened wide to welcome back the triumphant king. David prayed that the victorious King of all kings would be welcomed in Jerusalem with the same joyful celebrations.

Just as David welcomed the Lord God, his King, you must welcome God in your life through prayer and celebrate His presence with gratitude.

Creator God, I welcome You as eternal King in my life and thank You for Your mercy and love.

Amen

Give thanks to God for His comfort

Praise be to the God and Father of our Lord Jesus Christ, the Father of compassion and the God of all comfort, who comforts us in all our troubles, so that we can comfort those in any trouble with the comfort we ourselves have received from God. For just as the sufferings of Christ flow over into our lives, so also through Christ our comfort overflows.

– 2 Corinthians 1:3-5 –

Often, shortly after you have been through a harrowing situation in your life, and have found comfort, you meet someone who has to handle a similar situation.

It is God who leads us to these people because the comfort that we offer is sincere and they know that we have wrestled with a similar experience ourselves.

In this letter, Paul praises God for using the church of Corinth to *"comfort those in any trouble with the comfort we ourselves have received from God"*.

In prayer and with gratitude, consider all the ways in which God has comforted you in times of affliction and tell God that you are willing to let Him use you to bring comfort to others.

Gracious God, thank You for the comfort which You have granted me so undeservedly. Use me to comfort others in turn.

Amen

The incense of grateful prayer

O Lord, I call to you; come quickly to me. Hear my voice when I call to you. May my prayer be set before you like incense; may the lifting up of my hands be like the evening sacrifice. Set a guard over my mouth, O Lord; keep watch over the door of my lips. Let not my heart be drawn to what is evil, to take part in wicked deeds with men who are evildoers; let me not eat of their delicacies.
                                                                — Psalm 141:1-4 —

In this prayer, David draws on images of the temple as He calls on the Lord for help. He asks the Lord to regard his prayer as fragrant incense that rises from the altar to heaven.

This kind of incense was usually offered in the tabernacle, together with the burnt offerings. He also asks the Lord to accept *"the lifting up of his hands like the evening sacrifice"*. In days gone by, people often raised their hands when they prayed.

God accepts our prayers in His own unique way. He rejoices when we come to Him with requests and He is always willing to do what is best for us. Let the "incense" of your prayer rise up to God and trust Him to hear your prayer.

Hearer of prayers, let my prayer rise like incense to Your throne today.
Amen

Give thanks to God for His goodness

Give thanks to the LORD, for he is good; his love endures forever. Who can proclaim the mighty acts of the LORD or fully declare his praise?

– PSALM 106:1-2 –

There are times when we want to praise and thank God, but we cannot find the words to express what we want to say. This is the situation in which the Psalmist finds himself when he asks, "*Who can proclaim the mighty acts of the LORD or fully declare his praise?*"

In the light of God's holiness and goodness, the Psalmist lists all the instances when the people of Israel proved themselves to be unworthy of God's love. But because of His goodness, God did not destroy them. How could they ever sufficiently praise and thank God for all that He had done for them?

While you are pleading for God's mercy, remind yourself of one of the reasons why God has delivered us: so that we can join the hosts of people who constantly praise His holy name and thank Him for His goodness. How can we ever give sufficient praise and thanks to God!

Merciful and Holy God, who can ever find the words to truly praise and thank You for Your goodness and grace. Your love endures forever!

Amen

Bow in worship before the throne

All the angels were standing around the throne and around the elders and the four living creatures. They fell down on their faces before the throne and worshiped God, saying: "Amen! Praise and glory and wisdom and thanks and honor and power and strength be to our God for ever and ever. Amen!"

— REVELATION 7:11-12 —

In this excerpt from the Book of Revelation we are given a glimpse of God's heavenly throne room. In John's vision, he sees both the faithful, who have risen from the dead, and the impressive heavenly creatures, kneeling before the throne of God. They praise and thank God for all that He has done for them.

Such remarkable worship of God contrasts sharply with the familiarity that we often display towards God. We must remember that it is God we are addressing when we pray. When we draw near to God in prayer, we must remember that He is the Creator and Ruler of the universe. We dare not approach the Holy God frivolously.

The heavenly creatures described in Revelation express their submission to and reverence for God by turning their faces to the ground. Join them in your prayer today and show your utmost respect to your Creator.

Most Holy God, blessings and glory, wisdom and thanksgiving and reverence and power belong to You alone, both now and forever.

Amen

Praise be to the Lord God

Praise be to the LORD God, the God of Israel, who alone does marvelous deeds. Praise be to his glorious name forever; may the whole earth be filled with his glory. Amen and Amen.

– PSALM 72:18-19 –

The word "praise" in this psalm, comes from the Hebrew word that also means "blessing." We usually use this word in prayer when we ask for God's blessing for ourselves or for others. But Solomon calls on his fellow-worshipers to bestow a "blessing" on God. What he means is that they must praise and thank God for all that He has done for them.

This blessing crowns a prayer in which he glorifies God for all that He has done for Israel: He is the God who *"does marvelous deeds"*. He prays for God's blessing on his people and his government. How fitting that Solomon, who has received so much from the hand of God, would profess his gratitude to God by blessing the Name of God.

When you ask God today to bless your loved ones, make sure that you bless God for the wonderful ways in which He continually helps you and grants you success.

Eternal God and Almighty Father, I praise and thank You for all the wonderful deeds You have done for my loved ones and me. Praise be to Your glorious Name for ever!

Amen

Joy amidst tension

Righteous are you, O LORD, and your laws are right. The statutes you have laid down are righteous; they are fully trustworthy. My zeal wears me out, for my enemies ignore your words. Your righteousness is everlasting and your law is true. Trouble and distress have come upon me, but your commands are my delight. Your statutes are forever right; give me understanding that I may live.
— PSALM 119:137-139, 142-144 —

We often wonder where God fits into the stress and tension of our lives. It is only natural, given our limited and insufficient understanding of God, that such questions will present themselves to us. This prayer provides us with a wonderful model for bringing such issues before God.

The Psalmist begins his prayer by reminding himself of God's righteousness and trustworthiness. When we make God's strength and holiness the point of departure of our prayers, our daily struggle and stress are placed clearly in perspective. When we can no longer make any sense out of life, there is only one place to go: to God and His ways.

Commit yourself and your problems to God and trust Him. Ask Him to grant you joy in His statutes and commands.

Loving and Omniscient God, You know the things that cause tension and stress in my life. Help me to find joy in Your statutes.

Amen

Praise and thanksgiving in heaven

Whenever the living creatures give glory, honor and thanks to him who sits on the throne and who lives for ever and ever, the twenty-four elders fall down before him who sits on the throne, and worship him who lives for ever and ever. They lay their crowns before the throne and say: "You are worthy, our Lord and God, to receive glory and honor and power, for you created all things, and by your will they were created and have their being."

— Revelation 4:9-11 —

Some of us may have had the privilege of viewing the wealth and luxury of a king's palace, but no one can fully visualize what God's throne room must look like. Revelation provides us with a glimpse of it: a dazzling throne made of precious stones, a shining sea of glass, clear as crystal, the emerald glow of the rainbow, encircling the throne.

And yet the central element in John's description of God's throne room is the praise that is given to God. Elders, seraphs and exotic living creatures join the choir in a never-ending hymn of praise to the glory of God. They proclaim that the entire universe has been created for God's glory.

If it is true that the universe was created for God's glory, then our role is crystal clear. We must give God the glory, worship and thanksgiving due to Him. Join the heavenly host in praise and grateful worship.

Transcendent God and Father, You are worthy to receive thanksgiving and glory and honor and power, now and forever!

Amen

Fulfil your vows to God

O LORD, truly I am your servant; I am your servant, the son of your maidservant; you have freed me from my chains. I will sacrifice a thank offering to you and call on the name of the LORD. I will fulfill my vows to the LORD in the presence of all his people, in the courts of the house of the LORD – in your midst, O Jerusalem. Praise the LORD.

– PSALM 116:16-19 –

There are not many places in the world where slavery is still practiced. But in days gone by, a person could have been sold into slavery to pay for debts that he had incurred.

The author of this prayer praises God for freeing him from the cruelty and humiliation of slavery to sin. He responds to his liberation with a thank-offering to God. He expresses his joy by promising to call on his Savior at all times and to fulfil his vows to the Lord. He glorifies the Lord for the precious gift of deliverance.

God expects us to honor Him for our deliverance in a similar way, by dedicating our lives as living sacrifices to Him. Thank the Lord for delivering you from the bondage of sin and commit yourself anew to Him in prayer.

Savior and Redeemer, in the presence of all Your children, I fulfil my vows to You through the grace You give me.

Amen

Consider God's amazing deeds

I will extol the LORD with all my heart in the council of the upright and in the assembly. Great are the works of the LORD; they are pondered by all who delight in them. Glorious and majestic are his deeds, and his righteousness endures forever. He has caused his wonders to be remembered; the LORD is gracious and compassionate. He provides food for those who fear him; he remembers his covenant forever.

– PSALM 111:1-5 –

Our thoughts naturally return constantly to those things that we do not understand. We ponder on them and try to make sense out of them. The Psalmist encourages the faithful to ponder the amazing deeds of God.

We should, in public, as well as in the seclusion of our quiet time, express our thanks to God, so that other believers may be comforted by the reports of God's goodness towards us. *"He has caused his wonders to be remembered,"* the Psalmist testifies.

God provides us with food, He remembers His covenant, He reveals His love and power by bestowing upon us all sorts of gifts, *"Glorious and majestic are his deeds."*

Add your personal testimony to this chronicle of God's faithfulness in your personal prayers, as well as your prayers in the presence of the members of your congregation, so that God may be glorified.

Father God, how amazing are Your deeds! How can I even for a moment forget all the wondrous deeds that You have performed for me!

Amen

Hymn of thanksgiving for
the miracles of God's creation

The heavens declare the glory of God; the skies proclaim the work of his hands. Day after day they pour forth speech; night after night they display knowledge. There is no speech or language where their voice is not heard. Their voice goes out into all the earth, their words to the ends of the world. In the heavens he has pitched a tent for the sun, which is like a bridegroom coming forth from his pavilion, like a champion rejoicing to run his course.

– PSALM 19:1-5 –

The sun and the moon, the stars and the planets, reminded David of God's remarkable workmanship. God placed the stars in the heavens and set them moving in their orbits.

Unlike his pagan neighbors, David did not worship the sun, the moon, or the stars. He realized that these heavenly bodies worshiped their Creator, simply by doing that which they had been created to do. If only our ears were attuned to the song of praise with which Creation glorifies God!

Spend some time reflecting upon the complexity and detail of the world around you. Let your hymn of praise join the voices in creation and glorify your Creator.

God, Creator and Father, let me constantly proclaim Your glory and Your mighty deeds.

Amen

Distress call to God

I called on your name, O Lord, from the depths of the pit. You heard my plea: "Do not close your ears to my cry for relief." You came near when I called you, and you said, "Do not fear." O Lord, you took up my case; you redeemed my life.

— Lamentations 3:55-58 —

Parents go to great lengths to make sure that they choose the right names for their babies. A child's name is definitely important, but how much more important is God's name? His name reveals His character.

To call on God's name means to remember the nature of the God we call upon. Jeremiah had to endure the wrath of those who made light of the warnings of God's coming judgment. He called on the name of the Lord and requested God to represent him as both his Defender and Redeemer.

He pleaded with the Lord to act on his behalf and to rescue him. The Lord answered him through defending him and comforting him with these simple words, *"Do not be afraid!"*

What a privilege we have to be able to call on the name of the Lord as Jeremiah did! Our God answers those who call on His name; He calms their fears and defends their cause.

Merciful God, defend my cause and free me from my enemies who wrongfully accuse me.

Amen

Praise, thanksgiving and a humble request

But in your great mercy you did not put an end to them or abandon them, for you are a gracious and merciful God. Now therefore, O our God, the great, mighty and awesome God, who keeps his covenant of love, do not let all this hardship seem trifling in your eyes – the hardship that has come upon us, upon our kings and leaders, upon our priests and prophets, upon our fathers and all your people, from the days of the kings of Assyria until today.

– NEHEMIAH 9:31-32 –

The people of Israel completed the rebuilding of the walls of Jerusalem in 52 days. For the next few weeks, Nehemiah and the priests led the people in confession of guilt and reading the Book of the Law. He asked them to renew their relationship with the Lord and to give Him thanks and praise.

Nehemiah pointed out how many times the Lord had delivered His people and, how in turn, the people were disobedient to the Lord.

In today's prayer, he praises the Lord God for being true to His covenant, regardless of the sins of His people. Then he makes a humble plea for God to have mercy on His people and deliver them once again.

God steadfastly honors His promises. Let us, like Nehemiah, thank the Lord for His faithfulness when we place our requests before Him.

Gracious God, You were true to Your covenant and did not forsake me. Help me to be faithful to You and to obey You always.

Amen

Rejoice in God's strength

God came from Teman, the Holy One from Mount Paran. His glory covered the heavens and his praise filled the earth. His splendor was like the sunrise; rays flashed from his hand, where his power was hidden. Plague went before him; pestilence followed his steps. He stood, and shook the earth; he looked, and made the nations tremble. The ancient mountains crumbled and the age-old hills collapsed. His ways are eternal. The Sovereign LORD is my strength; he makes my feet like the feet of a deer, he enables me to go on the heights.

– HABAKKUK 3:3-6, 19 –

Habakkuk posed some difficult questions to God: Why does God remain silent when the wicked oppress the righteous? God's reply to Habakkuk was that He would return to establish justice. When He returns to reign over the earth, He will deliver His people and punish the godless.

Habakkuk's response was a prayer of grateful praise. He compares God's power to a great storm that lights up the night skies with brilliant flashes of lightning – a storm so fierce that mountains and hills collapse in its wake.

One of the reasons why we pray, is to understand this world of ours from God's perspective. Like Habakkuk, we can take our difficult questions to God, if we do so with sincerity. If we meditate on the Scriptures and reflect on God's good plan, we will be inspired to praise the Almighty with gratitude, as Habakkuk did.

Merciful and Righteous God, I rejoice in Your righteousness, because You have delivered me as well.

Amen

To kneel in gratitude before the King of nations

From you comes the theme of my praise in the great assembly; before those who fear you will I fulfill my vows. The poor will eat and be satisfied; they who seek the LORD will praise him – may your hearts live forever! All the ends of the earth will remember and turn to the LORD, and all the families of the nations will bow down before him, for dominion belongs to the LORD and he rules over the nations.

– PSALM 22:25-29 –

Presidents and kings often rule for long periods of time. But inevitably there comes a time when they lose power and disappear from the scene. A few generations later, they may even be forgotten by the majority of people.

And yet, there is one King whose sovereignty will never end. He will rule over all the nations for all eternity. From the ends of the earth, people will acknowledge His sovereignty and call out, *"For dominion belongs to the LORD and he rules over the nations."* Earthly kings come and go, but our Lord, the King of nations, rules forever.

Kneel down in gratitude before this Lord, the King of all kings. Praise and thank Him and worship His holy Name!

Sovereign King and Lord, You are King of all nations. I kneel in gratitude before You as one of Your redeemed subjects.

Amen

Pray when hope dims

Save me, O God, for the waters have come up to my neck. I sink in the miry depths, where there is no foothold. I have come into the deep waters; the floods engulf me. I am worn out calling for help; my throat is parched. My eyes fail, looking for my God. But I pray to you, O Lord, in the time of your favor; in your great love, O God, answer me with your sure salvation.

– Psalm 69:1-3, 13 –

The prayer of David that is recorded in this Psalm, is actually quite simple, "Lord save me, for I am sinking!" It is the cry of distress of a desperate person who cannot even consider saving himself. But David at least knew who to turn to for help.

Even though he was exhausted from calling out to God in prayer, he continued to call out to God – because he knew that God was the only one who was able to save him.

When waves of adversity threaten to overwhelm you with despair, keep on praying to God. Remember David's perseverance and continue to plead with God for His help.

Deliverer and Savior, I am exhausted from calling out in my need, but I will keep on praying in faith until You, in Your time, answer my prayer.

Amen

Glory be to the Creator of the universe!

But you, O God, are my king from of old; you bring salvation upon the earth. It was you who split open the sea by your power; you broke the heads of the monster in the waters. It was you who crushed the heads of Leviathan and gave him as food to the creatures of the desert. It was you who opened up springs and streams; you dried up the ever flowing rivers. The day is yours, and yours also the night; you established the sun and moon. It was you who set all the boundaries of the earth; you made both summer and winter.

– Psalm 74:12-17 –

When the forces of nature disrupt our world through volcanoes, floods, droughts and other disasters, we are filled with both awe and fear. There is no man with the power to control the seething waters of a flood or the burning lava of a volcano. But God controls even these impressive forces. He is the one who created the world, who set it turning on its axis, who placed the stars in the heavens.

The cycles of the seasons reflect His thoughts. The diversity of plant and animal species reflects His creative ingenuity. But God's greatest and most glorious work is the salvation that He offers to those who worship His Name and believe in His Son.

Indeed, we worship an omnipotent God! You, too, should praise Him and give thanks to Him.

Creator God and loving Father, You are my Savior who sacrificed Your Son for me as well.

Amen

When mockers attack me

Hear us, O our God, for we are despised. Turn their insults back on their own heads. Give them over as plunder in a land of captivity. Do not cover up their guilt or blot out their sins from your sight, for they have thrown insults in the face of the builders.

– NEHEMIAH 4:4-5 –

Nehemiah traveled all the way from Persia to lead his people in the re-building of the walls of Jerusalem. When the people finally began with the reconstruction, they were greeted by gangs of mockers. *"If even a fox climbed up on it he would break that wall of stones!"* (v. 3) mocked Tobiah, and Nehemiah's response was neither obvious nor to be expected.

He did not try to silence the mockers with a volley of sarcastic responses or accusations. He did not become angry or aggressive, but he turned to God in prayer. He asked that God would listen to accusations that were hurled against them.

Mockery, accusations and taunts should not prevent us from doing the work of God. We should rather, like Nehemiah, look to God to take care of those who mock us, and faithfully and silently continue to do His work and to complete the task that He has given us to do.

Holy Father listen to the mockers, and help me not to become revengeful. Help me always to look to You to find the courage I need to complete my task for You.

Amen

Give thanks to God for His unfailing love

Give thanks to the LORD, for he is good. His love endures forever. Give thanks to the God of gods. His love endures forever. Give thanks to the Lord of lords: his love endures forever. To him who alone does great wonders, his love endures forever. Who by his understanding made the heavens, his love endures forever. Who spread out the earth upon the waters, his love endures forever. Who made the great lights – his love endures forever.

– PSALM 136:1-7 –

From the pure air that we breathe to the sand beneath our feet – all of creation is God's gift to us. We owe Him our gratitude for the abundance of His gifts to us. In this prayer, the leader calls on the people to give thanks to God for every aspect of His creation. The people then respond with the repeated chorus, *"His love endures for ever."*

Allow this prayer leader of old to guide you in giving thanks to God today. Look at His creation surrounding you the sky, the twinkling stars shining down on you, the ground beneath your feet.

Let every aspect of God's creation remind you of His faithfulness towards you personally and how He provides for your needs: food, clothing and a roof over your head. Give thanks to Him with a hymn of praise for His infinite love and loyalty.

Faithful Creator God, Your loyal love endures for ever. I thank You for the countless blessings that undeservedly come to me from Your hand of grace.

Amen

Drink with gratitude from the well of salvation

With joy you will draw water from the wells of salvation. In that day you will say: "Give thanks to the LORD, call on his name; make known among the nations what he has done, and proclaim that his name is exalted. Sing to the LORD, for he has done glorious things; let this be known to all the world."

— ISAIAH 12:3-5 —

This excerpt is a joyous hymn of praise in the otherwise alarming prophesies of the prophet Isaiah. In this prayer, Isaiah shows how the Israelites will rejoice in God when He delivers them from their sins of disobedience.

Isaiah compares their change of heart to the quenching of one's thirst from an overflowing well. The amazing truth is that, after they have suffered the terrible consequences of sin, they develop a new sense of obedience to God. The hearts of these new believers overflow with thanksgiving to God for all that He has done for them.

Give thanks to the Lord in your prayer today because He has delivered you. Ask Him to refresh your withered soul from the well of salvation and to renew your spirit.

Wondrous King, You have done wonderful things for me and have delivered my soul from death. I praise and glorify Your beautiful Name.

Amen

Thanks for answered prayers

Open for me the gates of righteousness; I will enter and give thanks to the LORD. This is the gate of the LORD through which the righteous may enter. I will give you thanks, for you answered me; you have become my salvation.

— PSALM 118:19-21 —

This psalm portrays a victorious but battle-weary king who leads a host of grateful people through the gates of the temple to give thanks to God for His deliverance. In those times, the temple represented the dwelling place of God; the place to which His followers went to worship Him and to pray to Him.

Today we can enter into God's presence wherever we are: in a car, at our place of work, or in the aisles of a supermarket. Wherever we find the time to pray to Him or to praise and thank His Name, we will find His presence. We may rest assured in the knowledge that God hears and answers our prayers, regardless of where they are being said. This inspires us to pray much more.

Like the victorious king of this psalm, we should enter into God's presence and give thanks to Him for hearing and answering our prayers.

O Hearer of prayers, all flesh must come to You. You have always proved faithful in times of trouble. I praise and thank You for all my prayers that You have answered.

Amen

Request for help

I have chosen the way of truth; I have set my heart on your laws. I hold fast to your statutes, O LORD; do not let me be put to shame. I run in the path of your commands, for you have set my heart free.

— PSALM 119:30-32 —

Most of us do not like asking for help. We are inclined to think that we do not need help. "I can handle matters myself!" we say to ourselves.

In today's prayer, the Psalmist desires to be faithful to God. However, he confesses that he cannot obey God's statutes in his own strength. He needs God's help and he seeks it unashamedly.

Present your heart's desire to God in prayer and follow Him with your entire heart, soul and mind.

Commit yourself anew to Him and ask for His guidance and help in every situation that you have to handle in life.

Merciful Father, help me to obey Your statutes today and every day, and to call upon Your Name for help to do so.

Amen

Joy and gratitude for eternal blessing

"You, my God, have revealed to your servant that you will build a house for him. So your servant has found courage to pray to you. O LORD, you are God! You have promised these good things to your servant. Now you have been pleased to bless the house of your servant, that it may continue forever in your sight; for you, O LORD, have blessed it, and it will be blessed forever."

— 1 CHRONICLES 17:25-27 —

One evening, towards the end of David's rule, God spoke to him through a prophet and promised that his offspring would rule as kings forever. David's immediate reaction to this wonderful message was to give thanks to God immediately. He replied with a resounding "Yes!" to God's promise.

God's final fulfillment of this promise was realized through His Son, Jesus Christ, who was rightfully a descendant of David.

Through Jesus, the Living Christ, we have also had an eternal blessing bestowed upon us. We serve an immortal King who desires to bless us with all the riches of His kingdom.

Thank God today for the eternal blessings He gives you through Jesus Christ, His Son, every day.

Lord my God, thank You for the countless and eternal blessings that come my way through Your Son, Jesus the King.

Amen

Praise God for His victory

The LORD is the strength of his people, a fortress of salvation for his anointed one. Save your people and bless your inheritance; be their shepherd and carry them forever.

– PSALM 28:8-9 –

During David's reign, military victories were essential for the survival of the people of Israel. If David did not triumph over his enemies, they would have pillaged and destroyed the nation. David trusted in the God who had anointed him as king to give him victory.

The Hebrew word for "anointed one" is Messiah. David's psalm is a hymn of praise to the coming Messiah: Jesus Christ! He is the Anointed One of God! Jesus is also the Victor: He conquered death, sin and Satan! His victory is ours too, because He conquered the sin that kept us in bondage.

Think of all the ways in which Christ has enabled you to conquer those sins that used to rule your life. Thank God today for Christ's victories and also for those that you have achieved through Christ.

Gracious God, thank You that You made Your Anointed One victorious and, in so doing, delivered Your children. Your love endures forever!

Amen

The joy of those who trust in the Lord

Taste and see that the LORD is good; blessed is the man who takes refuge in him. Fear the LORD, you his saints, for those who fear him lack nothing. The lions may grow weak and hungry, but those who seek the LORD lack no good thing.
– PSALM 34:8-10 –

David invites us all, *"Taste and see that the LORD is good"*. When writing this psalm, David was once again overwhelmed by the goodness of God in his life. Although Saul was intent on killing David and Abimelech considered executing him, God saved David's life by allowing him to escape from both of them.

David's heart burst with joy because he saw God's power at work in his own life. Therefore, he invited others to come and experience the goodness and victory of God.

God has no doubt also revealed His goodness to you. What good things has God brought about in your life? Let David's prayer inspire you to find joy in the Lord today.

God of love and grace, I have personally experienced Your goodness. Thank You for abundantly providing for my needs every day.

Amen

December

Salvation and redemption for God's people

"Salvation is found in no one else, for there is no other name under heaven given to men by which we must be saved."

— Acts 4:12 —

There is no idea more soul-destroying than the belief that sinners can renew or redeem themselves, or that they simply show remorse and confess their sins when it suits them. It is imperative to be brought to the conviction of this truth. Only once people are convinced of their need for salvation and their inability to save themselves will they look for help from the only Source where it can be found: Jesus of Bethlehem. This, in essence, is what Advent and Christmas are all about.

B*ut because of his great love for us, God, who is rich in mercy, made us alive with Christ even when we were dead in transgressions – it is by grace you have been saved. And God raised us up with Christ and seated us with him in the heavenly realms in Christ Jesus, in order that in the coming ages he might show the incomparable riches of his grace, expressed in his kindness to us in Christ Jesus. For it is by grace you have been saved, through faith – and this not from yourselves, it is the gift of God – not by works, so that no one can boast.*

— Ephesians 2:4-9 —

Testify to God's saving grace

"This, then, is how you should pray: 'Our Father in heaven, hallowed be your name, your kingdom come, your will be done on earth as it is in heaven. Give us today our daily bread. Forgive us our debts, as we also have forgiven our debtors. And lead us not into temptation, but deliver us from the evil one.'"

– MATTHEW 6:9-13 –

When you go to a restaurant you do not just order "a plate of food". You request specific items. In the same way, Jesus' model prayer reminds us to state our specific request when asking something of God in prayer.

Use Jesus' prayer as a guide to specific prayer. Acknowledge that it is God, the Almighty, whom you approach: His Name must be revered by everyone wherever He is worshiped.

Commit yourself once again to His kingdom and His purpose. Confess your sins and pray that God will preserve you so that you will not give in to temptation.

Then ask the Lord for those things that you need every day. God is waiting lovingly to bestow His blessing upon you – if only you would ask.

Holy God, let Your will be done in my life every day so that You will be praised and glorified.

Amen

Lay your fears before God

But Moses said to God, "Who am I, that I should go to Pharaoh and bring the Israelites out of Egypt?" And God said, "I will be with you. And this will be the sign to you that it is I who have sent you: When you have brought the people out of Egypt, you will worship God on this mountain."

— EXODUS 3:11-12 —

After Moses had fled Egypt to escape the wrath of Pharaoh, he led a quiet life in Midian. However, God had a different plan for Moses. He wanted Moses to return to Egypt, confront Pharaoh and lead the Israelites from bondage to freedom.

When Moses heard this, he hesitated, *"Who am I, that I should go to Pharaoh … ?"* He also had the excuse that the people would not believe him and that he was not a good speaker because of his stuttering. God, however, had an answer to each of Moses' excuses. God promised to be with him and to empower him every step of the way.

What challenges has God given you? Honestly confess your uncertainty about the tasks God has entrusted to you and remember God's willingness to empower you every step of the way.

Omnipresent God and Father, be with me while I fulfill Your will, even though I may feel inferior to the task, wanting to ask, "Who am I, then?"

Amen

All good gifts come from heaven

David praised the LORD in the presence of the whole assembly, saying, "Praise be to you, O LORD, God of our father Israel, from everlasting to everlasting. Yours, O LORD, is the greatness and the power and the glory and the majesty and the splendor, for everything in heaven and earth is yours. Yours, O LORD, is the kingdom; you are exalted as head over all. Wealth and honor come from you; you are the ruler of all things. In your hands are strength and power to exalt and give strength to all. Now, our God, we give you thanks, and praise your glorious name."

— 1 CHRONICLES 29:10-13 —

Many of us work very hard in order to afford all kinds of things, then we feel inclined to say "I have earned it all through my own efforts and hard work. It is all mine!"

King David was one of the wealthiest people of his time, he possessed gold and silver in abundance and he was the ruler of the united kingdoms of Israel – he did not fall into the trap of thinking that all his possessions belonged to him. On the contrary, he acknowledged that everything in heaven and on earth belonged to the Lord. Therefore, David sacrificed many of his treasures in order to build the temple of the Lord.

Remember the grandeur and majesty of God and pray today with the same attitude that David had.

Merciful God, everything in heaven and on earth belongs to You, and from Your abundance and love You also provide for my needs.

Amen

Glory be to God for the gift of wisdom

During the night the mystery was revealed to Daniel in a vision. Then Daniel praised the God of heaven and said: "Praise be to the name of God for ever and ever; wisdom and power are his. He changes times and seasons; he sets up kings and deposes them. He gives wisdom to the wise and knowledge to the discerning. He reveals deep and hidden things; he knows what lies in darkness, and light dwells with him. I thank and praise you, O God of my fathers: You have given me wisdom and power, you have made known to me what we asked of you, you have made known to us the dream of the king."

— 1 DANIEL 2:19-23 —

While Daniel and his friends were in exile, they were chosen to act as advisors to King Nebuchadnezzar. One night, the king had a disturbing dream and he demanded that his wise men tell him what he had dreamed and also to interpret the dream. Should they be unable to do both, they would all be put to death – including Daniel and his friends.

Daniel and his friends reacted by consulting God in prayer. Daniel could not read the king's mind, but the omniscient God could. The Lord answered their prayers by revealing the dream, as well as its meaning to Daniel. Then Daniel praised and thanked God.

The same God who listened to Daniel and his friends, still listens to you today and would dearly love to answer your prayers.

Omniscient God, to You belong all wisdom and knowledge and power forever and ever. I praise and thank You for being a God who answers prayers.

Amen

The holy desire to be obedient to God

May he turn our hearts to him, to walk in all his ways and to keep the commands, decrees and regulations he gave our fathers. And may these words of mine, which I have prayed before the Lord, be near to the Lord our God day and night, that he may uphold the cause of his servant and the cause of his people Israel according to each day's need.

— 1 Kings 8:58-59 —

After King Solomon had devoted seven years to building the temple of God, he led the Israelites in the dedication of this beautiful building to God.

Firstly, he glorified and praised the Lord for keeping His promises and for settling the Israelites in the Promised Land. He thanked God for granting them the opportunity to build the temple.

God kept all the promises that He made to Solomon's father, David. What should the response of the Israelites be to their God? Solomon prayed that the Israelites would have the desire to obey the Lord's statutes so that His name may be glorified.

Pray today that your entire life will glorify God. Reflect upon your motives as to why you obey God and then pray for a heart like Solomon's.

Righteous God, grant me the desire to obey You and to do Your will at all times.

Amen

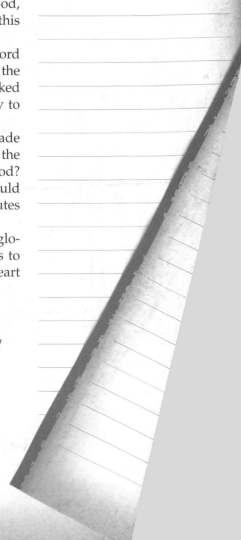

Thank God for His discipline

Blessed is the man you discipline, O Lord, the man you teach from your law; you grant him relief from days of trouble, till a pit is dug for the wicked. For the Lord will not reject his people; he will never forsake his inheritance. Judgment will again be founded on righteousness, and all the upright in heart will follow it.

– Psalm 94:12-15 –

It sometimes seems as though people who live according to God's decrees do not get anywhere in life, while those who don't spare God a second thought, seem to prosper.

If you also think this way, you are not alone. The Psalmist pondered over this issue and expressed it in prayer to God. This Psalmist had walked with God long enough to know that God is righteous in His judgment.

The Lord taught him, admonished him, and disciplined him, so that His will became second nature to him. If we have that kind of dynamic relationship with the Lord, we will eventually enjoy prosperity. The time will come when those who ignored or disregarded God's justness, will have to endure the tragic consequences of their wicked ways.

If you become discouraged, join the Psalmist and remember the works of God.

Righteous Judge, thank You for disciplining me so that Your will can become my pleasure and my joy. I want to follow You with joy and gratitude.

Amen

Wait patiently on God

Teach me your way, O LORD; lead me in a straight path because of my oppressors.
I am still confident of this: I will see the goodness of the LORD in the land of the
living. Wait for the LORD; be strong and take heart and wait for the LORD.
— PSALM 27:11, 13-14 —

David was no stranger to pressure and stress. He was surrounded by a host of enemies who wished for his downfall. But even during those desperate times, he beseeched God for help with words that prepared his own soul for God's timing.

Although David probably had his own thoughts on how God could solve his problems, he submitted himself to God's will and to the path that God had planned for him. He asked God to teach and lead him. Even though the temptation to take action spurred on by panic was undoubtedly present in David's mind, he guarded his heart and became quiet and waited patiently on God.

Too often we expect instant answers from God. However, God often uses our difficult circumstances to shape our character. Together with David, we can confidently state that *"I will see the goodness of the LORD."* However, God always has His own perfect timing and therefore we must wait patiently on the Lord – even in prayer.

Omniscient God, teach me how to live according to Your perfect plan and grant me the grace to wait patiently on You.

Amen

Jesus' praise for God's method of action

At that time Jesus said, "I praise you, Father, Lord of heaven and earth, because you have hidden these things from the wise and learned, and revealed them to little children. Yes, Father, for this was your good pleasure."

– MATTHEW 11:25-26 –

When Jesus lived on this earth, He often prayed within hearing distance of His disciples. It would be acceptable to suggest that by doing so, He wanted to teach them something.

In today's prayer, Jesus gives thanks to God for His wondrous ways. God is incomprehensible to many people in many ways, especially to those who think of themselves as self-sufficient, independent, and think that they know all they need to know. Often, the "wisdom" of the world is an assertion that they do not need God. Jesus, on the other hand, chooses to reveal His truth to the humble and the willing.

Praise the Lord for revealing His truth to all those who come to Him with the desire to learn from Him. May the Lord make our hearts tender and receptive so that we draw near to Him in humility and trust. True wisdom and knowledge can only be found in God.

I praise and thank You, Holy God, that You hide the truth from people who think that they are wise and learned, and that You actually reveal it to those who are humble.

Amen

God causes us to see

And Elisha prayed, "O LORD, open his eyes so he may see." Then the LORD opened the servant's eyes, and he looked and saw the hills full of horses and chariots of fire all around Elisha. As the enemy came down toward him, Elisha prayed to the LORD, "Strike these people with blindness." So he struck them with blindness, as Elisha had asked.

– 2 KINGS 6:17-18 –

Elisha, the prophet, had a bounty on his head. The king of Aram was tired of Elisha constantly warning the king of Israel about his attempt to ambush the Israelites. Therefore, the king of Aram decided to have Elisha killed. When Elisha's servant saw all the enemy troops massed against his master, he started to despair. But Elisha simply prayed that the servant's eyes be opened.

After God had answered Elisha's prayer, Elisha prayed for God to strike the enemy with blindness. Once again, God answered immediately and forcefully.

If ever you feel that you are being overwhelmed by forces that are arrayed against you, as was the case with Elisha's servant, pray for the Lord to open your eyes. Ask God to show you how He will protect you.

Please open my eyes, Almighty God, so that I may see how You protect me every day and in all circumstances.

Amen

God's amazing power

Sing to God, O kingdoms of the earth, sing praise to the LORD, to him who rides the ancient skies above, who thunders with mighty voice. Proclaim the power of God, whose majesty is over Israel, whose power is in the skies. You are awesome, O God, in your sanctuary; the God of Israel gives power and strength to his people. Praise be to God!

– PSALM 68:32-35 –

In this prayer, David tries to find images that would do justice to God's omnipotence and power. He uses the sun and the thunder to illustrate God's omnipotence. It is God's power that makes the sun shine and that gives the storm its mighty lightning bolts.

God also grants His people power and strength. Therefore, the Almighty is worthy of our worship. David's desire is for the entire congregation of God to unite their voices in a hymn of praise to His glory and to worship Him.

Like David, we too can receive God's power and strength. Find the time today to reflect upon God's omnipotence. Find images that reveal His wonderful power to you personally. Then glorify the God who has created those things.

God of grace, thank You that You still today give people power and strength to do Your will and to testify to Your grandeur.

Amen

Lift up your eyes to God for mercy

I lift up my eyes to you, to you whose throne is in heaven. As the eyes of slaves look to the hand of their master, as the eyes of a maid look to the hand of her mistress, so our eyes look to the LORD our God, till he shows us his mercy. Have mercy on us, O LORD, have mercy on us, for we have endured much contempt. We have endured much ridicule from the proud, much contempt from the arrogant.

– PSALM 123:1-4 –

One of the most difficult things we have to do in life, is to wait. We impatiently long to hold the finished product in our hands, or to achieve the goals that we have set immediately.

However, the Psalmist proves that it is best to wait on the Lord. Therefore, he is willing to wait for as long as it pleases God, to see His mercy revealed in his life. God has mercy on us, not because we deserve it, but because He loves us. And He will show us mercy in His own perfect time. Like slaves who keep their eyes fixed on the hand of their masters and mistresses for even the slightest sign, we must keep our eyes attentively on God and patiently wait on His help and guidance.

Lift your eyes to God and seek His mercy. Wait faithfully for Him to help you. Remember to give thanks to God for His goodness and mercy.

Merciful God, I keep my eyes fixed on You, because I know from experience where my help comes from.

Amen

Acknowledge the majesty of God

I know that the LORD is great, that our LORD is greater than all gods. The LORD does whatever pleases him, in the heavens and on the earth, in the seas and all their depths. Your name, O LORD, endures forever, your renown, O LORD, through all generations. For the LORD will vindicate his people and have compassion on his servants.

– PSALM 135:5-6, 13-14 –

It is difficult to portray true grandeur and majesty. The Psalmist compares the living God to the pagan gods who were worshiped in those times. There is simply no comparison: *"Our LORD is greater than all gods."* People think that gods control separate parts of the creation – such as a rain god, a god of the ocean, etc. – but our God *"does whatever pleases him, in the heavens and on the earth, in the seas and all their depths."*

Nothing is impossible to Him! And yet, God uses His omnipotence to help His people and to provide for all they need. He is willing to answer the prayers of those who call on Him. We worship a gracious and merciful God for whom nothing is impossible.

Find time in your prayers today to reflect upon the majesty of God and worship Him with your entire being.

Your grandeur, Creator God, cannot be put into words. I thank You for Your mercy shown to me by answering my prayers.

Amen

Prayer for discernment

Your righteousness is everlasting and your law is true. Trouble and distress have come upon me, but your commands are my delight. Your statutes are forever right; give me understanding that I may live.

— PSALM 119:142-144 —

The trials and tribulations of life often force us to turn somewhere for help. We tend to look for a sympathetic ear first of all when wrestling with a problem.

The Psalmist knew that it is best to turn to God for wisdom and discernment. He asked God, *"Give me understanding that I may live."* He knew that the living God's plan with him would preserve him from wrongful actions and would destroy the way of the foolish. Therefore, he delighted in God and committed himself to upholding His statutes.

Perhaps you are also wrestling with a difficult problem. God promises to grant us wisdom if we pray to Him for it (see Jas. 1:5.) Pray to God for discernment in your struggle and ask Him to teach you, so that you may apply His wisdom to your situation.

Heavenly Father, I am Your redeemed servant and I plead for wisdom and discernment in my testimony for You.

Amen

Prayer for an important decision

So they proposed two men: Joseph called Barsabbas (also known as Justus) and Matthias. Then they prayed, "Lord, you know everyone's heart. Show us which of these two you have chosen to take over this apostolic ministry, which Judas left to go where he belongs." Then they cast lots, and the lot fell to Matthias; so he was added to the eleven apostles.

– Acts 1:23-26 –

Important decisions, such as which job offer to accept or whom to marry, are the kind that cause us the most concern. We spend hours brooding over the advantages and disadvantages. Who would replace Judas to serve as an apostle? These early Christians wanted to make a choice in accordance with the will of God, therefore they prayed.

As a group, they nominated two people who were sincere followers of Jesus. But they realized that they did not know the hearts of the two candidates – only God would have that knowledge. Therefore, they entrusted the final choice to God in prayer.

There are virtually daily decisions that we must discuss with God in prayer. Ask for His wisdom and guidance when making your decision. Ask Him to reveal His choice to you.

Omniscient God, You know my heart and know how I wrestle with important decisions. Help me to make decisions in accordance with Your will.

Amen

Acknowledgement that God is at work

I will praise God's name in song and glorify him with thanksgiving. This will please the LORD more than an ox, more than a bull with its horns and hoofs. The poor will see and be glad – you who seek God, may your hearts live! The LORD hears the needy and does not despise his captive people. Let heaven and earth praise him, the seas and all that move in them.

— PSALM 69:30-34 —

Sometimes, when we are very depressed, we doubt whether there is anyone who hears our anguished cries. That is how David felt. His enemies surrounded him and gloated over his situation. However, David reminds himself that God does hear, *"The LORD hears the needy and does not despise his captive people."*

One day, the poor and the simple-hearted will shout for joy over the work of God's hands. David knew that God heard his beseeching call and that he would receive an answer. He could take joyful delight in this.

You may sometimes feel as though your difficult circumstances have robbed you of joy. Remember then that God is capable of hearing your cry of anguish. Look for ways in which you can recognize how God is already at work in your congregation and community. Sing a hymn of thanksgiving to Him, because *"the poor will see and be glad."*

Loving God and Father, I thank You with heartfelt gratitude for being at work in my life and in this world. I praise and thank You for it.

Amen

Prayer of an aged man

Even when I am old and gray, do not forsake me, O God, till I declare your power to the next generation, your might to all who are to come. Your righteousness reaches to the skies, O God, you who have done great things. Who, O God, is like you? Though you have made me see troubles, many and bitter, you will restore my life again; from the depths of the earth you will again bring me up. You will increase my honor and comfort me once again.

— PSALM 71:18-21 —

Whether the days of our lives are few or many, God never forsakes us. The author of this psalm had a long life. In his old age, he feels abandoned by his family and friends. However, in his despair, he turns to God and asks the Lord never to forsake him.

While reflecting upon his life, he realized that, through all his afflictions and all the troubles in his life, God was working with him. Now he wants to tell the next generation how wonderful God is.

Decide today to tell someone just how wonderful God's deeds are and share with others some stories of God's help, grace and mercy.

Merciful and wondrous God, You have performed such glorious deeds in my life. Help me, through Your Holy Spirit, to proclaim Your deeds.

Amen

Jesus gives thanks for a prayer answered

So they took away the stone. Then Jesus looked up and said, "Father, I thank you that you have heard me. I knew that you always hear me, but I said this for the benefit of the people standing here, that they may believe that you sent me."

— John 11:41-42 —

The raising of Lazarus from the dead gives us a unique insight into the prayer life of Jesus Christ. He knew that the Father always answered His prayers, therefore, when Lazarus' tomb was opened, He thanked God out loud.

He wanted to demonstrate to His followers that God had sent Him. When He told Lazarus to come out, He was not in the least surprised when Lazarus got up and came walking towards Him, but the bystanders were surprised: Was it really possible?

Jesus' prayer answered their question: God the Father had sent Jesus to them. The raising of Lazarus from the dead was physical proof of Jesus' divine power.

Jesus' prayer is also for our benefit. Reconfirm your faith in Jesus Christ and His power over death in your prayer today. Praise and thank Him for answering your prayers as well.

Resurrected Lord Jesus, I believe with all my heart that God sent You to our world. Thank You for also answering my prayers and for interceding with God for my needs.

Amen

Glory be to God who grants us success

"He raises the poor from the dust and lifts the needy from the ash heap; he seats them with princes and has them inherit a throne of honor. For the foundations of the earth are the LORD's; upon them he has set the world. He will guard the feet of his saints, but the wicked will be silenced in darkness. It is not by strength that one prevails; those who oppose the LORD will be shattered. He will thunder against them from heaven; the LORD will judge the ends of the earth. He will give strength to his king and exalt the horn of his anointed."

– 1 SAMUEL 2:8-10 –

Who would believe that this is the prayer of a mother who has just handed over her son to the LORD to become a priest! Instead of despairing about her child, Hannah praised the LORD, because He had blessed her with a son in the first place. In her eyes, her sacrifice was success, because she had always been a true follower of God.

Success always follows on one kind of sacrifice or another, and joy normally succeeds a time of suffering. Let Hannah's prayer remind you of the kind of faith that is required to survive times of suffering in your life. God will turn your suffering into success, your weakness into strength.

Cast your suffering, your sorrow and your weakness upon God in prayer. Ask Him to use these problems in your life to help others and to glorify Him.

Almighty God of love, I know that I cannot be successful in my own strength. Thank You for the power and strength that You grant me during times of affliction and sorrow.

Amen

A petition for success

"O LORD, let your ear be attentive to the prayer of this your servant and to the prayer of your servants who delight in revering your name. Give your servant success today by granting him favor in the presence of this man." I was cupbearer to the king.

— NEHEMIAH 1:11 —

Nehemiah, the cup-bearer to King Artaxerxes, understood that success often depends on a variety of factors, including the reaction of other people. Therefore, he approached God in prayer about his plan to return to Judah to rebuild the walls of Jerusalem. He knew that the success of his plan depended on God's influencing the heart of the king.

Once he had prayed, Nehemiah confidently explained his plan to the king. Nehemiah confessed, *"And because the gracious hand of my God was upon me, the king granted my requests"* (Neh. 2:8).

God is aware of our needs and He wants us to succeed in our plans, so that we may honor Him. Take your plans to the Lord in prayer. Declare yourself willing to honor His name through your plans and then pray with confidence for success.

Merciful Father, I find pleasure in honoring You in all that I do. Grant that I will be successful so that You will be glorified.

Amen

Simeon's praise to his Savior

"Sovereign Lord, as you have promised, you now dismiss your servant in peace. For my eyes have seen your salvation, which you have prepared in the sight of all people, a light for revelation to the Gentiles and for glory to your people Israel."

— Luke 2:29-32 —

The aged Simeon was not merely any Jewish citizen who sat around in the fading hope that the Messiah would come during his lifetime. He looked forward to it in fervent expectation. His attitude was supported by the Word. He understood what this little Baby, whom Joseph and Mary brought to the temple, meant to all the nations on earth. This Little Child was the Savior of the world.

Today, people still make the mistake of seeing only the crib, without hearing the message. They remember the remarkable baby Jesus, but they miss seeing God's presence around us.

While others merely saw a little child, Simeon saw *"a light for revelation to the Gentiles"*. He was ready to see God! While others might see Christmas merely as a time to enjoy their presents, the Christian sees it as a time to pay homage to the Light of the world!

Father God, I thank and praise You that You have given me the gift of a Savior. Thank You, Lord Jesus, that You are also the Light of my life.

Amen

Rejoice in our Savior

And Mary said: "My soul glorifies the Lord and my spirit rejoices in God my Savior, for he has been mindful of the humble state of his servant. From now on all generations will call me blessed, for the Mighty One has done great things for me – holy is his name."

— LUKE 1:46-49 —

Mary was several months pregnant when she visited the home of Elizabeth, a relative of hers. Elizabeth herself was about to give birth to an unexpected baby. Her child, who would be the future John the Baptist, leaped inside her womb when he heard the sound of Mary's voice. When Elizabeth told Mary this, Mary sung a hymn of praise.

Mary not only understood the grandeur of God, but she also believed that God had done great things for her. She understood that she was part of God's great plan. She knew that she did not deserve the privilege of giving birth to the Messiah, and she expressed her surprise about God's particular choice.

Mary's role was unique. She was the only woman who could have been the mother of our Savior. Nonetheless, our role is very similar to that of Mary. As Christians, our lives should be dwelling places for the Holy Spirit of Christ.

Holy Lord Jesus, thank You that You have done great things for me as well. I rejoice in You, my Redeemer and my Savior.

Amen

Hannah glorifies and praises God

The Lord brings death and makes alive; he brings down to the grave and raises up. The Lord sends poverty and wealth; he humbles and he exalts. He raises the poor from the dust and lifts the needy from the ash heap; he seats them with princes and has them inherit a throne of honor. For the foundations of the earth are the Lord's; upon them he has set the world.

– 1 Samuel 2:6-8 –

It would have been very easy for Hannah to become proud and develop a sense of self-importance when her son, Samuel, was born. She easily could have become revengeful and triumphant towards her arch-rival, Penninah.

Not only was Hannah blessed with a son, but she also had the love of the man to whom they were both married. For years on end she had been harassed by Penninah and she could have used this opportunity to pay Penninah back.

Instead, she offers her thanks and praise to God for having heard her prayers for a son; for having picked her up out of the dust of despair.

When confronted with a difficult problem, you must guard against becoming embittered. Do not utter bitter words in haste. Remember Hannah's prayer and use it as a model for yourself. Rather talk to God: He listens and He understands.

Oh Hearer of prayers, I praise and thank You for the countless times that You have picked me up out of the dust of despair and placed me on firm ground. I honor You for it.

Amen

Zechariah glorifies God for a promise fulfilled

Praise be to the Lord, the God of Israel, because he has come and has redeemed his people. He has raised up a horn of salvation for us in the house of his servant David (as he said through his holy prophets of long ago), salvation from our enemies and from the hand of all who hate us – to show mercy to our fathers and to remember his holy covenant, the oath he swore to our father Abraham: to rescue us from the hand of our enemies, and to enable us to serve him without fear in holiness and righteousness before him all our days.

– LUKE 1:68-75 –

Think back for a moment on how you rejoiced when you received a gift that had been promised to you. For Zechariah, it was God's promise to grant him a son. However, on the day of his son's birth, Zechariah had much more to rejoice in.

His son, who would later become John the Baptist, would announce the coming of the Messiah: the Savior whom God had promised to Israel such a long time ago. Yet another of God's promises was honored and there was yet another reason for jubilant joy. We can only imagine how much joy it must have brought to Zechariah to see the fulfillment of God's promises with his own eyes.

Reflect upon God's faithfulness and the fulfillment of His promises while preparing for Christmas.

Faithful God, we glorify You for the mighty Savior whom You have sent for our redemption – just as You promised.

Amen

Mary glorifies God for His grace

His mercy extends to those who fear him, from generation to generation. He has performed mighty deeds with his arm; he has scattered those who are proud in their inmost thoughts. He has brought down rulers from their thrones but has lifted up the humble. He has filled the hungry with good things but has sent the rich away empty. He has helped his servant Israel, remembering to be merciful to Abraham and his descendants forever, even as he said to our fathers.

— LUKE 1:50-55 —

I t is easy to take God's grace for granted. It is only through His grace that He grants our country good rains and good weather conditions so that we can produce food in abundance. It is only through His grace that we have food and clothes and a roof over our heads.

Too often we act like children who think that grace is only needed when they find themselves in trouble. Mary's prayer is proof that she knew how to rejoice in God's grace while enjoying His blessing.

Reflect in prayer upon God's abundant grace to you and your family during this festive season. Think how far God was willing to go to bestow His infinite grace on this world torn apart by sin.

Merciful Father, in Your grace You have performed mighty deeds for me. You have lifted up the humble and gave a Savior to us all. We glorify Your great Name.

Amen

Glory to God in the highest!

Suddenly a great company of the heavenly host appeared with the angel, praising God and saying, "Glory to God in the highest, and on earth peace to men on whom his favor rests."

– Luke 2:13-14 –

For the average person, life was not noticeably different on the night of Jesus' birth. Bars and taverns were busy serving clients. Shepherds crouched around their fires to keep warm while they kept watch over their sheep.

But in an isolated corner of Bethlehem, in the stable of a modest inn, a Baby lay in a manger. And when the shepherds were preparing for sleep, the angels gathered in a mighty choir and the silence of the night was broken by celestial hymns of praise. Imagine the shepherds' reaction: shock, fear and awe. They knew that they had to find this extraordinary Child whose birth the angels had announced.

While commemorating and celebrating the joyous birth of Christ on this day, make sure that you personally seek Jesus and find him, like the shepherds did on that very first Christmas night so many years ago. Use the angels' song as your prayer to rejoice in the birth of your Savior.

Glory to You, my God in the highest, but also in my heart. May all who seek You be blessed with peace.

Amen

Jesus prays for the world to know Him

"I have given them the glory that you gave me, that they may be one as we are one: I in them and you in me. May they be brought to complete unity to let the world know that you sent me and have loved them even as you have loved me. Father, I want those you have given me to be with me where I am, and to see my glory, the glory you have given me because you loved me before the creation of the world."

– John 17:22-24 –

While we remember the birth of Jesus this week, we must also remember why Jesus came to this world in the first place.

In this prayer, Jesus speaks about the purpose of His coming and asks that those who believe in Him will experience unity with God and among themselves. His prayer articulates all that He has achieved through His life: the establishing of our relationship with God and the possibility of unity among all people.

Jesus Christ became one with us so that we may become one with God. The Child whose birth we celebrate, grew up and became the One who invites us to become children of God in His Eternal Kingdom.

In this festive season, as you meditate on what the life, death and resurrection of Jesus mean to you personally, pray that you will reflect the love of Jesus.

Jesus of Bethlehem, through Your Spirit, help me to show love, so that the world may know that God has sent You to deliver us from sin and lovelessness.

Amen

Prospects of the wedding feast of the Lamb

Then I heard what sounded like a great multitude, like the roar of rushing waters and like loud peals of thunder, shouting: "Hallelujah! For our Lord God Almighty reigns. Let us rejoice and be glad and give him glory! For the wedding of the Lamb has come, and his bride has made herself ready. Fine linen, bright and clean, was given her to wear."

— REVELATION 19:6-8 —

The Scriptures, the revelation of the will of God for our lives, require certain responses of us. We must fall down in silence before His awe-inspiring presence, or we must rejoice with hymns of praise. The writer of Revelation was given a vision of the future day, when God's people – the bride – will celebrate their union with the Bridegroom: Jesus, the Lamb of God!

In John's vision, a voice coming from the throne of God, leads the people in a hymn of praise, *"Praise our God, all you his servants."* This impressive celebration commemorates the final reason for Jesus' coming to this world.

He came to redeem His people from the bondage of sin, so that they can participate joyfully in His eternal kingdom.

This vision of our happy and joyous union with Christ should remain in our mind's eye while we bear testimony to Jesus in this world.

Hallelujah, You reign, Lord our Almighty God. I rejoice in You and glorify Your Name.

Amen

God is a trustworthy ally

Praise be to the LORD my Rock, who trains my hands for war, my fingers for battle. He is my loving God and my fortress, my stronghold and my deliverer, my shield, in whom I take refuge, who subdues peoples under me. O LORD, what is man that you care for him, the son of man that you think of him?

— PSALM 144:1-3 —

I f a nation wants to declare war against a formidable enemy, diplomats are sent to its allies to recruit their support. No one wants to enter into battle without someone backing him. In this prayer, David declares God to be his ally. He calls God "my rock" and "my fortress", "deliverer" and "stronghold". He gives thanks to the Lord for his training in the art of warfare, which gives him the strength to fight.

In the confusion of the battlefield, David could trust in God to support him and to lead him to victory over his enemies. Nevertheless, he is still amazed about God's willingness to come to his rescue, *"O LORD, what is man that you care for him?"*

Give thanks to God today for all the times that He has delivered you.

I give thanks to You, Lord my God, that You are also my Rock, my Fortress and my Deliverer. I praise and thank You for Your protection during times of crisis in my life.

Amen

Draw near unto God with an honest heart

Hear, O LORD, my righteous plea; listen to my cry. Give ear to my prayer – it does not rise from deceitful lips. May my vindication come from you; may your eyes see what is right. Though you probe my heart and examine me at night, though you test me, you will find nothing; I have resolved that my mouth will not sin. And I – in righteousness I will see your face; when I awake, I will be satisfied with seeing your likeness.

– PSALM 17:1-3, 15 –

Like a child longing to see his father after he has been away for a long time, David longed to see God face to face. He wanted to praise and thank God for his deliverance. David knew that God is holy and that all who enter into His presence, must do so with a clean heart and a sincere and pure life.

In this prayer, David promises to walk in God's ways and he even asks God to examine his heart. David had undoubtedly sinned – he was even guilty of the murder of an innocent man.

But David did not hide his sins; he confessed them before God and asked God to cleanse him of sin so that he could enter God's presence with hymns of praise.

Pray to God to cleanse you from all sin.

Loving Father God, You know that my prayer comes from an honest heart. Probe my heart, know my thoughts and cleanse me of all sin through the blood of Jesus.

Amen

Solomon prays for wisdom

At Gibeon the LORD appeared to Solomon during the night in a dream, and God said, "Ask for whatever you want me to give you." Solomon answered, "You have shown great kindness to your servant, my father David, because he was faithful to you and righteous and upright in heart. You have continued this great kindness to him and have given him a son to sit on his throne this very day. Now, O LORD my God, you have made your servant king in place of my father David. But I am only a little child and do not know how to carry out my duties. Your servant is here among the people you have chosen, a great people, too numerous to count or number. So give your servant a discerning heart to govern your people and to distinguish between right and wrong. For who is able to govern this great people of yours?"

— 1 KINGS 3:5-9 —

Consider this man Solomon: the heir to the throne of one of the richest and most powerful nations of the time. When he became king he asked God for His help and wisdom, because, *"I am only a little child and do not know how to carry out my duties."*

With everything at his disposal, Solomon deliberately emphasized the power of prayer. Solomon honestly appraised his own abilities in the light of the scope of his duties as king of Israel. He concluded by calling out, *"For who is able to govern this great people of yours?"*

As the old year draws to a close, let Solomon's prayer for wisdom be your theme for the new year. Seek God's wisdom and let it guide you through the year ahead.

Hearer of prayers, I kneel in deep dependence before You and beseech You to grant me Your wisdom on my path through the year ahead.

Amen

Hymn of praise to God's faithfulness

I will sing of the LORD's great love forever; with my mouth I will make your faithfulness known through all generations. I will declare that your love stands firm forever, that you established your faithfulness in heaven itself.

— PSALM 89:1-2 —

Early during David's reign, God promised him that his descendants, his kingdom and his kingship *"shall endure for ever before me; your throne will be established for ever"* (see 2 Sam. 7:16). This prayer of Ethan's reminds us that God was fulfilling His promise to David. It was proof of God's eternal acts of love and His faithfulness to coming generations: a love and faithfulness that would endure for ever and ever.

Jesus Christ fulfilled God's promise to David. Jesus was a descendent of David by way of His father, Joseph. He was raised from the dead to reign forever at the right hand of God. (see Mk. 14:62-63; Acts 5:30-32.) God, in His love and grace, included us in His eternal kingdom.

Therefore, in your prayer time today, reflect upon God's faithfulness to you personally through Jesus Christ and then join Ethan in a hymn of praise to His glory to conclude the old year.

I thank You, Lord my God, for Your eternal faithfulness and love and I sing a hymn of praise to Your glory, because Your grace and love have carried me through yet another year.

Amen